The Official Collectors Guide

Dr. Stephen F. Hofer, Managing Editor

Bangzoom Publishers
14 Storrs Avenue
Braintree, MA 02184
www.bangzoom.com

TV GUIDE CONTRIBUTORS
Alan Appel
Barbara Bagge
Helene Curley
Michael Davis
Peggy Nolan
Karina Reeves
Steve Scebelo

Jim Kelley – Publisher
Leatrice Sherry – Design Director
Sharen Forsyth – Operations Manager
Chuck Barnard – Sales and Service Manager
Surrell Wells – Assistant to Sales and Service Manager
Peter Custer – Technical Consultant

ISBN 0-9772927-1-1 Copyright ©2006 by Bangzoom Publishers, a division of Bangzoom Software, Inc. All rights reserved. No part of this book may be reproduced or transmitted in any form or by any means, electronic or mechanical, including photocopying, recording, or by any information storage or retrieval system, without the written permission of the publisher.

Library of Congress Control Number: 2006900087

Printed in the United States of America

10 9 8 7 6 5 4 3 2 1

TABLE OF CONTENTS

Greetings from the midtown Manhattan editorial offices of *TV Guide*, the place where it's not only OK to watch television while you work, it's part of your job description.

For me, working at the magazine is the realization of a life-long ambition. My attachment to *TV Guide*, perhaps like yours, began as a child. My parents tell me that as a boy, I would race to the mailbox each week and turn to the Thursday listings. Zorro, a character and a series that was my obsession at age 5, aired at 8 pm Thursday on ABC during its debut season of 1957-58. It's no exaggeration to say that I gained as many reading-readiness skills from the listings pages of TV Guide as I did from Dr. Seuss. Certainly I had the letter "Z" down before I hit kindergarten.

Guy Williams portrayed the swashbuckling black-caped Robin Hood who blazed his way onto the April 26, 1958 cover. Photographed to make Zorro pop from the newsstand racks, Williams is in costume against a red backdrop, carving his calling card — a jagged Z — with his sword.

My mother used that issue as part of a centerpiece in celebration of my sixth birthday. (She also baked a chocolate-frosted devil's food cake with a Z across the top in white icing.)

To the denizens of the Editorial Department, that *Zorro* issue is considered as one of the great iconic covers in the digest's history. And we know from surfing eBay that it's a coveted collectible. It has been known to whip up cyclonic bidding frenzies, as do mint-condition copies of the *Guide*'s dazzling *Green Hornet* issue, featuring an airborne, leg-kicking Bruce Lee as Cato.

The holy grail of covers (at least at my house) is the September 25, 1953 *Superman* issue, featuring George Reeves as both Clark Kent and the Man of Steel. My heart skips a beat every time I venture into *TV Guide*'s library of bound volumes and turn to that edition.

I can spend hours in the stacks leafing through our past, lingering over the issues from the 1950s and '60s that mean so much to me now. But so do issues I worked on in the 2000s, especially the multiple-cover projects (24 different "Secret Stars" of *The Simpsons*! 35 *Star Trek* characters!) and the 3-D and lenticular covers (*Star Wars*! Elvis! NASCAR!). Those covers take a rightful place in our collectible history, along with regional sports covers we produced for fans of the NFL, Major League Baseball, the NHL and college basketball and football.

The four December 12, 2004 lenticular covers of *The Simpsons* with holographic ornaments.

Why did so many people save our magazine through the decades, boxing and shelving them in cool, dry places? Lots of reasons. But it seems to me that vintage issues of *TV Guide* are like little time machines. They provide a window to any given week, day or even hour of our past. They bring us back to happy times with family and friends and help us recapture the fleeting and the ephemeral.

Plus, compared to collecting vintage Corvettes or antique Harleys, *TV Guide*s are an affordable indulgence and a smart investment in an age when all it takes is a couple of clicks to track down a long-desired item.

Here's wishing you happy hunting in your search for *TV Guide*s of the past. And if you come across a killer copy of the *Superman* issue, duck into a phone booth and call me.

Michael Davis
Senior Editor, *TV Guide*

Collecting *TV Guide*® Magazines

TV Guide collecting typically began with interest in the subject on the cover, which was the star or stars of a television series. More recently, covers have featured movie and sports stars. Because of this, the concept of the split and series covers came into being. Since 1991, there have been hundreds of split covers: on any given week there may be as many as three dozen different covers. In the case of sports covers, the subjects are regional stars. For instance, on the week of September 3, 1994 covers, there were football favorites John Madden, Troy Aikman, John Elway, Dan Marino, Joe Montana, Barry Sanders, and Thurman Thomas all featured that same week. The sports figure on the cover appeared in the regional edition of *TV Guide*, which meant the Dan Marino cover would be purchased in Florida and the Joe Montana cover in California.

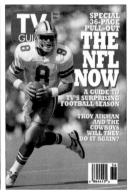
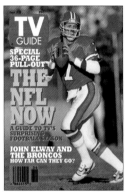

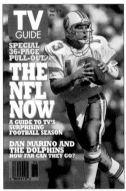
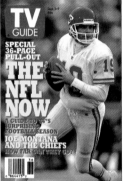
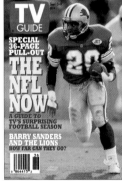
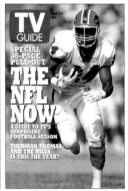

The covers of August 24, 1996, show the stars of the four *Star Trek* series; these series covers were distributed nationally and could feature television programs, movies, or sports teams, which could also be distributed just regionally.

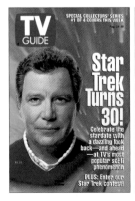
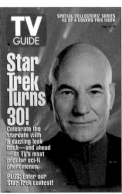

Take a look at the covers of September 28, 1996 (see page 163), and you will see the example of regional split covers and series covers all being produced for the same week — a Michael J. Fox *Spin City* national cover was tossed into the mix that week as well. As a collector, it is a daunting task to obtain all the issues of a split and/or series cover week. This is one of the challenges of collecting *TV Guide*.

An example of a most unusual split cover occurred on July 13, 1991, and it was not planned. That issue featured Michael Landon on the cover with the title, "What Michael Means to Us." Unfortunately, he died during the week the magazine was being printed, so a second cover was immediately issued with the title, "What Michael Meant to Us."

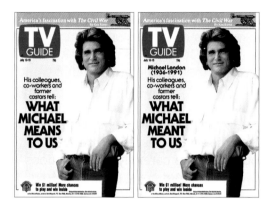

When *TV Guide* first appeared in April of 1953, there were only three national networks: NBC, CBS, and DuMont. The primetime schedule the magazine presented reflected the very limited program choices, so the articles featuring TV stars were the main attractions of the magazine. Another goal for the collector is to possess all the articles about a specific TV star or favorite program. This could be particularly challenging if that personality worked in numerous programs spanning many decades like Mary Tyler Moore.

TV Guide has presented over fifty years of television. Individual issues that represent a personal event such as a birthday or anniversary could be another focus of a *TV Guide* collection. These issues could also be used as unusual gifts for a person to remember what was on television at the time of a special event in his or her life.

So, whether your goal is to collect every issue ever produced, including regional, split, and series, or to be more focused in your collecting, you will join the ranks of intrepid souls who frequent yard sales, flea markets, and antique shops, as well as the attics and basements of relatives and friends, in search of the world's most collected magazine.

Finding, Rating, and Preserving Your Magazines

Older editions of *TV Guide* can be purchased at magazine dealers who may specialize or have many back editions for sale. More current back issues may be purchased at the store on the *TV Guide* website (www.tvguidestore.com). In addition to combing flea markets, antique stores, and the cellars of friends and family for back issues, you might contact local trash removal companies that clean out basements, attics, and garages. Tell the owner what you are looking for and offer to pay a fair price for any *TV Guide* magazines his employees may find. You can also put ads in the local newspapers under the "Wanted" section and, of course, there is eBay. Most collectors research items sold on eBay because of the millions of auctions that occur every day. You will find thousands of *TV Guide* back issues on this site. However, since you do not actually see the issue, you must rely on the seller's description, honesty, and ability to package your purchase carefully so that it does not get destroyed in shipping. You can often get great deals on eBay, but there is always a risk of the item not living up to its description. Finally, you can search for listings of dealers in used and collectible magazines over the Web.

April 3, 1953 – First national *TV Guide* cover and the most valuable.

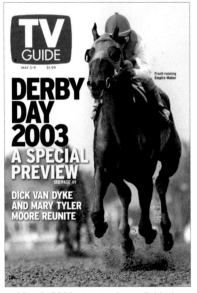

May 3, 2003 cover only available in Kentucky and Southern Ohio.

The picture or artwork on the cover determines the value of the individual magazine. The more popular the TV star, the higher the cost of that issue. Currently, Lucille Ball issues command higher prices than covers featuring any other TV star. The first issue of *TV Guide*, which features Desi Arnaz, Jr., is the most valuable of all. Some more recent regional covers also command higher prices. The Kentucky Derby issue of May 3, 2003, is an example of a limited regional split cover that was only distributed in Kentucky and Southern Ohio, while the national cover featured the stars of *JAG*.

The condition of the magazine is most important. The cover should be well centered, be free of a mailing label, and have strong colors. Folds, water stains, creases, chips, pen or pencil markings, and general wear and tear will reduce the overall value of the magazine. The early editions that were held together by staples should be tight and rust-free. A filled-in crossword puzzle reduces the value, as well. *TV Guide* magazines can be graded in the same way as comic books are graded. A true gem, mint condition magazine is usually worth more than the published value. Pristine examples of every issue of *TV Guide* do exist and there are dedicated collectors who pursue only these fine specimens. The problem becomes matching the collector with the person who has the issue.

As of today, following the April 3, 1953 "Lucy's Baby" issue, the three most valuable issues are the September 25, 1953 *Adventures of*

May 3, 2003 national cover.

Superman's George Reeves cover, the September 8, 1956 Elvis Presley cover, and the June 25, 1954 *The Howdy Doody Show*'s Bob Smith and Howdy Doody cover.

September 25, 1953 cover.

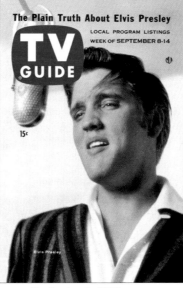

September 8, 1956 cover.

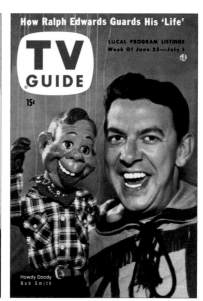

June 25, 1954 cover.

Since there are acids contained in the paper of magazines, keeping your *TV Guide* magazines sealed in plastic bags prevents air (oxygen) from interacting with the acid (oxidizing), which causes foxing or brown staining. The plastic material recommended for this application is archival, acid-free, lignin-free polyethylene, which is also used for food storage bags. You should never use PVC plastic bags or sheeting to protect your magazines. You can also put your collection into archival boxes. Special protective bags and boxes can be purchased from library supply distributors like Gaylord Bros., Inc. (www.gaylord.com — 800-448-6160) or Brodart (www.shopbrodart.com — 888-820-4377). Keep your collection out of direct sunlight or fluorescent light and NEVER use clear adhesive tape to repair tears. If you must repair your magazines, you will find the proper, acid-free tapes available at the sources mentioned above.

Metal edges on boxes provide strength.

CONDITION RATINGS	
MINT	No visible flaws.
NEAR MINT	Only a slight flaw that can be seen upon careful inspection.
VERY FINE	Several minor flaws in the color, edge or overall appearance.
FINE	May have visual distractions in color, centering, corner folds, and nicks. No major visible flaws. This is the lowest collectible category.

Issues with many flaws should be purchased as fillers until a
better quality sample can be found.

A Brief History of *TV Guide*® Magazine

In 1953, Walter H. Annenberg, head of family-owned Triangle Publications, which had interests in newspapers, magazines, and early television, considered the prospect of producing a national publication that would carry network and local television programs along the lines of a Philadelphia television magazine called *TV Digest*. After buying that magazine, Annenberg purchased New York's *TV Guide*, Chicago's *TV Forecast*, and other local publications serving the Boston, Philadelphia, Washington-Baltimore, Pittsburgh, Cleveland, Detroit, Harrisburg, and Wilkes-Barre markets. On April 3, 1953, the national *TV Guide*, which was to become the largest week-

November 25, 1950 issue of New York *TV Guide* autographed by Buffalo Bob Smith.

ly circulation magazine in the world, appeared on newsstands. From that beginning, its editors strove to make the magazine more than just a program guide or a fan magazine. It stood as the undisputed source for critical perspectives on not only television programs and their stars, but also of the very industry itself. It became an icon for that industry and a benchmark for the medium's impact upon society.

January 17, 1953 issue of *TV Forecast*.

Distinguished writers such as John Updike, Isaac Asimov, Arthur Miller, and John Cheever have contributed their views to its pages. Celebrity photographers like Phillippe Halsman and Gene Trindl have captured the faces of the stars it profiled. Major artists like Andy Warhol used his characteristic silkscreen technique for the March 5, 1966 cover featuring *Get Smart*'s Barbara Feldon. The subjects of caricatures by New York Times artist, Al Hirschfeld,

ranged from Bob Hope and Milton Berle to Peter Falk and Lassie. Charles Addams let his cartoon characters of Gomez and Morticia Addams dance with John Astin and Carolyn Jones of *The Addams Family* on the October 30, 1965 cover. His gridiron werewolf on the cover of the January 14, 1978 issue marked the first nighttime Super Bowl. Salvador Dali's unique vision foretold the future of television on the cover of June 8, 1968. And, as part of a series of covers for the December 22, 2001 issue, artists Jamie Wyeth and Peter Max gave their tributes to the American flag in the wake of the 9/11 tragedy.

October 30, 1965 cover by Charles Addams.

Lucille Ball and Desi Arnaz's baby, Desi Arnaz, Jr., graced the cover of the very first *TV Guide*. The week was April 3, 1953, and the cover headline dubbed him,"Lucy's $50,000,000 Baby." Lucy's photo was in a small box at the top of the page, and over the next 53 years, her likeness appeared 39 more times on the cover of the magazine. No other celebrity has come even close to her appearances — Johnny

Carson has appeared 28 times and Michael Landon and Mary Tyler Moore tied at 27 times apiece. Oprah Winfrey has made a respectable 23 cover appearances.

The digest form of *TV Guide* was printed weekly at seven publishing sites across the United States. At one time, there were over 180 different editions printed. The articles were the same, but the local programs differed from market to market. Editions were produced for Alaska and Hawaii, as well as for hotels and motels. Weekly, there were Eastern, Central, Mountain, and Pacific time zone editions.

Large format experimental version of May 4, 1991 issue.

TV Guide remained the largest circulation publication on a weekly basis for over 50 years. Its first-year sales reached almost a million-and-a half copies, and in the mid 70s it achieved a circulation of over 20 million. In recent years its circulation declined but it never dropped below nine million copies. The cover price rose from 15 cents in 1953 to $2.49 for its last digest-sized issue on October 9, 2005. Some special issues did, however, sell for $2.99.

The magazine experimented in 1991 with a larger, 7 1/2" x 10" format, in addition to the traditional digest-size of 5" x 7". The larger size was tested in Nashville, TN, Pittsburgh, PA, and Rochester, NY, and came out on March 30th of that year with Cheryl Ladd and Whitney Houston on the cover. For cable subscribers, starting in 1998, *TV Guide* brought out another large-size magazine, and this time the size expanded to 8" x 11". The articles were the same for both large-sized issues, and collectible values are also similar. There are, however, some notable exceptions that have proven to be twice as valuable to collectors. In 1991 those would include the first issue of March 30th, the two Michael Landon issues of July 13th and July 20th, the following week's 200th Edition Collectors Guide, Madonna's cover of August 3rd, and, finally, Kirk and Picard of *Star Trek* on August 31st. Commanding double the prices of regular issues in 1998 are the issues featuring Fall Previews, the cast of *Frasier*, the characters on *The Simpsons*,

Large format cable version of November 30, 2002 issue.

and the split wrestling issues featuring Hulk Hogan and Steve Austin on December 5, 1998.

Fall Preview issues are very popular among collectors. Published in September, the issues list and preview the new, primetime series before they debut. Usually, there is only one issue, but in 1990 there were three

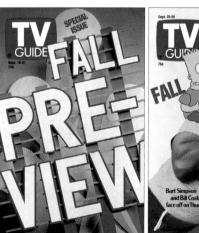

September 15, 22, and 29, 1990 Fall Preview issues.

consecutive weeks of Fall Preview issues. Starting in 1996, these preview issues were either preceded or followed by a "Returning Favorites" issue. 1994 was the year in which special

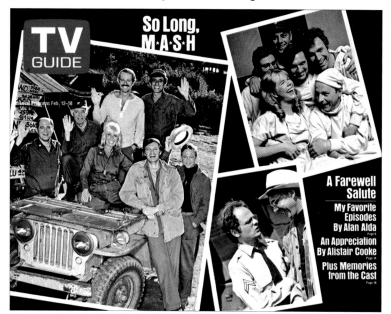

Winter Preview issues were published to highlight TV's "Second Season" of replacement programs. Preview editions for *TV Guide* collectors are somewhat like rookie cards in baseball — fans of a particular program usually like to have the first issue in which it appears in print.

Australian media mogul Rupert Murdoch purchased the magazine in 1988, and he brought in some new people to improve the features section in the book and to strengthen its circulation. In the early 1990s one of these circulation-improving strategies emerged, which was to make the collecting of *TV Guide* an even more formidable task. Multiple and split covers

First fold-out cover issue from February 12, 1983.

began to appear with some regularity. The first year was 1991 which saw two split covers: the January 26th issue featured both Cybill Shepherd and 50 Memorable Super Bowl Moments; Michael Landon's unforeseen death during the week of his cover appearance forced another. By 1996 there were over fifty different regional covers dealing with NASCAR, NFL teams, Major League Baseball, and college football teams playing bowl games on New Year's Day. Since that

year, there have been over five hundred additional split and multiple covers on *TV Guide*. The technique of using fold-out covers, first tried for *M*A*S*H* on February 12, 1983 was reintroduced for *Cheers* on May 15, 1993. Holographic elements were eventually brought into play to heighten the magazine's design appeal and to make collecting even more enjoyable.

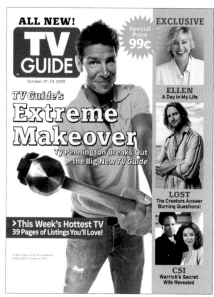

TV Guide has kept pace with a changing world and an evolving medium, providing guidance and entertainment news and profiles to two generations of Americans. It has enhanced the TV viewing experience by supplying information on close to a million TV series episodes and over 140,000 movies. It is a nationwide fixture on coffee tables not only because of its listings but also because of its presentation of the shows, the characters, the celebrities behind the characters, and the industry that puts them all together. The digest-sized guide may have ended on October 9, 2005, but the new *TV Guide* continues to maintain its position as an icon of American popular culture and will be sought vigorously by collectors as well.

October 17, 2005 –
The first big *TV Guide*.

Television Programs Through the Decades

The Forties

After World War II ended, the United States began a national recovery. Many returning servicemen had been trained in electronics during their time at war. The birth of television also began at this time. The National Broadcasting Company (NBC), Columbia Broadcasting System (CBS) and the DuMont Network began airing programs, first on an experimental basis, then consistently during the hours of 7 to 11pm, a period which was to become known as "primetime." Cities like New York, Boston, Baltimore, Washington, Chicago, and Los Angeles were the first sites with stations that could broadcast a small, black and white image to wooden boxes in these metropolitan areas.

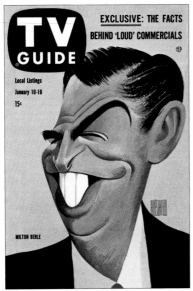

Milton Berle on the January 10, 1959 cover.

The first programs these networks began to broadcast were extensions of already popular radio shows translated into this new medium. Variety shows became the most prevalent type of evening entertainment. Among those popular shows were *Texaco Star Theatre* starring Milton Berle, *Toast of the Town* featuring the well-known syndicated New York gossip columnist, Ed Sullivan, *Arthur Godfrey's Talent Scouts* and *Arthur Godfrey and His Friends* hosted by the red-haired, ukulele-playing radio personality, and *Fireball Fun For All*, starring the comedy team of Ole Olsen and Chic Johnson. Joining these highest rated programs during the 1948-1949 TV season was *The Philco Television Playhouse*, a one-hour "live" drama program. This show and others like it which blossomed in the fifties produced programming ranging from original made-for-television shows to adaptations of well-known short stories and novels. And, 1949 brought the serialized radio drama to television with *The Goldbergs*, starring Molly Berg. Ms. Berg had conceived, written, produced, and starred in this engaging story of a Jewish family from the Bronx for twenty years, five to six times a week, for her faithful radio audience.

Network executives not only wanted to engage adult viewers, but they also knew that entertaining children would be commercially profitable. Starting on December 27, 1947, as *Puppet Playhouse*, Buffalo Bob Smith created a children's show that would have a long, successful run on the small screen. Howdy Doody, Mr. Bluster, Dilly Dally, Inspector John J. Phadoozel, and Flub-a-Dub were the marionette stars. They lived in Doodyville with their human friends Buffalo Bob, Princess Summer Fall-Winter Spring, Chief Thunderthud, and, of course, Clarabell the Clown played by Bob Keeshan, who later became Captain Kangaroo. Clarabell spoke no words, so his horn "honk" became well-known by all of the members of the "Peanut Gallery." Lasting many years, the *Howdy Doody Show* finally ended its long TV run, and on the last show, Clarabell finally spoke the words, "Goodbye, Kids!"

Many children's programs were built around the science-fiction theme. *Captain Video and His Video Rangers*, *Tom Corbett*, *Space Cadet*, and *Flash Gordon* were the more successful shows. Set in space, these programs used inexpensive costumes and sets, and kept the interest of young viewers day after day as they sat on the edge of their sofas.

The western drama, a form that interested both children and adults, came to television in 1949 with the adaptation of a radio series, which had produced close to 3,000 programs, called *The Lone Ranger*. With his faithful Indian companion, Tonto, at his side, the silver-bullet-firing, ex-lawman was to ride into and out of living rooms for the next eight years with a "Hi, ho, Silver, Away!"

The first attempt at TV network news was undertaken by NBC, CBS, and DuMont after the end of World War II. By 1948 Douglas Edwards was the anchorperson for CBS. One year later, NBC was airing the *Camel News Caravan* hosted by John Cameron Swayze. These programs were fifteen minutes in length and displayed news film footage as the anchor read the news.

On November 6, 1947, *Meet the Press*, the longest-running television show in broadcasting history began. It had started as a radio show in 1945 as *American Mercury Presents: Meet the Press*, originating from WRC-AM in Washington. Later, it was adapted for television by conservative magazine publisher Lawrence Spivak, who was a panelist and then its moderator until 1975.

By the end of the 1940s, black and white television was on its way to becoming the center of activity for the average American home. After the initial purchase of the family television set, the family could remain at home and be entertained nightly for only the cost of electricity to power the tube.

The Fifties

1950s were known as "The Golden Age of Television." During this period (1948 to 1956), the quality and range of live drama programs remains unsurpassed by any other period in television history. Leading the way in bringing the American stage into the new medium was *Playhouse 90*, followed closely by *Kraft Television Theater*, *The Ford Theater*, *Philco Television Playhouse*, *Goodyear Television Playhouse*, *NBC Television Playhouse*, *Studio One*, and *Actors Studio*.

One of the finest examples of "golden age" drama debuted on May 24, 1953. The program was NBC's *Philco Television Playhouse*; the teleplay was Paddy Chayefsky's acclaimed love story, "Marty." Rod Steiger played a lonely, middle-aged man trying to escape the controlling influence of a domineering mother. Nancy Marchand played the unattractive girl he meets at the Stardust Ballroom. Each character's liberation from desperately unhappy lives made this simple story an important dramatic triumph. The story was later made into a feature film, which won four Academy Awards.

Lucille Ball, Arthur Godfrey, Milton Berle, Imogene Coca, and Sid Caesar on the April 17, 1953 cover.

The variety shows, which dominated the early fifties, were always at the top of the "Most Watched" list. They drew heavily from vaudeville, with many of the actors having comedic, vaudeville experience. Shows like *Texaco Star Theatre*, *Your Show of Shows*, *The Colgate Comedy Hour*, *The Jackie Gleason Show*, *The Bob Hope Show*, and *The Ed Sullivan Show*, always topped the Nielsen ratings.

Ed Sullivan on the June 19, 1953 cover.

"Mr. Television" or "Uncle Miltie" owned Tuesday nights during the fifties. While *The Milton Berle Show* welcomed wacky skits and famous guests, Milton Berle remained the star attraction of the show. The wildly popular *Your Show of Shows* starring Sid Caesar and Imogene Coca gave many comic geniuses, including Woody Allen, Mel Brooks, Neil Simon and Carl Reiner, their start in the business.

In 1951, a new format of primetime television — the situation comedy — quickly became a staple in TV programming. One of the shows that started it all was called *I Love Lucy*, which starred Lucille Ball and her real-life husband Desi Arnaz. The duo played Lucy Ricardo and her bandleader husband, Ricky Ricardo, and they lived and worked in New York City. The series focused on Lucy's hilarious attempts at getting into show business by any means. The supporting cast featured Vivian Vance and William Frawley as the Ricardos' landlords and closest friends, Ethel and Fred Mertz. Lucille Ball made the transition to television gracefully, and *I Love Lucy* rose to the number one rated show in 1952. Going down in history as one of the medium's most successful television shows, *I Love Lucy* lasted ten years with Lucy always finding herself in an outlandishly funny situation.

NBC's *Today Show*, the first and longest-running morning network show, debuted in 1952 with host Dave Garroway and chimpanzee, J. Fred Muggs, as cohost. Two years later, Steve Allen was the first

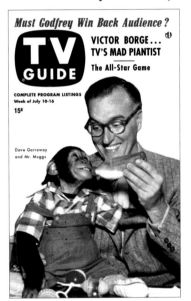

host on the *Tonight Show*, a music, comedy, talk program. From 1957-1962 Jack Paar firmly established the show's late-night audience, but he left the show suddenly after a network censor bleeped his use of the initials "WC" for "water closet" (meaning bathroom). He returned after two months but did finally leave the show two years later. Johnny Carson took over and for the next twenty years audiences were to hear Ed McMahon's introductory words, "Here's Johnny!"

The police drama *Dragnet* starring Jack Webb as Sergeant Joe Friday of the Los Angeles Police Department reached number two in the ratings in 1954. This series lasted eighteen years and made the phrase "Just the Facts, Ma'am" famous. It set the bar extremely high for police dramas that followed.

Appearing on a regular basis in December of 1952, *The Ernie Kovacs Show* pushed the visual medium of television to its limit. Many believed that Kovacs was one of the most innovative contributors in the early days of television and was often noted as being well ahead of his time.

Cohosts of *Today* on the July 10, 1953 cover.

Accompanied by his beautiful wife, Edie Adams, sponsored by Muriel cigars, and ably assisted by the three apes of the Nairobi Trio, Ernie Kovacs played such incredibly clever tricks with the medium that he was to have a profound influence on comedy shows that followed. Johnny Carson's Carnac the Magnificent was born from Kovacs' character "The Question Man," and *Laugh-In*'s sight gags carried on the tradition of Kovacs' visual cleverness. When Chevy Chase accepted his Emmy for his work on *Saturday Night Live*, he thanked Ernie Kovacs.

The Jackie Gleason Show starred Jackie Gleason as Ralph Kramden on "The Honeymooners," the most popular sketch on the program. Comedian Art Carney paired with Gleason and played the role of Ed Norton, one of New York's most popular sewer workers. This comedic duo, with wives played by Joyce Randolph and Audrey Meadows, created more uproariously funny problem situations from which they rarely emerged victorious.

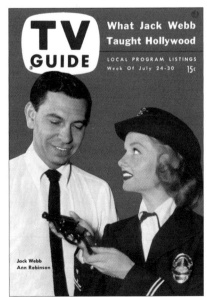

Jack Benny made his first television appearance in 1950, and slowly moved his popular radio show onto television. His well-known aversion to spending money, his intentionally bad violin playing, and his on-going celebration of his 39th birthday, entertained viewers for fifteen years. Benny's valet Eddie "Rochester" Anderson was one of the first African-American roles in primetime, and he often bested his employer with his wit. Other series regulars included Don Wilson, Mary Livingstone, and Dennis Day.

Jack Webb and Ann Robinson on the July 24, 1954 cover.

You Bet Your Life also moved from radio into television in 1950 and kept audiences laughing for over ten years. It was hosted by "the one, the only — Groucho!" Contestants found it hard to keep a straight face when answering questions by the always-clever Groucho Marx, supported by his

announcer, George Fenneman, and a bespectacled duck that would often drop down from above with $100 for anyone who said the pre-determined "secret word." The quiz part of the show was almost inconsequential compared with the big-money quiz shows of its day. It was Groucho's quick wit that created the hilarious banter with each pair of contestants — one usually being an attractive woman — and made the show one of the funniest on television.

Groucho Marx on the
March 19, 1954 cover.

The $64,000 Question, emceed by Hal March and sponsored by Revlon, was the first quiz show that offered unheard of cash prizes. On Tuesday nights practically everyone in America (the show had an 84.8% audience share) tuned in to CBS to see if contestants could answer eleven questions correctly in order to win the top prize. The enormous success of this program gave rise to *The $64,000 Challenge* from the same producers and *Twenty-One* produced by Dan Enright and hosted by Jack Barry. Popular university English professor, Charles Van Doren, admitted to being given answers to the questions, creating a scandal that rocked the whole television industry. After producers were found guilty of "fixing" the show, *Twenty-One* and all similar programs were quickly pulled from the air. This single event rippled across the country, causing Americans to lose confidence and trust in the television shows they watched. It was years before quiz shows could return to the medium.

Hal March on the
September 22, 1956 cover.

The Perry Como Show's warm atmosphere always welcomed singers and guests, while Art Linkletter launched his skit-based show, *People Are Funny*, and humiliated his guests by making them do outrageous things for the amusement of his audience, much like the prank shows *Jackass* and *Punk'd* of today.

The Nat King Cole Show debuted in November of 1956, but only lasted six months due to low ratings and failure of sponsors to keep the show on the air. Cole was the first African-American to star in a primetime network variety program. The NBC network kept the show on the air during the summer of 1957. However, the show was pulled by December 1957.

At the end of the decade, television was dominated by western programming. Top-rated shows included *Gunsmoke*, *Wagon Train*, *Have Gun Will Travel*, *The Rifleman*, *Wanted: Dead or Alive*, *Maverick* and *Tales of Wells Fargo*.

Late in 1959, CBS aired a sci-fi series that each week took the viewers on a trip to *The Twilight Zone*. Created by the inventive host, Rod Serling, *The Twilight Zone*'s "Fifth Dimension" allowed the sci-fi fans to travel through time and space. Presented in black and white, these weekly adventures lasted until 1964. Serling returned to television in 1970 with another sci-fi series called *Night Gallery*. The show, which aired from 1970 to 1973, was not as successful as the original series.

Politics came into living rooms with the 1952 Presidential campaign between retired General Dwight D. Eisenhower and former Illinois Governor Adlai Stevenson. And Eisenhower's Vice Presidential candidate Richard Nixon, who had been accused of taking political payoffs in the form of money and the gift of a dog named "Checkers," used television to convince voters that, "...the kids, like all kids, love the dog, and...regardless of what they say about it, we're gonna keep it."

Delivering the news on television came of age in 1954 with the televising of the Army-McCarthy hearings. Daily viewers could now see the Senator from Wisconsin attacking accused Communists in high places.

From *The Lone Ranger* to *The Rocky and Bullwinkle Show*, the fifties provided television entertainment that brought growing numbers of fans into the medium year after year. It was the depth of its drama, the inventiveness of its comedy, and the incredible demands of its live performances that secured television entertainment's influential position in impacting American culture.

The Sixties

At the start of the 1960s, there was a major change in the TV ratings process. More detailed and complete viewer information helped network vice-presidents of programming make more accurate predictions of what shows would be most successful during primetime viewing for each network. Network programming departments began to concentrate on the quantity of those viewers, rather than the quality of the shows.

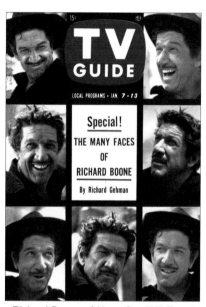

Richard Boone of *Have Gun Will Travel* on the January 7, 1961 cover.

The 1960s' programs continued with the popular western theme. *Gunsmoke*, starring James Arness, Amanda Blake, and Milburn Stone premiered on CBS in September of 1955 and would not complete its network run until September of 1975. Other popular westerns that appeared in the top ten programs throughout the 60s were *Wagon Train* (NBC), *Have Gun Will Travel* (CBS), *Rawhide* (CBS), and *Bonanza* (NBC).

As the decade began to unfold, network executives aimed primetime situation comedy programs at a younger viewing audience. *The Beverly Hillbillies* focused on a backwoods family that struck it rich in oil and moved to Hollywood, tasting the life of luxury with their new-found wealth. *The Dick Van Dyke Show*, costarring Mary Tyler Moore, charmed viewers with the depiction of an All-American family, while *The Andy Griffith Show* and *Green Acres* centered on old-fashioned, small town living. *Bewitched*'s Elizabeth Montgomery cast a spell over Americans with a twitch of her nose, and Jim Nabors comically portrayed life in the Marine Corps in *Gomer Pyle, USMC*. These shows along with others like *Hogan's Heroes*, *The Lucy Show*, *Family Affair*, and *Mayberry RFD* remained favorites with young viewers.

The cast of *The Beverly Hillbillies* on the November 10, 1962 cover.

Doctor programs proved to be very popular in the 60s. *Dr. Kildare*, starring Richard Chamberlain, began the tradition in 1961 on NBC, followed the next year by *Ben Casey* on ABC. At the end of the decade, Robert Young, as *Marcus Welby, M.D.*, began a long run as the star in one of the top-ten-watched television programs. Unfortunately, the events seen on television screens early in the decade were more emotionally stirring than a TV scriptwriter could ever imagine. The full extent of the medium's power was realized on Friday, November 22, 1963. First-hand reports from downtown

Dallas, Texas, interrupted afternoon programming with word that President John F. Kennedy had been shot. As the world watched, CBS anchor, Walter Cronkite, reported that at 2:00 pm. Eastern time, President Kennedy had died. All of the networks covered this terrible event, and the nation came to a stop. As the weekend unfolded, the nation saw the arrest of Lee Harvey Oswald, the finding of the alleged weapon, the location of the sniper at the time of the shooting, the plane returning to Washington D.C., and the preparations for J.F.K's funeral. On Sunday, November 24, the nation was again shocked as Jack Ruby murdered Lee Harvey Oswald on live television. A nation mourned as viewers witnessed John-John salute his father's casket. Later in the decade, television brought the tragedies of Martin Luther King's and Robert Kennedy's assassinations into living rooms as well.

The Fugitive, airing on ABC, was a fixture from 10 to 11 pm on Tuesday nights. The show starred David Janssen as Dr. Richard Kimble, who ran from police as he tracked a one-armed man for over four years. Its first episode aired September 17, 1963, and the final episode was August 29, 1967. The series started in black and white and ended in living color. And regarding the introduction of color to television, the premier of *Walt Disney's Wonderful World of Color* in September, 1961, was, perhaps, the single greatest influence in persuading consumers to go out and buy color television sets.

Cartoon characters spanned history — from the stone-aged *Flintstones* to the futuristic family in *The Jetsons*, and one studio, run by William Hanna and Joseph Barbera, was responsible for the majority of cartoon programming. *The Ruff and Reddy Show*, NBC-TV (1957-1960), was their first, and *The Huckleberry Hound Show*,

January 25, 1964 issue dedicated to 11/22 to 11/25/1963.

starring a dim-witted, hound dog with a Southern drawl was their next offering, and it was the first fully-animated series made specifically for television. *The Yogi Bear Show*, sponsored by Kellogg's cereals, spun off from *Huckleberry Hound* in 1961 and followed the quest for picnic baskets by the "smarter than the average bear" (not really) and his side-kick and conscience, Boo-Boo Bear. These popular cartoons stayed on the air for many years and are still enjoyed by young viewers of today on the Cartoon Network.

In 1962 a Chicago Cubs baseball game was viewed in Europe via satellite TV. Using Telstar, viewers half way around the world were able to see the "live" sports action from Wrigley Field in Chicago. As satellite television grew, immediate worldwide coverage of events was soon able to take place anytime, anywhere.

CBS debuted its news magazine, *60 Minutes*, in 1968 and by the end of the next decade it was ranked as one of the top five programs ever viewed on television. Along with *Cheers* and *All in the Family*, it has been the number one television program five times. The CBS news team put together by producer Don Hewitt consisted of Mike Wallace, Harry Reasoner, Morley Safer, Dan Rather, and Andy Rooney. The program featured television journalists doing in-depth coverage on news stories and issues; topics ranged from politics to the arts — any story with mass appeal, particularly where a cover-up needed to be uncovered.

Fred Flintstone on the
June 13, 1964 cover.

Following the dreams of President Kennedy, the "Race to Space" occupied the end of the decade, and America's space program moved forward rapidly. On July 20, 1969, Astronaut Neil Armstrong took the first human step from the ladder of the Eagle to the surface of the moon. Walter Cronkite reported the event as it transpired 230,000 miles from Earth. Man stepped onto the moon on television. Apollo XIII was more widely seen and the words, "Houston, we have a problem!" were clearly heard around the globe. Audiences focused nervously on their television sets as three Americans tried to return safely from space.

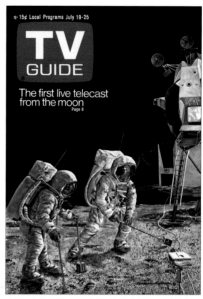

The July 19, 1969 "first live telecast from the moon" cover.

The Children's Television Workshop, a non-profit production company, produced a landmark program under the supervision of Joan Ganz Cooney in New York City on November 10, 1969. She engaged the talents of a young puppeteer named Jim Henson to "create a family of Muppet characters" who would join a group of human friends to populate *Sesame Street*. From this invitation were born Big Bird, Oscar, Ernie & Bert, Cookie Monster and many more endearing creatures. And so began the program's commitment to quality programming to educate — while entertaining — over 120 million children in over 130 countries around the world. *Sesame Street* was to become a true national treasure.

The 1960s reached its conclusion with expanding news coverage from the trenches of Vietnam. For the next five years, Americans were able to follow the Vietnam conflict from the safety of their homes via nightly news presentations.

The Seventies

Although the series began in the late 1960s, *Rowan and Martin's Laugh-In* was still a trendsetter in 1970s primetime television. This number one rated, fast-paced, slapstick comedy made waves in America with Goldie Hawn dancing in a bikini and psychedelic body paint, Arte Johnson tipping over on a tricycle, Ruth Buzzi swinging a mean pocket book, and Henry Gibson reciting poetry — all the madness held together by Dan Rowan and Dick Martin. John Wayne and President Richard M. Nixon were just a few of the show's famous guests. Also in the comedy-variety category was *The Flip Wilson Show* which was popular in the ratings from 1970 through 1974.

Dan Rowan and Dick Martin on the March 28, 1970 cover.

Flip's character, Geraldine Jones, uttered one of *TV Guide*'s Top Twenty Catchphrases: "The devil made me do it!" *The Sonny & Cher Comedy Hour* appeared as a summer replacement in 1971, thanks to the vision of CBS programming head, Fred Silverman, and became a ratings hit. The show always began with very funny, good-natured verbal sparring between the couple; unfortunately, their own personal break-up in 1974 caused the cancellation of this popular show.

In 1971 CBS took a huge risk and broadcast a new brand of irreverent satire called *All In The Family*, which starred Carroll O'Connor as the brash and bigoted Archie Bunker; Jean Stapleton as wife Edith; Sally Struthers as "daddy's little girl"; and Rob Reiner as the "meathead" son-in-law. By the 1972-1973 season, it was the most viewed show on television. Despite the controversy it raised, *All in the Family* continued to be the number one rated show until 1976. *Maude* starring Bea Arthur spun off in 1972 with her controversial, tell-it-like-it-is type of comedy that also offended some of its audience. *The Jeffersons*, another spin-off in 1975, featured Sherman Hemsley as

George Jefferson, wealthy owner of seven dry cleaning stores. This show enjoyed great popularity into the mid 80s. Other sitcoms exploring race relations were *Sanford and Son*, *Chico and The Man*, and *Good Times*.

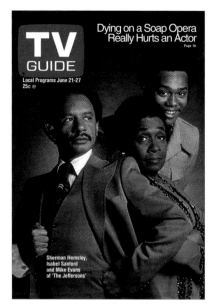

Cast members of *The Jeffersons* on the June 21, 1975 cover.

The "family drama" made a strong appearance in the early 70s with two, long-running shows that continued into the next decade; both were adapted from novels. *Little House on the Prairie* starring Michael Landon was based on the stories of Laura Ingalls Wilder, chronicling the saga of a loving family somewhere in the American West during the 1870s. Landon's wife was played by Karen Grassle and his three daughters were portrayed by Lindsay and Sidney Greenbush, Melissa Gilbert, and Melissa Sue Anderson. *The Waltons*, adapted by Earl Hamner, Jr. from his novel *Spencer's Mountain*, also profiled the close bonds of a family in rural Virginia facing adversity during the Depression. The show became so popular that in its first season, it received Emmy Awards for Outstanding Drama Series, Best Dramatic Actor (Richard Thomas) and Actress (Michael Learned), Best Supporting Actress (Ellen Corby) and Best Dramatic Writing (John McGreevey). Distinguished stage actor, Ralph Waite, played the father, John Walton, and talented character actor, Will Geer played Grandpa Walton.

Popular crime dramas which began in the 60s continued into this decade like *Hawaii Five-0*, *Mannix*, *Ironside*, and *Mod Squad*. New dramas created in the 70s included *Kojak*, *Adam 12*, *The Rookies*, *Police Woman*, and *The Rockford Files*. *The Streets of San Francisco*, starring Karl Malden and Michael Douglas in his first major acting role, was produced by Quinn Martin, who was responsible for such successful shows as *The Untouchables* (1959-1963), *The Fugitive* (1963-1967), *The F.B.I.* (1965-1974), *Cannon* (1971-1976), and *Barnaby Jones* (1972-1980). Less successful Quinn Martin series included Robert Lansing's *Twelve O'Clock High*, *Dan August* starring Burt Reynolds, and *Banyon* with Robert Forster in the title role.

Peter Falk on the May 5, 1973 cover.

Peter Falk created one of the longest-lasting TV characters in television history: the rumpled-raincoat-wearing Lieutenant Columbo. Writers Richard Levinson and William Link (*The Fugitive*, *Alfred Hitchcock Presents*) wrote a stage play entitled "Prescription: Murder," which was adapted into a TV movie in 1967 with Falk in the lead. In 1971 NBC approved a two-hour *Columbo* pilot ("Ransom for a Dead Man") and so began a series of 120 and 90 minute programs which was to last — off and on — for over thirty years. The first episode of the true series, "Murder by the Book," was directed by Steven Spielberg and written by Steven Bochco, who wrote five *Columbo* programs before he went on to produce *Hills Street Blues*.

The Brady Bunch, never a ratings winner but a pop culture classic, merged a mother with three daughters with a father with three sons, added a dog and a maid and though it only ran for five years, it will live forever in re-runs. Surprisingly, this show was the first to feature a married couple sharing a bed on television. *Three's Company*'s John Ritter, Suzanne Somers and Joyce DeWitt invited primetime viewers to come and knock on their door, while *Mork and Mindy* aptly showcased the early genius of Robin Williams.

Happy Days starred Ron Howard who returned to television after playing Opie in *The Andy Griffith Show* a decade-and-a-half earlier. Set in the fifties in Milwaukee, Wisconsin, the show centered on

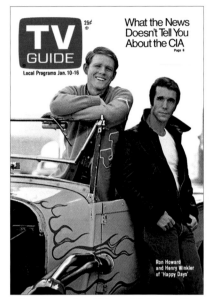

Ron Howard and Henry Winkler on the January 10, 1976 cover.

Richie Cunningham, his family and friends, and breakout star The Fonz (played by Henry Winkler); it quickly vaulted to the number one show in 1976. *Happy Days* became a powerful, popular series for ten seasons, and launched the equally successful spin-off, *Laverne and Shirley*, starring Penny Marshall and Cindy Williams.

The show that gave rise to three spin-offs was *The Mary Tyler Moore Show*, which ran from 1970-1977 and was produced by Mary and her then-husband Grant Tinker (MTM Enterprises). It also emphasized the changing role of the career woman in society who takes control of her own destiny. The action of the show was divided between the newsroom of WJM-TV, a mediocre Minneapolis TV station — thanks to the empty-headed news reading by Ted Knight's character Ted Baxter — and Mary Richard's apartment, where her at-home friends got the push into their own series: Valerie Harper's *Rhoda* and Cloris Leachman's *Phyllis* emerged. In the newsroom only Lou Grant, played by Ed Asner, went on to his own show. *Lou Grant*, however, was a major departure from its predecessor because it was a one hour drama featuring Asner as a serious journalist working as city editor for the "L.A. Tribune." The program tackled difficult social issues facing journalists in contemporary society and went on to win Emmy Awards in 1979 and 1980 as the outstanding drama series. MTM Enterprises continued to produce other hit shows like *Hill Street Blues*, *The Bob Newhart Show*, *St. Elsewhere*, and *WKRP in Cincinnati*.

Producer James L. Brooks and director James Burrows led a group of talented employees of MTM Enterprises into a new venture: a blue collar program set in the Sunshine Cab Company in New York City. Danny DeVito, Andy Kaufman, Judd Hirsch, Christopher Lloyd, Tony Danza and Marilu Henner kept *Taxi* running from 1978 to 1982 on ABC and from 1982-1983 on NBC.

The cast of *M*A*S*H* on the February 24, 1973 cover.

M*A*S*H, a show that took place at The Mobile Army Surgical Hospital unit 4077th, made an incredible impact on viewers; although in its first year (1972), it was almost cancelled. It took place at the front of the Korean conflict, lasting almost four times as long as the actual event. Humor was brought to a new level by the bizarre and hilarious antics of the cast, offering constant comic relief from the horror of the war that served as its backdrop. When the final episode aired on February 28, 1983, it was seen by 106 million viewers, and remains the highest rated episodic program ever.

The early 70s saw the initial season of what became an American mainstay for over thirty years: *ABC Monday Night Football*. The show's producer, Roone Arledge, worked with the National Football League to select a match-up of teams and present them live each week on network television. The first three announcers to cover the games were Howard Cosell, Keith Jackson, and former NFL player Don Meredith, referred to as "Dandy Don" by Cosell. The program first aired on September 21, 1970, with a game between the New York Jets and the Cleveland Browns. Beginning with the 2006 season, *Monday Night Football* will air on ESPN.

The 1978 fall season of new programs presented viewers with television's first night-time soap opera.

Dallas was set in South Fork Ranch outside of Dallas, Texas, and centered on the Ewing clan, detailing their struggles with family, finance, vendettas and romantic situations on a weekly basis. At the conclusion of the 1979-1980 season, the star of the series, J.R. Ewing, portrayed by Larry Hagman, had been shot. For the entire summer of 1980, everyone was asking "Who Shot J.R.?" There were several endings filmed, each with a different shooter. On November 21, 1980, Kristin Shepard (played by Mary Crosby) was revealed as the shooter. The ratings skyrocketed and soon J.R. recovered. This series remained on television until 1991.

Mary Crosby, Larry Hagman, and Linda Gray on the March 8, 1980 cover.

The outstanding series of the decade was the highly acclaimed miniseries *Roots.* Broadcast first for eight days in January of 1977, and again in 1978, the series traced the roots of Alex Haley from Africa in the 1750s to his great-great grandson in Tennessee. The enormous scope of the series was a first for primetime television. *Roots* had a profound effect on future primetime series, as well as the evolution of the mini-series into the next decade.

No discussion of television in the 70s would be complete without discussing the daring experiment in live television conceived and developed by Dick Ebersol, Director of Late Night Programming at NBC, and Producer Lorne Michaels. *Saturday Night Live* first aired on October 11, 1975. The first guest host was comedian, George Carlin. The original cast — the "not ready for prime time players" — consisted of Chevy Chase (1975-1976), John Belushi (1975-1979), Dan Aykroyd (1975-1979), Garrett Morris (1975-1980), Jane Curtin (1975-1980), Laraine Newman (1975-1980), and Gilda Radner (1975-1980). Bill Murray, Paul Shaffer, Eddie Murphy, Joe Piscopo, Julia Louis-Dreyfus, Damon Wayans, Joan Cusack, Robert Downey Jr., Dennis Miller, Phil Hartman, Jon Lovitz, Mike Myers, David Spade, Chris Farley, Adam Sandler, Chris Rock, Rob Schneider, Will Ferrell, and Norm MacDonald (to name a few) got their starts on *SNL.* The show was irreverent, politically incorrect, inventive, and generally outrageous. It brought viewers back to television's roots of live comedy, and placed enormous stress upon its writers and performers. This weekly tension sometimes elevated the show's skits to the level of comedy classics — sometimes not. Chevy Chase left the show for Hollywood after one year and was replaced by Bill Murray. The original cast, along with Murray and Lorne Michaels, left the show by the end of the 1979-1980 season, and *SNL* was to struggle to stay funny and to keep its audience until Michaels returned to produce the show again in 1985. With the possible exception of how *Sesame Street* has continued to impact its audience, no other show in the history of television has had such an effect on its viewers and on popular culture as has *Saturday Night Live.*

The cast of *Saturday Night Live* on the July 29, 1978 cover.

The 70s brought television to new heights. The decade's sitcoms, nighttime dramas, news programs, sports, and comedy/variety shows raised the bar significantly for entertaining audiences in the years to come.

The Eighties

The 1980s began with at least one television set in 98 percent of all American homes. The average amount of time that the television was turned on exceeded six hours per day, with many of the

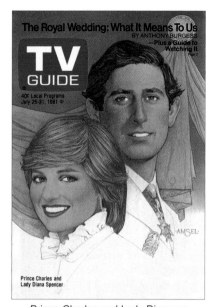

Prince Charles and Lady Diana on the July 25, 1981 cover.

evening hours filled with nighttime soap operas. The formats of daytime soap operas had been transposed to primetime television. Shows featuring love, tension, deceit, manipulation, murder and scandal kept viewers glued to the screen week after week. *Dallas*, *Knot's Landing*, *Dynasty*, and *Falcon Crest* were all overwhelmingly popular.

President Ronald W. Reagan took the oath of office on the 20th of January in 1981. As he completed the oath of office, the American hostages from the takeover of the American Embassy 444 days earlier were released. The news was captured by television cameras as the hostages made their way home back to the United States.

After reporting the news of the day for decades, Walter Cronkite, one of the most trusted icons of American television, retired from his CBS anchor desk. During the summer of 1981, Diana Spencer married the most eligible bachelor in England, Prince Charles Phillip Arthur George Windsor of Wales. Known

from that point on as Princess Diana, "the people's princess" quickly surpassed her husband as one of the most popular people in the world. Not able to escape the lenses of the army of photographers wherever she traveled — a cruel twist of fate that eventually led to her demise — Princess Diana ruled the television waves here in America like no other British royal.

Bill Cosby and Phylicia Ayers-Allen on the September 7, 1985 cover.

In March of 1981, President Ronald Reagan was nearly killed after being shot by John Hinkley on the streets of Washington, D.C. The videotape was shown over and over for careful analysis. For the next several days, television coverage focused solely on the recovering president. Reagan returned to the White House, and the news machine moved on.

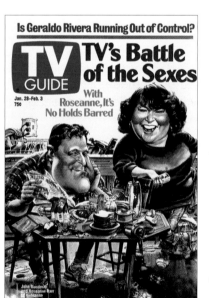

John Goodman and Roseanne Barr on the January 28, 1989 cover.

One of the most popular hit shows of the eighties was *The Cosby Show* (running from 1984-1992) starring none other than Bill Cosby as Dr. Cliff Huxtable. Set in a fashionable section of Flatbush (Brooklyn), this long-running series details the daily life of a well-to-do African-American family. This wonderful staple of eighties television focused on a strong father figure who instilled strong family values and morals. Other family-based sitcoms of the eighties included *Family Ties*, *Married With Children*, *ALF*, *Who's The Boss?*, and *Full House*.

In contrast to the loving, functional family situation created in *The Cosby Show*, we see the exact opposite in *Roseanne*. Beginning in 1988, Roseanne Barr made the transition from doing stand-up comedy to playing the title character with her trademark cynicism. John Goodman played her husband, Dan Conner. The show's popularity was instant. Like *All In The Family* and *The Honeymooners*, *Roseanne* captured the essence of day-to-day problem solving by average working people, but this time it was done with comic sarcasm. When her kids had left for school, she would often shout, "Quick! Change the locks." The series lasted almost a decade and was in the top five rated programs each year.

On September 30, 1982, television viewers who tuned in to NBC at 9 pm Eastern time saw the first episode in what was to become a long-running hit series: *Cheers*. Set in Boston at a neighborhood bar, *Cheers* had a colorful cast of characters, including Sam "MayDay" Malone (Ted Danson), Diane (Shelley Long), Carla (Rhea Perlman), Norm (George Wendt), Cliff (John Ratzenberger) and Coach (Nicholas Colasanto) and quickly won the hearts of viewers. For eleven seasons the antics and situations at *Cheers* entertained millions of fans. Joining the original cast was Woody Harrelson as bartender Woody Boyd, Kirstie Alley playing Rebecca Howe, Bebe Neuwirth as Dr. Lilith Sternin and, finally, Kelsey Grammer as Dr. Frasier Crane. Grammer went on to reprise the role of Frasier Crane in the *Cheers* spin-off, *Frasier*, and played the character of Frasier for 20 consecutive years, a record for an American, non-soap opera actor. Despite its debut episode finishing dead last in the Nielsen ratings, the series went on to become an overwhelming success.

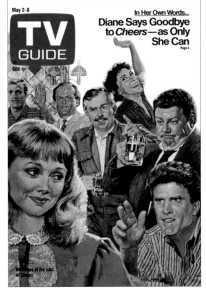

The cast of *Cheers* on the
May 2, 1987 cover.

In 1985 promoter Vince McMahon, aided by gladiators like Hulk Hogan and Rowdy Roddy Piper, transformed pro wrestling, under the banner of the World Wrestling Federation (WWF), from regional syndication to national fascination. McMahon's idea was to position wrestling as more entertainment than sport, and his ground breaking event "WrestleMania" was first held at Madison Square Garden on March 31, 1985. The program was offered through cable stations on a pay-per-view basis, thus launching pro wrestling on television as an enterprise more profitable than ever before.

Another daring undertaking, but this time at the network level, was the introduction of a cable outlet offering music-related material aimed at adolescents and young adults. The MTV network was founded on August 1, 1981. MTV's combination of music videos, music industry news, profiles of performers, promotion of rock concerts, and youth-focused commentaries and criticisms established MTV as a driving force in pop culture. It did on a large scale what Dick Clark's *American Bandstand* had done at the program level for almost thirty years.

Other popular shows in the eighties included *Alice*, *Charlie's Angels*, *Newhart*, *Diff'rent Strokes*, *The Facts of Life*, *Moonlighting*, *MacGyver*, *Miami Vice*, *The Love Boat*, *Knight Rider*, *The A-Team*, *Dukes of Hazzard*, *Magnum P.I.*, *Cagney and Lacey*, and *Murder, She Wrote*. Although these programs and other top shows of the 80s were entertaining, it is difficult to single many out as radical, pioneering, or truly original as many were in previous decades.

Television in the eighties featured people who might live next door to the viewer. The family, mostly functional, was brought to center stage. A "safe" approach to primetime shows proved to be a successful strategy in the ratings game, something that had become increasingly important to the networks.

The Nineties

The world changed politically as the decade began. The movement for democracy in the Soviet Union had been initiated in the late 1980s. The world watched as the Eastern blocks of former Communist countries began to experience democracy and freedom for the first time. From our television sets, we were able to watch as the Berlin Wall crumbled before our very eyes.

Congress passed the Children's Television Entertainment Act of 1990, which required that networks reduce the amount of commercials played during programs viewed by American children. This meant that there would be fewer interruptions during Saturday morning cartoon fare that the major television networks had been airing since the 1950s.

Primetime programming still offered the sitcoms that were successfully bringing in large rating numbers. The problem now faced by the original networks was cable television. Cable had grown from its early years when it was known as "community antenna television" and simply offered television to rural residents who lived in mountainous regions of the country. By the 1990s over fifty percent of the country was now wired for cable television. Television watching choices for any hour of any day were in the hundreds, if not thousands. Re-runs of older network primetime shows, home shopping, sci-fi, sports, weather, news, and new movies now could be selected by the cable subscriber.

The September 28, 1991 cover — one of *TV Guide*'s yearly Parents' Guides.

The Gulf War television coverage was live and showed war at its worst. Fortunately, the war was over quickly and TV could return its focus to lighter fare.

Aaron Spelling, who is now regarded as one of the most prolific producers in the history of television, created many memorable dramas of the seventies and eighties, including *Starsky and Hutch*, *Charlie's Angels*, *Fantasy Island*, *The Love Boat*, *Hart to Hart*, *Dynasty*, and *T.J. Hooker*. He put his mark on the nineties with the popular television shows *Beverly Hills 90210*, which spanned the decade and *Melrose Place*, which spun off in 1992 and ran through 1999.

1992 saw a first in presidential debates. It was to be a three-way debate as the major independent candidate Ross Perot was involved. The results were reported in November of 1992 and Governor William Jefferson Clinton was elected President.

Luke Perry and Jason Priestly on the December 14, 1991 cover.

Cable television continued to grow. News was broadcast on a 24 hour a day, 7 days a week basis. Music channels provided a constant stream of the latest videos produced by pop, rock, rap, and country performers. Sci-fi, comedy, religion, cooking, shopping-at-home, classic television, foreign language, and sports were all available with only several clicks of the remote control. The choices seemed limitless. While events of the world were being broadcast live, the cable channels continued with the hourly grind of their specialized entertainment.

The nineties also saw the conclusion of *Cheers* and the beginning of *Seinfeld*. This new concept of a sitcom — a carefully scripted show about nothing — became the most watched series in 1994. Jerry Seinfeld, Julia Louis-Dreyfus, Jason Alexander, and Michael Richards, four friends living, working, and surviving in New York City, provided humor on a new level. Popular episodes of *Seinfeld* included "The

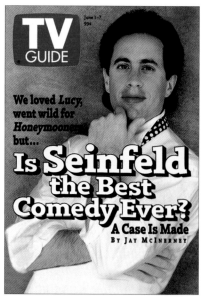

Jerry Seinfeld on the June 1, 1996 cover.

Bubble Boy," "The Soup Nazi," and "The Puffy Shirt." One very relevant episode (No. 71) even focused on George Costanza's father, Frank (played by Jerry Stiller), collecting *TV Guide* magazines.

Everyone's favorite friends kicked off in 1994, making Ross, Rachel, Monica, Chandler and Joey household names. *Friends* had a long list of mega-stars appearing as guest stars, including Julia Roberts, Tom Selleck, Sean Penn, Bruce Willis, and Brad Pitt. *Friends* and *Seinfeld* also gave rise to the multi-million dollar paychecks for the actors.

The Simpsons on the March 17, 1990 cover.

Although the first show aired on December 17, 1989, the decade of the nineties and beyond belongs to one of the most popular television show of all-time, *The Simpsons*. Creator Matt Groening examines a mostly dysfunctional nuclear family living in the fictional town of Springfield. The show is drawn using the extremes of satire, irony, and parody; it is at once outrageous and heartwarming, politically scathing and insanely vulgar. In a word it is brilliant. There are so many jokes and sight gags packed into one program that it takes many viewings to catch all the subtleties within the broad comedy. The success of the series lies in the characters: Homer is lazy, dim, and incompetent at just about everything he does including his job as safety inspector at a nuclear power plant run by the Scrooge-like Mr. Burns. Marge, Homer's faithful wife has tall, blue hair. Maggie, the youngest, doesn't speak, and Lisa is the smartest person in her class at school, and, possibly in all of Springfield. But the role of the incomparable anti-hero, the greatest of underachievers, belongs to Bart Simpson, the perpetual prankster who is clever enough to know right from wrong, but prefers wrong. Other notable Springfield characters include Krusty the Clown, Mayor Quimby, Apu Nahasapeemapetilon, and Moe Szyslak. So popular is this series that celebrities welcome the opportunity to provide voices for the characters. Elizabeth Taylor spoke Maggie's only words, and Prime Minister Tony Blair even added his voice to one show. It appears that there will always be a *Simpsons*.

The retirement of a legend and the undisputed king of late-night took place when Johnny Carson announced that he was leaving *The Tonight Show*. The final show, Thursday, May 21, 1992, was one of remembering the humor he had so carefully given audiences for over thirty years. There were tears shed as Bette Midler closed the show by singing, "One for the Road." Johnny's last words to his audience were as follows: "And so it has come to this. I am one of the lucky people in the world. I found something that I always wanted to do and I have enjoyed every single minute of it. I bid you a very heartfelt goodnight."

Daytime television took a back seat to the "trial of the decade," when O.J. Simpson was charged with the murder of his former wife. Television covered the entire sequence of events from arrest to acquittal and *TV Guide* put O.J. Simpson on the cover for a second time on July 30, 1994.

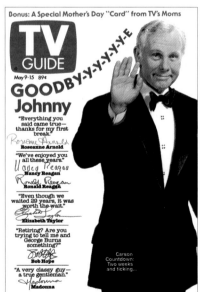

Johnny Carson on the May 9, 1992 cover.

Another political saga was broadcast live to America with the impeachment hearings presented against President Bill Clinton. Testimony after testimony was heard and seen as the weeks passed. After all the words and pictures, the impeachment failed to get the necessary vote in the U.S. Senate. And, sadly, just as the world viewed Princess Diana's royal wedding on TV, it viewed her funeral as well.

Everybody Loves Raymond starring Ray Romano, with Patricia Heaton as his wife, started its long run mid-decade, but it didn't make it into the top 10 programs until 1999. The rest of the talented cast included Doris Roberts and Peter Boyle as Raymond's parents and Brad Garrett as his brother. The great comic tension comes about because Raymond's parents and brother live across the street and constantly intrude into his life.

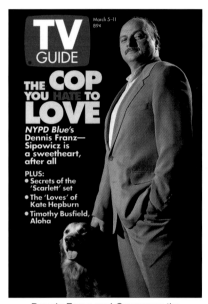

Dennis Franz and Caesar on the March 5, 1994 cover.

Perhaps, the most daring show of the decade was Steven Bochco's gritty *NYPD Blue*. Before the show began a warning message appeared on the screen that "viewer discretion is advised" because of strong language and nudity. In fact, many ABC stations refused to carry the program initially. However, the program's popularity was almost immediate. The cast changed over the seasons with the exception of the enduring Detective (later Sergeant) Andy Sipowicz played by Dennis Franz. David Caruso started in the series but left to pursue a movie career. Sharon Lawrence, Jimmy Smits, Rick Schroder, Esai Morales, and Nicholas Turturro (to name just a few) all contributed admirably to the program.

Several other television series began in the 1990s that had long broadcast runs. Among these were *Home Improvement*, *The X-Files*, *Frasier*, the medical drama *ER*, and the crime drama *Law & Order*. All of these endured the ratings wars, providing comedy and drama to millions of viewers.

Reality TV began with programs like *Candid Camera* in the 50s; *America's Funniest Home Videos* was its grandchild in the 90s. In the former, the producers set up potentially comic situations which would make unsuspecting subjects look ridiculous. The latter allowed people to send in videos of ridiculous situations of their own making. PBS captured real interpersonal drama in its 70s series, *An American Family*. It profiled the Loud family over a period of seven months culminating in the divorce of the mother and father. *The Real World,* which debuted in 1992, is widely recognized as the first reality show of its kind. Seven young people from all over the country, each with distinctly different personalities, moved into a New York apartment to subject themselves to the constant scrutiny of TV cameras, and so began a new genre of television programming which did not require actors or scriptwriters.

The 90s ended with the introduction of a cable program (HBO) dominating all other dramas on television. *The Sopranos* starring James Gandolfini as Tony Soprano, a "waste management consultant" who has problems with both of his families, was a break-out hit. Edie Falco plays his wife and Lorraine Bracco his therapist. The writing was exceptional and the supporting cast, particularly on Tony's "business" side, was superb.

The 20th Century ended with few problems of computers crashing, electrical power failing, and other dire predictions by Y2K doomsday forecasters. A new era of television began in the 21st Century. Viewers then were anxious to see what was to entertain in the next millennium.

The cast of *The Sopranos* on the January 8, 2000 foldout cover.

The 2000s

What started with *The Real World* continued in force in the year 2000. Reality shows permeated primetime. Audiences loved them, and producers loved them even more because there were no

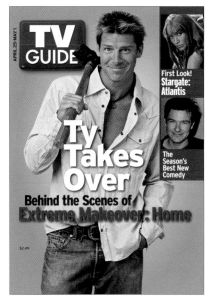

scripts and no actors. Many successful television programs do not make any profits for the production companies until after the series goes into syndication because of the high production costs, particularly actors' salaries. For example, in the final seasons of *Friends* each of the stars received $1,000,000 per episode. Setting up races and competitions and videotaping the results costs significantly less, so this type of program can show an immediate profit. ABC put plastic surgeons to work starting in 2002 to change the looks and the lives of the individuals it chose for an *Extreme Makeover*. The producers gave the show itself a new life with *Extreme Makeover: Home Edition* in 2004. *The Amazing Race*, *Survivor*, *American Idol*, *The Apprentice*, and *Big Brother* are all examples of this popular phenomenon.

Ty Pennington on
the April 25, 2004 cover.

On October 6, 2000, *CSI* premiered on CBS and introduced a compelling new twist on the crime drama format, the "procedural", which proceeded to dominate the Nielsen ratings. *CSI* inspired a small army of other cop-show procedurals, including its own tropical spin-off *CSI: Miami* and a Big Apple version, *CSI: NY*. *CSI* was the first crime drama in the history of television to be ranked No. 1 for the season, finishing first three times. The series focuses on Las Vegas criminologists who use scientific methods to solve grisly murders, and stars William Petersen as Gil Grissom and Marg Helgenberger as Catherine Willows. Other popular procedurals in the early 2000s included *Cold Case*, *NCIS*, *Without a Trace*, and *Numb3rs*, all of which aired on CBS.

In 2002, Trekkies celebrated the 35th anniversary of *Star Trek*, and were thrilled to see thirty-five different *Star Trek* covers on *TV Guide*. Each of the *Star Trek* series was presented with the major stars and villains on the covers. The original series continues to live in syndication on the cable television channels.

Cable TV's contribution to comedy at the beginning of the new century was *Curb Your Enthusiasm*. Larry David, who was responsible for producing *Seinfeld*, created and starred in this extremely clever series about a fictioinalized version of himself. The highly successful show has won both Emmys and Golden Globe awards. A very funny network comedy program, although it was adapted from a British comedy show of the same name, is *The Office*, which premiered in 2005. Steve Carell, formerly of *The Daily Show*, plays an annoying boss who offends just about every one of his employees with his ignorance and insensitivity. The result is hilarious.

William Petersen and Marg Helgenberger
on the February 23, 2002 cover.

The primetime soap *Desperate Housewives* became a mega hit for ABC in 2004. The darkly comic view of suburban unrest on Wisteria Lane provides steamy viewing during each episode. The highly competitive female members of the cast consisting of Teri Hatcher, Felicity Huffman, Marcia Cross, Nicollette Sheridan, and Eva Longoria greatly add to the enormous interest in the show.

One of the hottest new shows on the planet began in 2004 and airs on Wednesday nights on ABC. *Lost* has taken the collective breath of the nation as we watch the 48 survivors of a plane crash struggle each week for survival. Bloggers compete with theories about the mystical nature of the show's events, an official magazine has emerged, a huge fan club has formed, and conventions of avid followers are spreading across the country. The show's creators, J. J. Abrams who produced

Cast members of *Lost* on the
August 28, 2005 cover.

Alias and Damon Lindelof who developed *Party of Five*, have bound together a band of relatively unknown actors, with the possible exceptions of Matthew Fox as Dr. Jack Shepherd and Terry O'Quinn as John Locke, who will most likely survive on this mysterious island for many years to come. Newcomer Evangeline Lilly as Kate and heartthrob Josh Holloway as Sawyer are standouts.

With the enormous strides made in technology, television is changing rapidly. The seemingly continuous avalanche of technological advances has given viewers increasing control over when, where and how they can view their favorite programs. Digital video recorders such as TiVo permit the pausing of programs or saving them for later viewing. Huge plasma TV sets allow the audience to view shows in home theater environments and make the words "small screen" inappropriate. When it comes to truly small screens, cell phones and portable video playback devices such as the video iPod allow people to take shows with them and watch wherever and whenever they want. Broadband internet connections make video much easier to download and view on computer screens. As 2006 began, all the major networks announced partnerships that will make selections of their programs available for viewing on many more devices beyond traditional television sets.

To deal with these changes, *TV Guide* magazine chose a new way of maintaining its responsibility to television viewers and to the medium itself, by re-launching in its new large-size format in October 2005. The new *TV Guide* magazine provides the most comprehensive coverage about television for the modern consumer, providing in-depth feature coverage of popular television programs along with high-quality reviews and recommendations. TV Guide adds valuable and entertaining insight, and thoughtful information about shows, characters and trends in the television landscape.

Today's TV Guide has kept up with the changing television times by expanding beyond the magazine and offering TV Guide brand products that reach consumers on their computers, through their cable or satellite set-top boxes, and through their TiVo, digital recorder or television set, all with one simple goal in mind — to simplify and enhance viewers' television watching experience. From TV Guide Channel and TV Guide Spot to TVGuide.com, TV Guide Interactive and TV Guide On Screen, TV Guide provides information and insight where viewers need it, in the manner that most appeals to them.

The brand that has always been the authority on all things television now goes beyond what's on, to guide viewers to what's hot, what's new, and what's best.

TV GUIDE The Fifties

"There may be a place for pay-as-you-see television, but if it comes we'd like to see it as *part* of television – not as the whole darned thing."
TV Guide, As We See It
October 1, 1955

"Lassie can act with her rear end."
Lassie's Cloris Leachman
March 1, 1958

"I think I'm getting better. At least I haven't been getting any more letters telling me to get off my own program."
Ed Sullivan
January 22, 1955

"It's time somebody told the public what those of us in the business already know: The award gimmick has gotten badly out of hand and not one award in 50 is really of serious value."
Steve Allen
July 6, 1957

1953

April 03 1953
Desiderio Alberto Arnaz IV
and Lucille Ball of
I Love Lucy

April 10 1953
Jack Webb of
Dragnet

April 17 1953
Lucille Ball, Arthur Godfrey,
Milton Berle, Imogene Coca,
and Sid Caesar

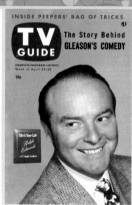

April 24 1953
Ralph Edwards of
This Is Your Life

May 01 1953
Eve Arden of
Our Miss Brooks

May 08 1953
Arthur Godfrey of
Arthur Godfrey and His Friends

May 15 1953
David Nelson and
Ricky Nelson of
Ozzie and Harriet

May 22 1953
Red Buttons of
The Red Buttons Show

May 29 1953
Queen Elizabeth II – How You'll
See Elizabeth Crowned

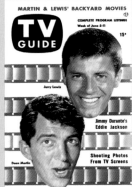

June 05 1953
Jerry Lewis and Dean Martin –
Martin & Lewis Backyard Movies

June 12 1953
Eddie Fisher of
Coke Time

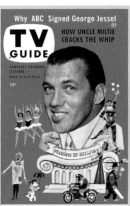

June 19 1953
Ed Sullivan of
The Ed Sullivan Show

June 26 1953
Dinah Shore of
The Dinah Shore Show

July 03 1953
Perry Como of
The Perry Como Show

Lucille Ball and Desi Arnaz incorporated the birth of their second child, Desi Jr., into their show *I Love Lucy*. The series began in 1951 and in 1957 the duo switched to *The Lucy-Desi Comedy Hour*. After the demise of that series, they divorced. Desi Arnaz died on 12/2/1986 and Lucille Ball died on 4/26/1989.

July 10 1953
Dave Garroway and
Mr. Muggs of
Today

July 17 1953
Lucille Ball and
Desi Arnaz of
I Love Lucy

July 24 1953
Groucho Marx of
You Bet Your Life

July 31 1953
Max Liebman, Sid Caesar,
and Imogene Coca of
Your Show of Shows

August 07 1953
Ray Milland of
The Ray Milland Show

August 14 1953
Patti Page of
The Scott Music Hall

August 21 1953
Mary Hartline and
Claude Kirchner of
Super Circus

August 28 1953
Jayne Meadows of *I've Got a
Secret* and Audrey Meadows of
The Jackie Gleason Show

September 04 1953
Marion Lorne and
Wally Cox of
Mr. Peepers

September 11 1953
Joan Caulfield and
Ralph Edwards of
This Is Your Life

September 18 1953
Fall Preview:
1953-1954 Shows

September 25 1953
George Reeves of
Superman

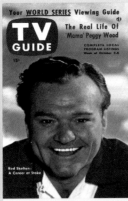

October 02 1953
Red Skelton of
The Red Skelton Show

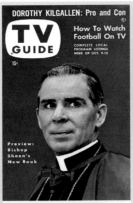

October 09 1953
Bishop Fulton J. Sheen of
Life Is Worth Living

October 16 1953
1953 T-Venus Winners

October 23 1953
Arthur Godfrey of
Arthur Godfrey and His Friends

October 30 1953
Buelah the Witch, Kukla,
and Ollie of
Kukla, Fran, and Ollie

November 06 1953
Warren Hull of
Strike It Rich

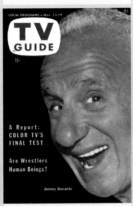

November 13 1953
Jimmy Durante

November 20 1953
Dorothy McGuire and
Julius La Rosa of
Arthur Godfrey and His Friends

November 27 1953
Lugene Sanders of
The Life of Riley

December 04 1953
Loretta Young of
The Loretta Young Show

December 11 1953
Jack Webb of
Dragnet

December 18 1953
Bob Hope: On The Run

December 25 1953
Perry Como, Patti Page
and Eddie Fisher

1954

January 01 1954
Bing Crosby – Why Bing Crosby
Is Turning To TV

Arthur Godfrey joined CBS Radio in 1945 and hosted *Arthur Godfrey's Talent Scouts* which began to broadcast on radio and television simultaneously in 1948 until 1958. From 1949 to 1959, he also hosted a daily variety show. He was inducted into the Radio Hall of Fame in 1988. Arthur Godfrey died on 3/16/1983.

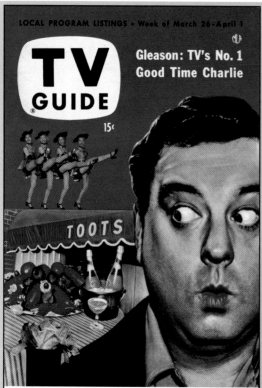

LOCAL PROGRAM LISTINGS • Week of March 26–April 1

TV GUIDE 15¢

Gleason: TV's No. 1 Good Time Charlie

TOOTS

Jackie Gleason was a TV staple in the 50's. His show, *The Honeymooners,* began as a sketch segment on variety shows (most notably *The Jackie Gleason Show*) and only had one season of half-hour shows in 1955. Jackie Gleason died on 6/24/1987 from cancer.

January 08 1954
Joan Caulfield of
My Favorite Husband

January 15 1954
Martha Raye of
The Martha Raye Show

January 22 1954
Jayne Meadows, Henry Morgan,
and Joan Bennett of
I've Got a Secret

January 29 1954
Robert Montgomery of
Robert Montgomery Presents

February 05 1954
Jack Benny of
The Jack Benny Program

February 12 1954
Red Buttons of
The Red Buttons Show

February 19 1954
Ann Sothern of
Private Secretary

February 26 1954
Liberace of
The Liberace Show

March 05 1954
Marion Marlowe and
Frank Parker of
Arthur Godfrey and His Friends

March 12 1954
Maria Riva

March 19 1954
Groucho Marx of
You Bet Your Life

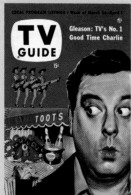

March 26 1954
Jackie Gleason of
The Jackie Gleason Show

April 02 1954
Eve Arden of
Our Miss Brooks

April 09 1954
Charlie Applewhite and
Milton Berle of
The Milton Berle Show

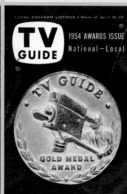

April 16 1954
1954 Awards Issue

April 23 1954
Lucille Ball of
I Love Lucy

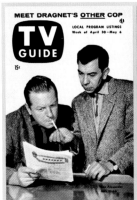

April 30 1954
Ben Alexander
and Jack Webb of
Dragnet

May 07 1954
Harriet Nelson, Ricky Nelson,
and David Nelson of
Ozzie and Harriet

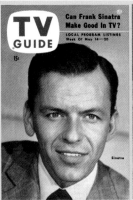

May 14 1954
Frank Sinatra – Can
Frank Make Good In TV?

May 21 1954
Patricia Benoit and
Wally Cox of
Mr. Peepers

May 28 1954
Gale Storm of
My Little Margie

June 04 1954
Arthur Godfrey – What Is
Godfrey's Hold On Women?

June 11 1954
Ben Blue and
Alan Young of
The Saturday Night Revue

June 18 1954
Rise Stevens and
Ed Sullivan of
The Ed Sullivan Show

June 25 1954
Bob Smith and
Howdy Doody of
Howdy Doody

July 02 1954
Joan Davis and
Jim Backus of
I Married Joan

July 09 1954
Arlene Francis of
What's My Line?

July 17 1954
Roy Rogers of
The Roy Rogers Show

July 24 1954
Jack Webb and
Ann Robinson of
Dragnet

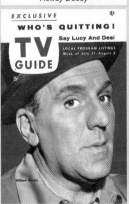

July 31 1954
William Bendix of
Life of Riley

August 07 1954
Perry Como of
The Perry Como Show
and Friends

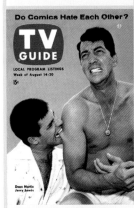

August 14 1954
Jerry Lewis and Dean Martin –
Do Comics Hate Each Other?

August 21 1954
Jayne Meadows of *I've Got
a Secret* and Steve Allen of
The Steve Allen Show

August 28 1954
Roxanne of
Beat the Clock

September 04 1954
Eddie Fisher of
Coke Time

September 11 1954
Betty Hutton of
Satins and Spurs

September 18 1954
Liberace of
The Liberace Show

September 25 1954
Fall Preview:
1954-1955 Shows

October 02 1954
Teresa Wright and
Dick Powell of
Climax!'s *The Long Goodbye*

October 09 1954
Lucille Ball of
I Love Lucy

October 16 1954
Red Buttons of
The Red Buttons Show

October 23 1954
Walt Disney of
Disneyland

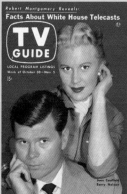

October 30 1954
Barry Nelson and
Joan Caulfield of
My Favorite Husband

November 06 1954
Gracie Allen and
George Burns of
The Burns and Allen Show

November 13 1954
Joanne Rio and
Liberace of
The Liberace Show

November 20 1954
Bebe Daniels and
Ralph Edwards of
This Is Your Life

November 27 1954
Peter Lawford and
Marcia Henderson of
Dear Phoebe

December 04 1954
George Gobel of
The George Gobel Show

December 11 1954
Marion Marlowe of
Arthur Godfrey and His Friends

December 18 1954
Imogene Coca of
The Imogene Coca Show

December 25 1954
The Nelson Family of
Ozzie and Harriet

1955

January 01 1955
Loretta Young of
The Loretta Young Show

January 08 1955
Arthur Godfrey – Why Godfrey
Doesn't Quit

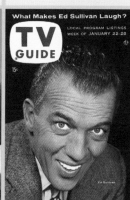

January 15 1955
Bill Cullen, Jayne Meadows, Henry
Morgan, Faye Emerson, and Garry
Moore of *I've Got a Secret*

January 22 1955
Ed Sullivan of
The Ed Sullivan Show

How Gleason Got Berle's Job

TV GUIDE
LOCAL PROGRAM LISTINGS
WEEK OF JAN. 29 - FEB. 4
15¢

January 29 1955
Martha Raye of
The Martha Raye Show

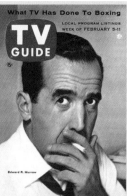

What TV Has Done To Boxing

TV GUIDE
LOCAL PROGRAM LISTINGS
WEEK OF FEBRUARY 5-11
15¢

February 05 1955
Edward R. Murrow of
Person to Person

The Eisenhowers And Television

TV GUIDE
LOCAL PROGRAM LISTINGS
WEEK OF FEBRUARY 12-18
15¢

February 12 1955
Snooky Lanson, Dorothy Collins,
Russell Arms, and Gisele
MacKenzie of *Your Hit Parade*

LOCAL PROGRAM LISTINGS • WEEK OF FEBRUARY 19-25

TV GUIDE
Round-The-World TV:
Around The Corner?
15¢

February 19 1955
Sid Caesar of
Caesar's Hour's

Custard Pie Famine Hits TV

TV GUIDE
LOCAL PROGRAM LISTINGS
WEEK OF FEB. 26-MARCH 4
15¢

February 26 1955
Steve Allen and
Judy Holliday of
Goodyear Playhouse

A LESSON IN LIVING
How Liberace Faced Greatest Challenge

TV GUIDE
LOCAL PROGRAM LISTINGS
WEEK OF MARCH 5-11
15¢

March 05 1955
Liberace of
The Liberace Show

How YOU Control TV Programs

TV GUIDE
LOCAL PROGRAM LISTINGS
WEEK OF MARCH 12-18
15¢

March 12 1955
Dinah Shore of
The Dinah Shore Show

The Chordettes: 'Who's Mr. Godfrey?'

TV GUIDE
LOCAL PROGRAM LISTINGS
WEEK OF MARCH 19-25
15¢

March 19 1955
Art Carney of
The Honeymooners

Your Program For The Oscar Awards

TV GUIDE
LOCAL PROGRAM LISTINGS
WEEK OF MAR 26-APRIL 1
15¢

March 26 1955
Gale Gordon and
Eve Arden of
Our Miss Brooks

LOCAL PROGRAM LISTINGS • WEEK OF APRIL 2-8

TV GUIDE
How Television
Aids The F.B.I.
15¢

April 02 1955
Tony Martin of
The Tony Martin Show

Batter Up! TV Baseball Picture in '55

TV GUIDE
LOCAL PROGRAM LISTINGS
WEEK OF APRIL 9-15
15¢

April 09 1955
Gloria Marshall and
Bob Cummings of
The Bob Cummings Show

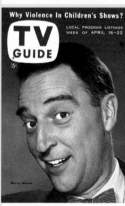

Why Violence In Children's Shows?

TV GUIDE
LOCAL PROGRAM LISTINGS
WEEK OF APRIL 16-22
15¢

April 16 1955
Garry Moore of
The Garry Moore Show

Frank Parker: A Phony Romance Ends

TV GUIDE
LOCAL PROGRAM LISTINGS
WEEK OF APRIL 23-29
15¢

April 23 1955
Gale Storm of
My Little Margie

Our Readers Pick Their Favorite Shows

TV GUIDE
LOCAL PROGRAM LISTINGS
WEEK OF APRIL 30-MAY 6
15¢

April 30 1955
Buddy Ebsen and
Fess Parker of
Disneyland's Davy Crockett

IS THIS THE END FOR GODFREY?
See Page 3

TV GUIDE
LOCAL PROGRAM LISTINGS
WEEK OF MAY 7-13
15¢

May 07 1955
Robin Morgan and
Peggy Wood of
Mama

How Perry Como Found Peace Of Mind

TV GUIDE
LOCAL PROGRAM LISTINGS
WEEK OF MAY 14-20
15¢

May 14 1955
Perry Como of
The Perry Como Show

Kefauver: 'Reduce Crime On TV!'
...See Page 10

TV GUIDE
LOCAL PROGRAM LISTINGS
WEEK OF MAY 21-27
15¢

May 21 1955
Audrey Meadows and
Jackie Gleason of
The Honeymooners

What Becomes Of Ralph Edwards' Guests?

TV GUIDE
LOCAL PROGRAM LISTINGS
WEEK OF MAY 28-JUNE 3
15¢

May 28 1955
Ralph Edwards of
This Is Your Life

The McGuire Sisters That Godfrey Built

TV GUIDE
LOCAL PROGRAM LISTINGS
WEEK OF JUNE 4-10
15¢

June 04 1955
Eddie Fisher of
Coke Time

Meet The Other Liberace

TV GUIDE
LOCAL PROGRAM LISTINGS
WEEK OF JUNE 11-17
15¢

June 11 1955
Gail Davis of
Annie Oakley

The Truth About Those Fan Clubs

LOCAL PROGRAM LISTINGS
WEEK OF JUNE 18–24

15¢

June 18 1955
Danny Thomas of
Make Room for Daddy

SPECIAL SUMMER PREVIEW ISSUE

LOCAL PROGRAM LISTINGS • WEEK OF JUNE 25–JULY 1

June 25 1955
Barbara Nichols, Sid Caesar,
and Cliff Norton of
One-Nighter

Guess Who's The Boss Of Your TV Set !

LOCAL PROGRAM LISTINGS
WEEK OF JULY 2–8

15¢

July 02 1955
Tommy Rettig and Lassie of *Lassie*
with Lee Aaker and Rin Tin Tin of
Rin Tin Tin

The Cop And The $64,000 Question

LOCAL PROGRAM LISTINGS
WEEK OF JULY 9–15

15¢

July 09 1955
Patti Page of
The Patti Page Show

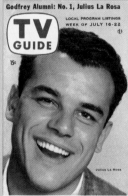

Godfrey Alumni: No. 1, Julius La Rosa

LOCAL PROGRAM LISTINGS
WEEK OF JULY 16–22

15¢

July 16 1955
Julius La Rosa of
The Julius La Rosa Show

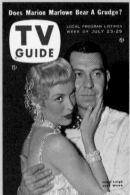

Does Marion Marlowe Bear A Grudge?

LOCAL PROGRAM LISTINGS
WEEK OF JULY 23–29

15¢

July 23 1955
Janet Leigh and
Jack Webb of
Pete Kelly's Blues

What The Mariners Think Of Godfrey

LOCAL PROGRAM LISTINGS
WEEK OF JULY 30–AUG. 5

15¢

July 30 1955
Lucille Ball and Desi Arnaz with
Barbara and Margaret Whiting of
Those Whiting Girls

Story Behind Davy Crockett's Pal

LOCAL PROGRAM LISTINGS
WEEK OF AUGUST 6–12

August 06 1955
Art Linkletter of
House Party and Friend

All Of A Sudden—Movies Love TV

LOCAL PROGRAM LISTINGS
WEEK OF AUGUST 13–19

15¢

August 13 1955
Roxanne and
Bud Collyer of
Beat the Clock

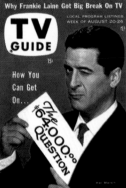

Why Frankie Laine Got Big Break On TV

LOCAL PROGRAM LISTINGS
WEEK OF AUGUST 20–26

15¢

August 20 1955
Hal March of
The $64,000 Question

Country Music Invades Television

See Page 10

LOCAL PROGRAM LISTINGS
WEEK OF AUG. 27–SEPT. 2

15¢

August 27 1955
Groucho Marx of
You Bet Your Life

Miss America's Final Fling On TV

LOCAL PROGRAM LISTINGS
WEEK OF SEPTEMBER 3–9

15¢

September 03 1955
Jody and Johnny Carson of
The Johnny Carson Show

THE TRUTH BEHIND:
Godfrey's Feud With The Press

LOCAL PROGRAM LISTINGS
WEEK OF SEPTEMBER 10–16

15¢

September 10 1955
Arthur Godfrey of
Arthur Godfrey and His Friends

Godfrey And The Reporters: Round 2
— See Page 13

LOCAL PROGRAM LISTINGS
WEEK OF SEPTEMBER 17–23

15¢

September 17 1955
Milton Berle and
Esther Williams of
The Milton Berle Show

SPECIAL ISSUE

LOCAL PROGRAM LISTINGS
WEEK OF SEPT. 24–30

15¢

FALL PREVIEW
1955-56 SHOWS

September 24 1955
Fall Preview:
1955-1956 Shows

Scientists Explain Gleason's 'Pow In Kisser'

LOCAL PROGRAM LISTINGS
WEEK OF OCTOBER 1–7

15¢

October 01 1955
Mickey Mouse of
The Mickey Mouse Club

Country Music Invades Television

See Page 10

LOCAL PROGRAM LISTINGS
WEEK OF AUG. 27–SEPT. 2

TV GUIDE

15¢

GROUCHO'S GUESTS

Groucho Marx

The **Marx Brothers** made their first film in 1921. A silent short called *Humor Risk*, it was never released and all copies were destroyed by the Marxes. In 1950, **Groucho** moved his radio show, *You Bet Your Life*, to TV where it ran until 1961. He authored many books before his death from pneumonia on 8/19/1977.

October 08 1955
George Burns and
Gracie Allen of
The Burns and Allen Show

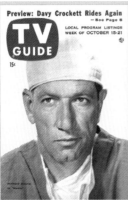

October 15 1955
Richard Boone of
Medic

October 22 1955
Peggy King and
George Gobel of
The George Gobel Show

October 29 1955
Phil Silvers of
You'll Never Get Rich

November 05 1955
Nanette Fabray of
Caesar's Hour

November 12 1955
Liberace of
The Liberace Show

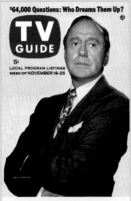

November 19 1955
Jack Benny of
The Jack Benny Program

November 26 1955
Martha Raye of
The Martha Raye Show

The Mickey Mouse Club premiered on October 1, 1955 and quickly became a children's favorite. It reappeared in 1977 as *The New Mickey Mouse Club* and in 1989 as *MMC*. It has launched the careers of many celebrities. **Mickey Mouse**, created by **Walt Disney**, appeared in the first sound cartoon in 1928.

December 03 1955
Mary Healy and
Peter Lind Hayes of
The Peter Lind Hayes Show

December 10 1955
Lucille Ball of
I Love Lucy

December 17 1955
Robert Montgomery of
Robert Montgomery Presents

December 24 1955
Merry Christmas

December 31 1955
Cleo of
The People's Choice

1956

January 07 1956
Arthur Godfrey of
Arthur Godfrey and His Friends
and Goldie

January 14 1956
Loretta Young of
The Loretta Young Show

Lawrence Welk: TV's Newest Sensation

January 21 1956
Lawrence Welk of
The Lawrence Welk Show

The Secrets Behind Those Commercials!

January 28 1956
Janis Paige of
It's Always Jan

Better Than Ever – New Movies For TV!

February 04 1956
Judy Tyler of *Howdy Doody*
and Ed Sullivan of
The Ed Sullivan Show

Top Stars In TV's Biggest Slugfest

February 11 1956
Perry Como of
The Perry Como Show

How TV Can Improve Your Bowling

February 18 1956
Jimmy Durante of
The Jimmy Durante Show

Phil Silvers' Army: Our Secret Weakness

February 25 1956
Gisele MacKenzie of
Your Hit Parade

An Intimate Glimpse Of Lawrence Welk

March 03 1956
Lynn Dollar and
Hal March of
The $64,000 Question

How La Rosa Shields His Romance

March 10 1956
Frances Rafferty and
Spring Byington of
December Bride

Programs For Emmy And Oscar Awards

HOW NOT TO GET ON
'$64,000 QUESTION'

March 17 1956
Maurice Evans and Lilli Palmer in
*Hallmark Hall of Fame's
Taming of the Shrew*

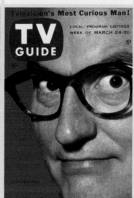

Television's Most Curious Man!

March 24 1956
Dave Garroway of
Today

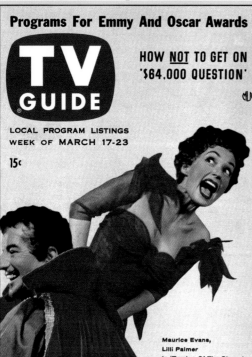

Programs For Emmy And Oscar Awards

HOW **NOT** TO GET ON
'$64.000 QUESTION'

LOCAL PROGRAM LISTINGS
WEEK OF MARCH 17-23

15¢

Maurice Evans,
Lilli Palmer
In 'Taming Of The Shrew'

Hallmark Hall of Fame premiered on Christmas Eve
in 1951 and since then has attracted more big screen
stars than almost any other show. In its 50+ years of
quality programming, with presentations like *The
Taming of the Shrew* and *Dial M for Murder*, it has won
over 100 awards including four Humanitas Prizes.

Godfrey's New Friends—Humility Galore

March 31 1956
Arlene Francis and
John Daly of
What's My Line?

The Amazing Story
Of 'Grand Ole Opry'

April 07 1956
Jayne Meadows, Garry Moore,
and Faye Emerson of
I've Got a Secret

Baseball: More Games For You On TV

April 14 1956
Grace Kelly: TV Invites You
To Her Wedding

April 21 1956
Nanette Fabray of
Caesar's Hour

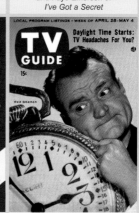

Daylight Time Starts:
TV Headaches For You?

April 28 1956
Red Skelton of
The Red Skelton Show

Dr. Spock: Your Child And Television

May 05 1956
George Gobel and
Mitzi Gaynor of
The George Gobel Show

May 12 1956
Bernadette O'Farrell and
Richard Green of
The Adventures of Robin Hood

May 19 1956
Phil Silvers and
Elisabeth Fraser of
The Phil Silvers Show

May 26 1956
Alice Lon and
Lawrence Welk of
The Lawrence Welk Show

June 02 1956
Sid Caesar and
Janet Blair of
Caesar's Hour

June 09 1956
Patti Page of
The Patti Page Show

June 16 1956
Elinor Donahue, Robert Young,
Lauren Chapin, and Billy Gray of
Father Knows Best

June 23 1956
Steve Allen of
The Steve Allen Show

June 30 1956
Bob Cummings of
Love That Bob!

July 07 1956
Lassie

July 14 1956
Gordon and Sheila MacRae of
The Gordon MacRae Show

July 21 1956
Bill Lundigan and
Mary Costa of
Climax!

July 28 1956
Gail Davis of
Annie Oakley

August 04 1956
Jackie Cooper and Cleo of
The People's Choice

August 11 1956
Democratic Convention

August 18 1956
GOP Convention

August 25 1956
Esther Williams

September 01 1956
Alice Lon of
The Lawrence Welk Show

September 08 1956
Elvis Presley – The Plain Truth
About Elvis Presley

September 15 1956
Fall Preview:
1956-1957 Shows

September 22 1956
Hal March of
The $64,000 Question

September 29 1956
Jackie Gleason of
The Honeymooners

October 06 1956
Gale Storm of
Oh! Susanna

October 13 1956
The Nelson Family of
Ozzie and Harriet

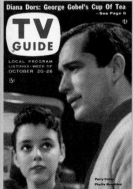

October 20 1956
Phyllis Goodwind and
Perry Como of
The Perry Como Show

October 27 1956
Alfred Hitchcock of
Alfred Hitchcock Presents

November 03 1956
Edward R. Murrow of
Person to Person

November 10 1956
Loretta Young of
The Loretta Young Show

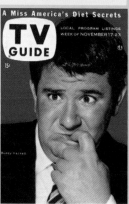

November 17 1956
Buddy Hackett of
Stanley

November 24 1956
Nanette Fabray of
High Button Shoes

December 01 1956
Gracie Allen and
George Burns of
The Burns and Allen Show

December 08 1956
Victor Borge of
The Victor Borge Show

December 15 1956
Dinah Shore of
The Dinah Shore Chevy Show

December 22 1956
Merry Christmas

December 29 1956
Jeannie Carson of
Hey, Jeannie

1957

January 05 1957
Arthur Godfrey of
Arthur Godfrey and His Friends

January 12 1957
Lucille Ball of
I Love Lucy

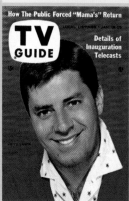

January 19 1957
Jerry Lewis of
The Jerry Lewis Show

January 26 1957
Bob Hope

February 02 1957
Jane Wyman of
Jane Wyman Theater

February 09 1957
Hugh O'Brian of
Wyatt Earp

February 16 1957
Jane Wyatt and
Robert Young of
Father Knows Best

February 23 1957
Charles Van Doren of
Twenty-One

March 02 1957
Dorothy Collins and
Gisele MacKenzie of
Your Hit Parade

March 09 1957
Arthur Godfrey and
Pat Boone of
Arthur Godfrey and His Friends

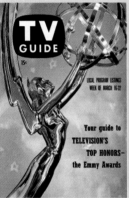

March 16 1957
Your Guide To Television's
Top Honors –
The Emmy Awards

March 23 1957
Ernie Ford of
The Ford Show

March 30 1957
Julie Andrews in
Rodgers and Hammerstein's
Cinderella

The first game show was *Truth or Consequences* which debuted on 7/1/1941. The FCC declared the date to be Day One of American commercial television. **Herb Stempel**, a contestant on *Twenty-One*, is responsible for revealing that the quiz show was fixed when he was forced to lose to **Charles Van Doren**.

April 06 1957
Lawrence Welk of
The Lawrence Welk Show

April 13 1957
Nanette Fabray of
Salute to Baseball

April 20 1957
Loretta Young of
The Loretta Young Show

April 27 1957
Groucho Marx of
You Bet Your Life

May 04 1957
Hal March and
Robert Strom of
The $64,000 Question

May 11 1957
James Arness of
Gunsmoke

May 18 1957
Esther Williams of
Lux Video Theatre

May 25 1957
Sid Caesar of
Casesar's Hour

June 01 1957
Ida Lupino and
Howard Duff of
Mr. Adams and Eve

June 08 1957
Lassie

June 15 1957
Red Skelton of
The Red Skelton Show

June 22 1957
Jack Bailey of
Queen for a Day

June 29 1957
Gale Storm of
Oh! Susanna

July 06 1957
Dorothy Kilgallen, Bennett Cerf,
Arlene Francis, and John Daly of
What's My Line?

July 13 1957
Gail Davis of
Annie Oakley

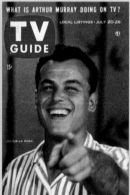

July 20 1957
Julius La Rosa of
The Julius La Rosa Show

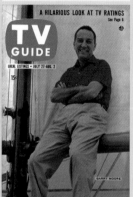

July 27 1957
Garry Moore of
I've Got A Secret

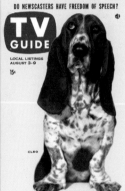

August 03 1957
Cleo of
The People's Choice

August 10 1957
Ann B. Davis and
Bob Cummings of
Love That Bob!

August 17 1957
Phil Silvers of
The Phil Silvers Show

August 24 1957
Marjorie Lord and
Danny Thomas of
The Danny Thomas Show

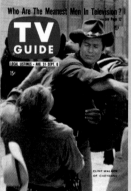

August 31 1957
Clint Walker of
Cheyenne

September 07 1957
Janette Davis and
Arthur Godfrey of
Arthur Godfrey and His Friends

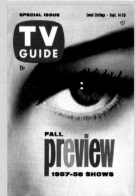

September 14 1957
Fall Preview:
1957-1958 Shows

September 21 1957
Pat Boone of
The Pat Boone Show

September 28 1957
Gracie Allen and
George Burns of
The Burns and Allen Show

October 05 1957
Joan Caulfield of
Sally

October 12 1957
This Is The Week To Watch

THE FACTS ABOUT
GUNSMOKE'S 'CHESTER'

Local Listings · January 25-31

Sid Caesar,
Imogene Coca:
Together Again

Sid Caesar began performing as a saxophonist. During World War II, he was assigned to a Coast Guard musician post where producer **Max Liebman** overheard him joking with the band. Thus began his long career as a comedian. He starred in numerous TV shows and appeared in many films and plays.

October 19 1957
Loretta Young of
The Loretta Young Show

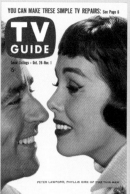

October 26 1957
Peter Lawford and
Phyllis Kirk of
The Thin Man

November 02 1957
Lucille Ball of
I Love Lucy

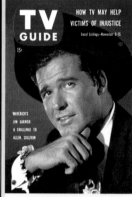

November 09 1957
James Garner of
Maverick

November 16 1957
Patti Page of
The Patti Page Show

November 23 1957
Mary Martin in
Annie Get Your Gun

November 30 1957
Alfred Hitchcock of
Alfred Hitchcock Presents

December 07 1957
Dinah Shore of
The Dinah Shore Show

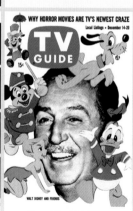

December 14 1957
Walt Disney of
Disneyland

December 21 1957
Greetings

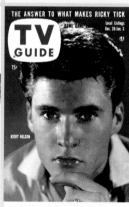

December 28 1957
Ricky Nelson of
Ozzie and Harriet

1958

January 04 1958
Lawrence Welk of
The Lawrence Welk Show

January 11 1958
Gisele MacKenzie of
Your Hit Parade

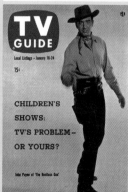

January 18 1958
John Payne of
The Restless Gun

January 25 1958
Sid Caesar and
Imogene Coca of
Sid Caesar Invites You

February 01 1958
Walter Winchell of
The Walter Winchell File

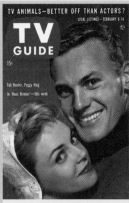

February 08 1958
Peggy King and Tab Hunter in
*Hallmark Hall of Fame's
Hans Brinker*

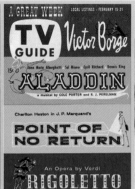

February 15 1958
A Great Week

February 22 1958
Rosemary Clooney of
The Rosemary Clooney Show

March 01 1958
Lassie

March 08 1958
Arthur Godfrey of
Arthur Godfrey and His Friends

March 15 1958
Amanda Blake and
James Arness of
Gunsmoke

March 22 1958
Perry Como of
The Perry Como Show

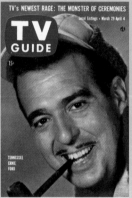

March 29 1958
Tennessee Ernie Ford of
The Ford Show

April 05 1958
Gale Storm of
The Gale Storm Show

April 12 1958
Hugh O'Brian of
Wyatt Earp

April 19 1958
Polly Bergen of
The Polly Bergen Show

April 26 1958
Guy Williams of
Zorro

May 03 1958
Shirley Temple of
Shirley Temple Theatre

May 10 1958
Richard Boone of
Have Gun, Will Travel

May 17 1958
Danny Thomas of
The Danny Thomas Show

May 24 1958
Dick Clark of
American Bandstand

May 31 1958
Phyllis Kirk of
The Thin Man

June 07 1958
Pat Boone of
The Pat Boone Show

June 14 1958
Jane Wyatt and
Robert Young of
Father Knows Best

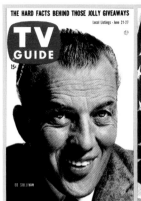

June 21 1958
Ed Sullivan of
The Ed Sullivan Show

June 28 1958
Jerry Mathers of
Leave It to Beaver

July 05 1958
Bill Cullen of
The Price Is Right

July 12 1958
Lucille Ball of
The Lucy-Desi Comedy Hour

July 19 1958
Dale Robertson of
Wells Fargo

July 26 1958
Paula Raymond and
Marvin Miller of
The Millionaire

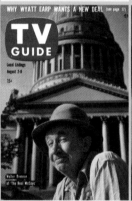

August 02 1958
Walter Brennan of
The Real McCoys

August 09 1958
Steve Lawrence and Eydie Gorme
of *The Steve Lawrence and Eydie
Gorme Show*

August 16 1958
Robert Horton and
Ward Bond of
Wagon Train

August 23 1958
Edie Adams and
Janet Blair of
The Chevy Show

August 30 1958
Bud Collyer, Polly Bergen,
and Kitty Carlisle of
To Tell the Truth

September 06 1958
Arthur Godfrey of
Arthur Godfrey and His Friends

September 13 1958
Kathy, Dianne, Peggy, and Janet
Lennon, and Lawrence Welk of
The Lawrence Welk Show

September 20 1958
Fall Preview
1958-1959 Shows

September 27 1958
Garry Moore of
I've Got a Secret

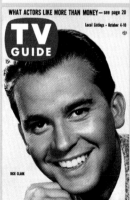

October 04 1958
Dick Clark of
American Bandstand

October 11 1958
Barrie Chase and
Fred Astaire of
An Evening with Fred Astaire

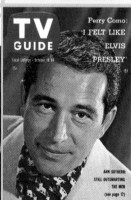

October 18 1958
Perry Como of
The Perry Como Show

October 25 1958
George Burns of
The George Burns Show

November 01 1958
Jack Paar of
The Jack Paar Show

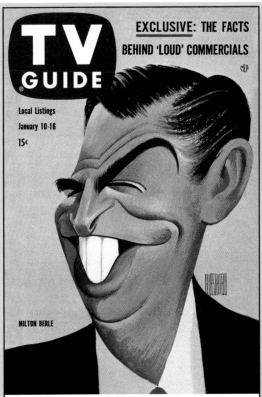

EXCLUSIVE: THE FACTS BEHIND 'LOUD' COMMERCIALS

Local Listings January 10-16

15¢

MILTON BERLE

Milton Berle (aka "Uncle Miltie" and "Mr. Television") made his first television appearance on an experimental broadcast in 1929. Along with appearing in many TV shows and films, he authored three books - two autobiographies and a compilation of jokes he collected over his 80 year career. He died on 3/27/2002.

November 08 1958
Loretta Young of
The Loretta Young Show

November 15 1958
Warner Anderson and
Tom Tully of
The Lineup

November 22 1958
Ronald and Nancy Reagan in
*General Electric Theater's A
Turkey for the President*

November 29 1958
Victor Borge of
Comedy and Music

December 06 1958
James Arness of
Gunsmoke

December 13 1958
Danny Thomas of
The Danny Thomas Show

December 20 1958
Special Holiday Issue

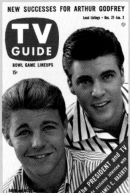

December 27 1958
David Nelson and
Ricky Nelson of
Ozzie and Harriet

1959

January 03 1959
Lola Albright and
Craig Stevens of
Peter Gunn

January 10 1959
Milton Berle of
The Milton Berle Show

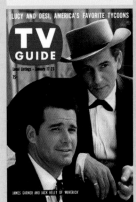

January 17 1959
James Garner and
Jack Kelly of
Maverick

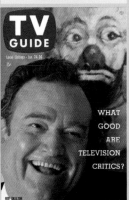

January 24 1959
Red Skelton of
The Red Skelton Show

January 31 1959
George Gobel of
The George Gobel Show

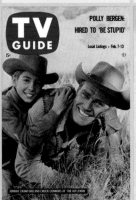

February 07 1959
Johnny Crawford and
Chuck Connors of
The Rifleman

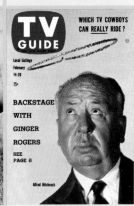

February 14 1959
Alfred Hitchcock of
Alfred Hitchcock Presents

February 21 1959
Barbara Hale and
Raymond Burr of
Perry Mason

February 28 1959
Richard Boone of
Have Gun, Will Travel

March 07 1959
Walter Brennan of
The Real McCoys

March 14 1959
Arthur Godfrey of
Arthur Godfrey and His Friends

March 21 1959
Ann Sothern of
The Ann Sothern Show

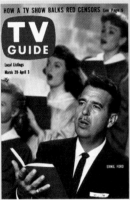

March 28 1959
Ernie Ford of
The Ford Show

April 04 1959
Efrem Zimbalist Jr. and
Roger Smith of
77 Sunset Strip

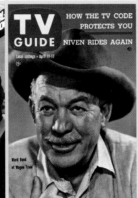

April 11 1959
Ward Bond of
Wagon Train

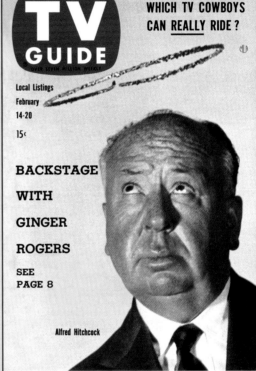

Alfred Hitchcock's first job in film was as a title
designer at the Paramount-Lasky Studios in London.
He directed his first American movie, *Rebecca*, in
1940 and his last was *Family Plot* in 1976. He started
Alfred Hitchcock Presents in 1955, the same year he
became a U.S. Citizen. He died on 4/28/1980.

April 18 1959
Dinah Shore of
The Dinah Shore Show

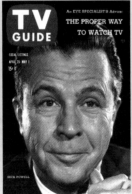

April 25 1959
Dick Powell

May 02 1959
Hugh O'Brian of
Wyatt Earp

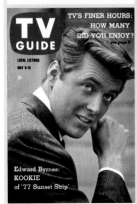

May 09 1959
Edward Byrnes of
77 Sunset Strip

May 16 1959
Loretta Young of
The Loretta Young Show

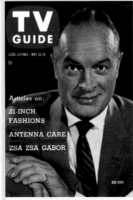

May 23 1959
Bob Hope

May 30 1959
Steve McQueen of
Wanted: Dead or Alive

June 06 1959
Gale Storm of
Oh! Susanna

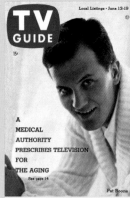

June 13 1959
Pat Boone of
The Pat Boone Show

June 20 1959
Robert Young and
Lauren Chapin of
Father Knows Best

June 27 1959
Lloyd Bridges of
Sea Hunt

July 04 1959
Jon Provost and Lassie of
Lassie

July 11 1959
Lola Albright and
Craig Stevens of
Peter Gunn

July 18 1959
Janet Blair of
The Blair and Raitt Show

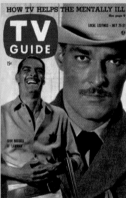

July 25 1959
John Russell of
Lawman

August 01 1959
Dave Garroway of
Today

August 08 1959
Donna Reed of
The Donna Reed Show

August 15 1959
Lawrence Welk of
The Lawrence Welk Show

August 22 1959
Bess Myerson, Henry Morgan,
Betsy Palmer, and Bill Cullen of
I've Got A Secret

August 29 1959
Dick Clark of
American Bandstand

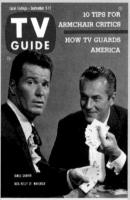

September 05 1959
James Garner and
Jack Kelly of
Maverick

September 12 1959
Arthur Godfrey of
Arthur Godfrey and His Friends

September 19 1959
Fall Preview:
1959-1960 Shows

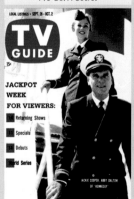

September 26 1959
Abby Dalton and
Jackie Cooper of
Hennessey

October 03 1959
June Allyson of
The June Allyson Show

October 10 1959
Robert Taylor of
The Detectives

October 17 1959
Ingrid Bergman in
The Turn of the Screw

October 24 1959
Jay North of
Dennis the Menace

October 31 1959
Fred Astaire and
Barrie Chase of
Astaire Time

November 07 1959
Jack Benny of
The Jack Benny Program

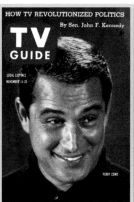

November 14 1959
Perry Como of
The Perry Como Show

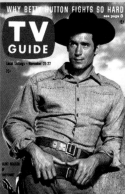

November 21 1959
Clint Walker of
Cheyenne

November 28 1959
Art Carney: Special This Week

December 05 1959
Dwayne Hickman, Gayle Polayes,
and Joan Chandler of
Dobie Gillis

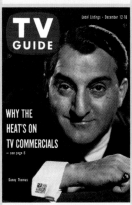

December 12 1959
Danny Thomas of
The Danny Thomas Show

December 19 1959
Merry Christmas

December 26 1959
Loretta Young of
The Loretta Young Show

"One of these days, Alice, one of these days... bang... zoom…to the moon." Ralph Kramden, *The Honeymooners*

Memorable TV Show Quotes from the 1950s

"When another comedian has a lousy show, I'm the first one to admit it."
Jack Benny, *The Jack Benny Program*

"We've been framed. Never trust animated people." Pokey, *The Gumby Show*

"Gifts are symbols that say 'I love you', and you returned Daddy's love to a department store." Mary Stone, *The Donna Reed Show*

"Ever since we said 'I do', there have been so many things that we don't."
Lucy Ricardo, *I Love Lucy*

"I don't have anything against education – as long as it doesn't interfere with your thinking!"
Ben Cartwright, *Bonanza*

"You see, to be a straight man you have to have a talent, you have to develop this talent, then you gotta marry her like I did."
George Burns, *The George Burns and Gracie Allen Show*

Ricky Ricardo: "I'm terrible at remembering names."
Tallulah Bankhead: "Oh, so am I. That's why I call everybody 'darling.'"
The Lucy-Desi Comedy Hour

Mouseketeers: "Now it's time to say goodbye to all our company, M-I-C..."
Jimmie: "See you real soon."
Mouseketeers: "K-E-Y..."
Jimmie: "Why? Because we like you!"
Mouseketeers: "M-O-U-S-E!"
The Mickey Mouse Club

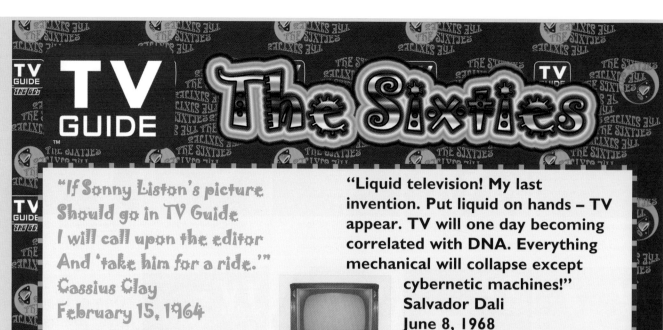

TV GUIDE — The Sixties

"If Sonny Liston's picture
Should go in TV Guide
I will call upon the editor
And 'take him for a ride.'"
Cassius Clay
February 15, 1964

"IF THIS SERIES GOES FIVE YEARS, I WILL BE 33 AND RICH. THEN I CAN STOP AND DO SOMETHING I'D ENJOY MORE. I WANT TO BE A SCHOOLTEACHER."
I SPY'S BILL COSBY
OCTOBER 23, 1965

"Liquid television! My last invention. Put liquid on hands – TV appear. TV will one day becoming correlated with DNA. Everything mechanical will collapse except cybernetic machines!"
Salvador Dali
June 8, 1968

"Emma Peel isn't fully emancipated. Steed pats me from time to time like a good horse."
The Avengers' Diana Rigg
January 21, 1967

1960

January 02 1960
James Arness, Amanda Blake, Dennis Weaver, and Milburn Stone of *Gunsmoke*

January 09 1960
Jane Wyatt and Elinor Donahue of *Father Knows Best*

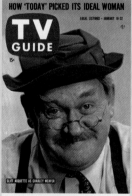

January 16 1960
Cliff Arquette of *The Charley Weaver Show*

January 23 1960
Kathleen Nolan and Walter Brennan of *The Real McCoys*

January 30 1960
Garry Moore of *The Garry Moore Show*

February 06 1960
Richard Boone of *Have Gun, Will Travel*

February 13 1960
Craig Stevens and Lola Albright of *Peter Gunn* with John Vivyan and Pippa Scott of *Mr. Lucky*

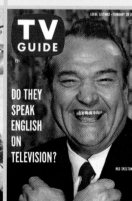

February 20 1960
Red Skelton of *The Red Skelton Show*

February 27 1960
Robert Stack of *The Untouchables*

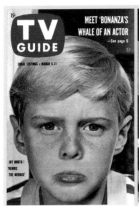

March 05 1960
Jay North of
Dennis The Menace

March 12 1960
Chuck Connors of
The Rifleman

March 19 1960
Raymond Burr and
Barbara Hale of
Perry Mason

March 26 1960
Donna Reed of
The Donna Reed Show

April 02 1960
Ernie Ford of
The Ford Show

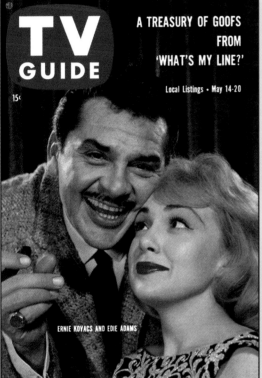

Ernie Kovacs was a television pioneer. His live TV shows contained ad-libbed routines, video effect experiments, and allowed the viewers to see behind the set. In 1957, he broadcast a half-hour show consisting only of sound effects and music, without dialogue. He died in a car accident on 1/13/1962 in Los Angeles.

April 09 1960
Efrem Zimbalist Jr. of
77 Sunset Strip

April 16 1960
Ann Sothern of
The Ann Sothern Show

April 23 1960
Robert Crawford, John Smith,
Robert Fuller, and Hoagy
Carmichael of *Laramie*

April 30 1960
June Lockhart, Jon Provost,
and Lassie of
Lassie

May 07 1960
*Frank Sinatra's Welcome
Home Party for Elvis Presley*

May 14 1960
Ernie Kovacs and
Edie Adams of
The Ernie Kovacs Show

May 21 1960
Gene Barry of
Bat Masterson

May 28 1960
Poncie Ponce and
Connie Stevens of
Hawaiian Eye

June 04 1960
Darren McGavin of
Riverboat

June 11 1960
Noreen Corcoran, John Forsythe,
and Sammee Tong of
Bachelor Father

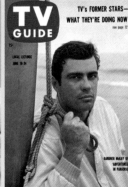

June 18 1960
Gardner McKay of
Adventures in Paradise

June 25 1960
Dan Blocker, Lorne Greene, Pernell
Roberts, and Michael Landon of
Bonanza

July 02 1960
Lawrence Welk of
The Lawrence Welk Show

July 09 1960
David Brinkley and
Chet Huntley of
NBC News

July 16 1960
Lucille Ball of
The Lucy-Desi Comedy Hour

July 23 1960
John Daly of
What's My Line?

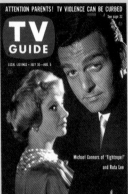

July 30 1960
Ruta Lee and
Michael Connors of
Tightrope

August 06 1960
Esther Williams in *Esther Williams
at Cypress Gardens*

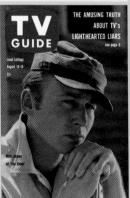

August 13 1960
Nick Adams of
The Rebel

August 20 1960
Betsy Palmer of
I've Got a Secret

August 27 1960
Roger Smith, Efrem Zimbalist Jr.,
Edd Byrnes, and Richard Long of
77 Sunset Strip

September 03 1960
Arlene Francis of
What's My Line?

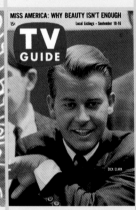

September 10 1960
Dick Clark of
American Bandstand

September 17 1960
June Allyson and Dick Powell

September 24 1960
Fall Preview:
1960-1961 Shows

October 01 1960
Dinah Shore of
The Dinah Shore Chevy Show

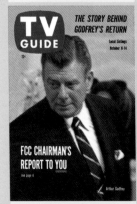

October 08 1960
Arthur Godfrey of
Candid Camera

October 15 1960
Marion Lorne and
Carol Burnett of
The Garry Moore Show

October 22 1960
Debbie Reynolds

October 29 1960
Danny Kaye in a Special
This Week

November 05 1960
Loretta Young of
Letter to Loretta

November 12 1960
Fred MacMurray of
My Three Sons

November 19 1960
Ward Bond of
Wagon Train

November 26 1960
Abby Dalton of
Hennesey and Friends

December 03 1960
Shirley Temple of
The Shirley Temple Show

December 10 1960
Amanda Blake and
James Arness of
Gunsmoke

December 17 1960
Sebastian Cabot, Anthony George,
and Doug McClure of
Checkmate

December 24 1960
Christmas

December 31 1960
Dorothy Provine of
The Roaring 20's

1961

January 07 1961
Richard Boone of
Have Gun, Will Travel

January 14 1961
Perry Como of
The Perry Como Show

January 21 1961
Barbara Stanwyck of
The Barbara Stanwyck Show

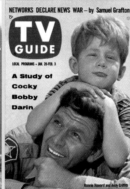

January 28 1961
Ron Howard and
Andy Griffith of
The Andy Griffith Show

February 04 1961
Eric Fleming and
Clint Eastwood of
Rawhide

February 11 1961
Lola Albright and
Craig Stevens of
Peter Gunn

February 18 1961
Nanette Fabray of
Westinghouse Playhouse

February 25 1961
Dorothy Collins, Allen Funt,
and Arthur Godfrey of
Candid Camera

March 04 1961
Raymond Burr of
Perry Mason

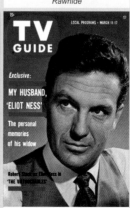

March 11 1961
Robert Stack of
The Untouchables

March 18 1961
Marjorie Lord of
The Danny Thomas Show

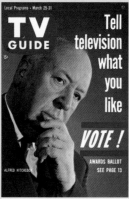

March 25 1961
Alfred Hitchcock of
Alfred Hitchcock Presents

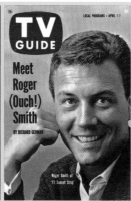

April 01 1961
Roger Smith of
77 Sunset Strip

April 08 1961
Lori Martin and King of
National Velvet

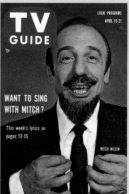

April 15 1961
Mitch Miller of
Sing Along with Mitch

April 22 1961
Garry Moore of
The Garry Moore Show

April 29 1961
Rod Taylor of
Hong Kong

May 06 1961
Donna Reed of
The Donna Reed Show

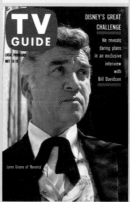

May 13 1961
Lorne Greene of
Bonanza

May 20 1961
Walter Brennan and
Richard Crenna of
The Real McCoys

May 27 1961
Ronald Reagan and
Dorothy Malone of
G. E. Theater

June 03 1961
Paul Burke and
Horace McMahon of
Naked City

June 10 1961
Nanette Fabray and Efrem
Zimbalist Jr. – Two of the
Award Show Stars

June 17 1961
Lawrence Welk of
The Lawrence Welk Show

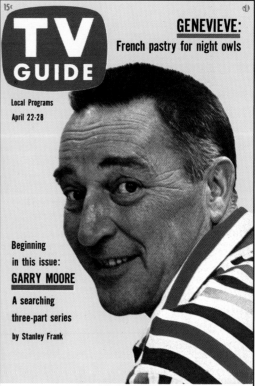

June 24 1961
John McIntire and
Robert Horton of
Wagon Train

July 01 1961
Betty, Wilma, Fred,
and Barney of
The Flintstones

July 08 1961
Harry Morgan and
Cara Williams of
Pete and Gladys

The Garry Moore Show started as a daily hour variety show on radio in 1949, and in June 1950 became a daily live half-hour TV show. Two months later it changed to a weekly hour show. Many top comedians made their first TV appearances on Moore's show. **Garry Moore** died on 11/28/1993 from emphysema.

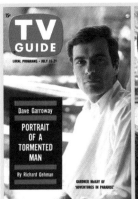

July 15 1961
Gardner McKay of
Adventures in Paradise

July 22 1961
Martin Milner and
George Maharis of
Route 66

July 29 1961
Bob Keeshan of
Captain Kangaroo

August 05 1961
Fred MacMurray, William Frawley,
and Stanley Livingston of
My Three Sons

August 12 1961
The World of Soap Opera

August 19 1961
Troy Donahue of
SurfSide 6

August 26 1961
Hugh Downs of
The Jack Paar Show

September 02 1961
Dwayne Hickman and
Bob Denver of
Dobie Gillis

September 09 1961
Sebastian Cabot, Anthony George,
and Doug McClure of
Checkmate

September 16 1961
Fall Preview:
1961-1962 Shows

September 23 1961
Mitch Miller of
Sing Along with Mitch

September 30 1961
Carol Burnett of
The Garry Moore Show

October 07 1961
Walter Cronkite of *CBS Reports*
with President
Dwight D. Eisenhower

October 14 1961
Red Skelton of
The Red Skelton Show

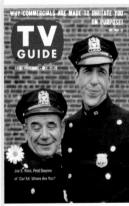

October 21 1961
Joe E. Ross and
Fred Gwynne of
Car 54, Where Are You?

October 28 1961
This is the Week to Watch

November 04 1961
Dorothy Provine of
The Roaring 20's

November 11 1961
Mr. and Mrs. Robert Stack

November 18 1961
Garry Moore, Durward Kirby,
and Marion Lorne of
The Garry Moore Show

November 25 1961
Amanda Blake and
James Arness of
Gunsmoke

December 02 1961
Joey Bishop of
The Joey Bishop Show

December 09 1961
Mary Tyler Moore and
Dick Van Dyke of
The Dick Van Dyke Show

December 16 1961
Raymond Massey and
Richard Chamberlain of
Dr. Kildare

December 23 1961
Merry Christmas

December 30 1961
Cynthia Pepper of
Margie

First employed in television as a game show host,
Jack Paar took over as *The Tonight Show* host in 1957
after guest hosting **Jack Benny**'s radio show. He was
so widely received that it was eventually renamed *The
Jack Paar Show* and it can be said that he reinvented
the talk show format. He died on 1/27/2004.

1962

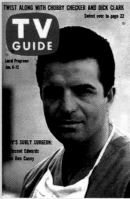

January 06 1962
Vincent Edwards of
Ben Casey

January 13 1962
Bobby Buntrock, Shirley Booth,
and Friend of
Hazel

January 20 1962
Chuck Connors of
The Rifleman

January 27 1962
Myrna Fahey of
Father of the Bride

February 03 1962
Mark Richman of
Cain's Hundred

February 10 1962
Mrs. John F. Kennedy – A TV
Tour of the White House

February 17 1962
Danny Thomas of
The Danny Thomas Show

February 24 1962
Troy Donohue of
Surfside 6

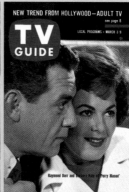

March 03 1962
Raymond Burr and
Barbara Hale of
Perry Mason

March 10 1962
Jack Paar of
The Jack Paar Show

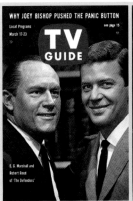

March 17 1962
E.G. Marshall and
Robert Reed of
The Defenders

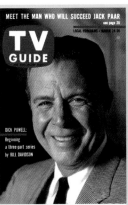

March 24 1962
Dick Powell of
The Dick Powell Show

March 31 1962
Alan Young and
Mister Ed of
Mister Ed

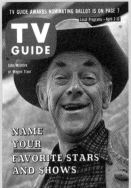

April 07 1962
John McIntire of
Wagon Train

April 14 1962
George Maharis and
Martin Milner of
Route 66

April 21 1962
Connie Stevens of
Hawaiian Eye

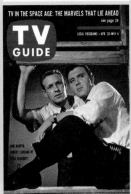

April 28 1962
Robert Lansing and
Ron Harper of
87th Precinct

May 05 1962
Sheila James and
Dwayne Hickman of
The Many Loves of Dobie Gillis

May 12 1962
Don Knotts of
The Andy Griffith Show

May 19 1962
Paul Burke of
Naked City

May 26 1962
Fred MacMurray and
Stanley Livingston of
My Three Sons

June 02 1962
Mary Tyler Moore of
The Dick Van Dyke Show

June 09 1962
Efrem Zimbalist Jr. of
77 Sunset Strip

June 16 1962
Raymond Massey and
Richard Chamberlain of
Dr. Kildare

June 23 1962
Arlene Francis of
What's My Line?

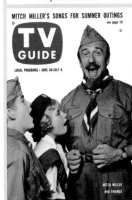

June 30 1962
Mitch Miller of
Sing Along with Mitch and Friends

July 07 1962
David Brinkley of
NBC News

July 14 1962
Sebastian Cabot and
Anthony George of
Checkmate

July 21 1962
Donna Reed of
The Donna Reed Show

July 28 1962
Barbara Benne and
Bill Cullen of
The Price Is Right

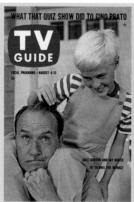

August 04 1962
Gale Gordon and
Jay North of
Dennis The Menace

August 11 1962
Robert Stack of
The Untouchables

August 18 1962
The Cast of
I've Got A Secret

August 25 1962
Lawrence Welk of
The Lawrence Welk Show

September 01 1962
Connie Stevens and
Troy Donohue of
Hawaiian Eye

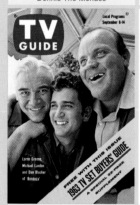

September 08 1962
Lorne Greene, Michael Landon,
and Dan Blocker of
Bonanza

September 15 1962
Fall Preview:
1962-1963 Shows

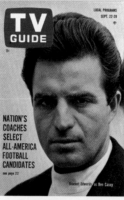

September 22 1962
Vincent Edwards of
Ben Casey

September 29 1962
Lucille Ball of
The Lucy Show

October 06 1962
Shirley Booth and
Don DeFore of
Hazel

October 13 1962
Jackie Gleason of
The Jackie Gleason Show

October 20 1962
Loretta Young of
The Loretta Young Show

October 27 1962
Richard Rust and
Edmond O'Brien of
Sam Benedict

November 03 1962
Stanley Holloway of
Our Man Higgins

November 10 1962
Donna Douglas, Max Baer Jr.,
Irene Ryan, and Buddy Ebsen of
The Beverly Hillbillies

November 17 1962
Jack Lord of
Stoney Burke

November 24 1962
Jacqueline Kennedy – The World
of Jacqueline Kennedy

December 01 1962
Marty Ingles and
John Astin of
I'm Dickens, He's Fenster

December 08 1962
Dick Van Dyke of
The Dick Van Dyke Show

December 15 1962
Zina Bethune and
Shirl Conway of
The Nurses

December 22 1962
Merry Christmas

December 29 1962
Edie Adams

1963

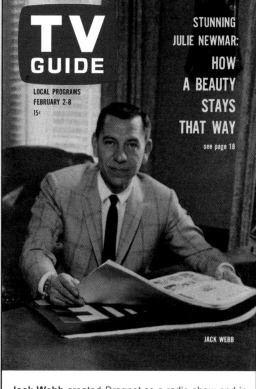

STUNNING
JULIE NEWMAR:
HOW
A BEAUTY
STAYS
THAT WAY
see page 18

JACK WEBB

Jack Webb created *Dragnet* as a radio show and in 1951 it moved to TV where the program ran until 1959. It was resurrected from 1967 to 1970, and made into a movie in 1987. *Dragnet* showed up on TV again in 1989 and 2003 with new stars but only ran for one season each time. Jack Webb died on 12/23/1982.

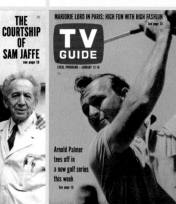

January 05 1963
Bettye Ackerman, Vincent Edwards, and Sam Jaffe of *Ben Casey*

January 12 1963
Arnold Palmer – Tees Off in a New Golf Series This Week

January 19 1963
Joe E. Ross and Fred Gwynne of *Car 54, Where Are You?*

January 26 1963
George Maharis and Martin Milner of *Route 66*

February 02 1963
Jack Webb of *Dragnet*

February 09 1963
Ernest Borgnine of *McHale's Navy*

February 16 1963
Princess Grace – Takes You on a Tour of Monaco

February 23 1963
Carol Burnett of *The Garry Moore Show*

March 02 1963
Wendell Corey and Jack Ging of *The Eleventh Hour*

March 09 1963
Donna Douglas and Buddy Ebsen of *The Beverly Hillbillies*

March 16 1963
Richard Chamberlain of *Dr. Kildare*

March 23 1963
Andy Williams of *The Andy Williams Show*

March 30 1963
Michael Landon, Dan Blocker, Lorne Greene, and Pernell Roberts of *Bonanza*

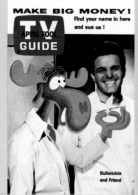

April 01 1963
Bullwinkle with
Vincent Edwards of
Ben Casey

April 06 1963
Lucille Ball of
The Lucy Show

April 13 1963
Richard Egan of
Empire

April 20 1963
Red Skelton of
The Red Skelton Show

April 27 1963
Bill Talman and
Raymond Burr of
Perry Mason

May 04 1963
Roberta Shore, Lee J. Cobb,
and James Drury of
The Virginian

May 11 1963
Don Knotts, Ron Howard,
and Andy Griffith of
The Andy Griffith Show

May 18 1963
E.G. Marshall and
Robert Reed of
The Defenders

May 25 1963
Lawrence Welk of
The Lawrence Welk Show

June 01 1963
Dorothy Loudon and
Garry Moore of
The Garry Moore Show

June 08 1963
Johnny Carson of
The Tonight Show

June 15 1963
Rick Jason and
Vic Morrow of
Combat

June 22 1963
Durward Kirby, Allen Funt,
and Marilyn Van Derbur of
Candid Camera

June 29 1963
Donna Reed and
Carl Betz of
The Donna Reed Show

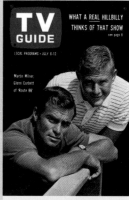

July 06 1963
Glenn Corbett and
Martin Milner of
Route 66

July 13 1963
Gloria Neil, Vic Damone,
and Quinn O'Hara of
The Lively Ones

July 20 1963
Dennis Weaver and
James Arness of
Gunsmoke

July 27 1963
The Odd Science of Picking
Game-Show Contestants

August 03 1963
Morey Amsterdam and
Richard Deacon of
The Dick Van Dyke Show

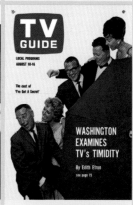

August 10 1963
The Cast of
I've Got a Secret

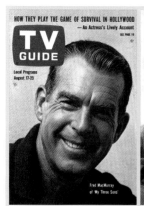

August 17 1963
Fred MacMurray of
My Three Sons

August 24 1963
June Lockhart, Lassie, and
Jon Provost of
Lassie

August 31 1963
Richard Boone of
The Richard Boone Show

September 07 1963
Irene Ryan and
Donna Douglas of
The Beverly Hillbillies

September 14 1963
Fall Preview:
1963-1964 Shows

September 21 1963
Richard Chamberlain of
Dr. Kildare

September 28 1963
Inger Stevens of
The Farmer's Daughter

October 05 1963
Phil Silvers of
The New Phil Silvers Show

October 12 1963
Ben Gazzara and
Chuck Connors of
Arrest and Trial

October 19 1963
Judy Garland of
The Judy Garland Show

October 26 1963
Lee J. Cobb and
Roberta Shore of
The Virginian

November 02 1963
Bill Bixby and
Ray Walston of
My Favorite Martian

November 09 1963
Carol Burnett in
Calamity Jane

Airing from 1955 to 1975, *Gunsmoke* is the longest running prime time drama ever and was in the Top 20 for most of its run. It was the first "adult western" and laid the groundwork for shows like *Bonanza* and *The Big Valley*. With only a few cast changes in its 20 years and 600+ episodes, *Gunsmoke* remains a true classic.

November 16 1963
James Franciscus and
Dean Jagger of
Mr. Novak

November 23 1963
Gene Barry, Joan Staley, Eileen
O'Neill, and Sharyn Hillyer of
Burke's Law

November 30 1963
George C. Scott of
East Side/West Side

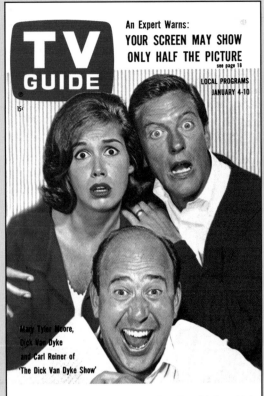

An Expert Warns:
YOUR SCREEN MAY SHOW
ONLY HALF THE PICTURE
see page 18

TV GUIDE

LOCAL PROGRAMS
JANUARY 4-10

Mary Tyler Moore,
Dick Van Dyke
and Carl Reiner of
'The Dick Van Dyke Show'

Dick Van Dyke won a Tony for *Bye Bye Birdie*, which
he left for a starring role in *The Dick Van Dyke Show*.
Mary Tyler Moore started a fashion fad by wearing
Capri pants on the show. Creator **Carl Reiner** based
many episodes on actual events. Usually filmed with a
live audience, the series ran from 1961 to 1966.

December 07 1963
John McIntire and
Robert Fuller of
Wagon Train

December 14 1963
Frank Sinatra, Rosemary Clooney,
Dean Martin, Kathryn Crosby,
and Bing Crosby

December 21 1963
Merry Christmas

December 28 1963
Patty Duke of
The Patty Duke Show

1964

January 04 1964
Mary Tyler Moore, Dick Van
Dyke, and Carl Reiner of
The Dick Van Dyke Show

January 11 1964
Marjorie Lord, June Lockhart,
Amanda Blake, and Barbara Hale

January 18 1964
Pernell Roberts and
Kathie Browne of
Bonanza

January 25 1964
America's Long Vigil

February 01 1964
Danny Kaye and
Laurie Ichinio of
The Danny Kaye Show

February 08 1964
Linda Kaye, Pat Woodall, Jeannine
Riley, and Bea Benaderet of
Petticoat Junction

February 15 1964
Mr. and Mrs. Andy Williams

February 22 1964
David Janssen of
The Fugitive

February 29 1964
Shirl Conway and
Zina Bethune of
The Nurses

March 07 1964
Richard Chamberlain of
Dr. Kildare

March 14 1964
Irene Ryan, Donna Douglas,
and Buddy Ebsen of
The Beverly Hillbillies

March 21 1964
Don Knotts, Andy Griffith,
and Jim Nabors of
The Andy Griffith Show

March 28 1964
Lawrence Welk of
The Lawrence Welk Show

April 04 1964
Vincent Edwards of
Ben Casey

April 11 1964
Bill Bixby and
Ray Walston of
My Favorite Martian

April 18 1964
Dean Jagger and
James Franciscus of
Mr. Novak

April 25 1964
Danny Thomas of
The Danny Thomas Show

May 02 1964
William Windom and
Inger Stevens of
The Farmer's Daughter

May 09 1964
Vic Morrow and
Rick Jason of
Combat

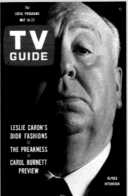

May 16 1964
Alfred Hitchcock of
Alfred Hitchcock Presents

May 23 1964
Mary Tyler Moore of
The Dick Van Dyke Show

May 30 1964
Ernest Borgnine, Tim Conway,
and Joe Flynn of
McHale's Navy

June 06 1964
Amanda Blake of
Gunsmoke

June 13 1964
Fred Flintstone of
The Flintstones

June 20 1964
Donna Reed of
The Donna Reed Show

June 27 1964
Mr. and Mrs. Johnny Carson

July 04 1964
Raymond Burr of
Perry Mason with
Erle Stanley Gardner

July 11 1964
The Anchor Men

July 18 1964
Doug McClure, Roberta Shore,
and James Drury of
The Virginian

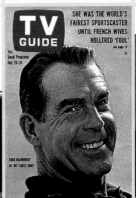

July 25 1964
Fred MacMurray of
My Three Sons

August 01 1964
Hugh Downs, Maureen O'Sullivan,
Frank Blair, and Jack Lescoulie of
Today

BURKE'S ASSISTANT: HE HAS LAWS TOO
SEE PAGE 15

August 08 1964
Gene Barry and
Gary Conway of
Burke's Law

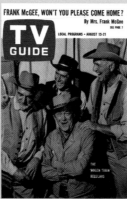

FRANK McGEE, WON'T YOU PLEASE COME HOME?
By Mrs. Frank McGee

August 15 1964
Frank McGrath, Terry Wilson,
Robert Fuller, and John McIntire
of *Wagon Train*

THIS WEEK: THE DEMOCRATIC CONVENTION
— COMPLETE DETAILS

August 22 1964
E.G. Marshall of
The Defenders

HOW ACTORS CASH IN ON TV's BIGGEST JACKPOT

August 29 1964
Patty Duke, William Schallert,
and Jean Byron of
The Patty Duke Show

Exclusive:
NEWTON MINOW'S
PROPOSALS FOR
RESHAPING TV

September 05 1964
Lucille Ball of
The Lucy Show

THE SUCCESSFUL COP WHO NEVER GETS HIS MAN
See Page 15

September 12 1964
David Janssen and
Barry Morse of
The Fugitive

SPECIAL ISSUE
TV GUIDE
FALL PREVIEW
1964·1965
SHOWS

September 19 1964
Fall Preview:
1964-1965 Shows

SOPHIA LOREN'S ROME: FACTS, FUN, FASHIONS
1964 ALL-AMERICA PREVIEW

September 26 1964
Dan Blocker of
Bonanza

THE MAD BUSINESS OF RUNNING FOR PRESIDENT
By Edward P. Morgan

October 03 1964
Mia Farrow of
Peyton Place

COMPLETE DETAILS OF OLYMPICS COVERAGE

October 10 1964
Gig Young, Charles Boyer,
and David Niven of
The Rogues

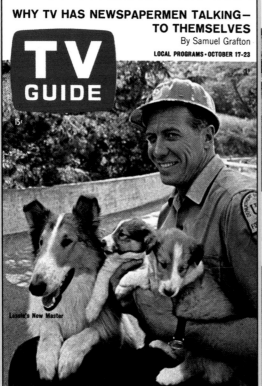

WHY TV HAS NEWSPAPERMEN TALKING—
TO THEMSELVES
By Samuel Grafton
LOCAL PROGRAMS · OCTOBER 17-23

Lassie's New Master

A short story in the *Saturday Evening Post* in 1938
was the birth of *Lassie*. Books, movies, a radio show,
and the classic TV show followed. Although the
character **Lassie** is a female, all six of the collies
that portrayed her were male. *Lassie* won the Best
Children's Series Emmy award in 1955.

WHY TV HAS NEWSPAPERMEN TALKING—
TO THEMSELVES
By Samuel Grafton

October 17 1964
Ray Bray and Lassie of
Lassie

GLINT IN EYE, GUN IN HAND, TONGUE IN CHEEK—
'THE MAN FROM U.N.C.L.E.'

October 24 1964
Robert Vaughn of
The Man from U.N.C.L.E.

DETAILS ON HOW TV WILL COVER THE ELECTION

October 31 1964
John Astin and
Carolyn Jones of
The Addams Family

WHAT RATINGS CAN AND CANNOT DO
By A.C. Nielsen Jr.

November 07 1964
Italy's Daniela Bianchi and
Richard Chamberlain in
Kildare Trilogy

THE MAN WOMEN LOVE TO HATE

She's sweet,
She's lovable,
She's reformed.
CARA WILLIAMS

November 14 1964
Cara Williams of
The Cara Williams Show

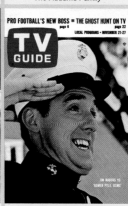

PRO FOOTBALL'S NEW BOSS ■ THE GHOST HUNT ON TV

November 21 1964
Jim Nabors of
Gomer Pyle, USMC

November 28 1964
Elizabeth Montgomery of
Bewitched

December 05 1964
Laurie Sibbald and
Sammy Jackson of
No Time For Sergeants

December 12 1964
Julie Newmar of
My Living Doll

December 19 1964
Merry Christmas

December 26 1964
Juliet Prowse

1965

January 02 1965
Al Lewis, Fred Gwynne, and
Yvonne DeCarlo of
The Munsters

January 09 1965
Lois Roberts, Sheila James,
Joan Staley, and Kathleen Nolan of
Broadside

The *Big Broadcast of 1938* was **Bob Hope**'s first film appearance. In 1940, with **Bing Crosby** and **Dorothy Lamour**, he commenced his series of *Road to…* movies. In the 40's he began to spend much of his time entertaining soldiers overseas and appeared in many NBC specials with the troops. Bob Hope died on 7/27/2003 from pneumonia.

January 16 1965
Bob Hope, an American
Institution

January 23 1965
Chuck Connors of
Branded

January 30 1965
Inger Stevens in Sweden

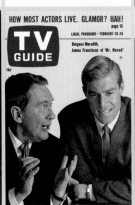

February 06 1965
Jackie Gleason of
The Jackie Gleason Show

February 13 1965
Andy Williams of
The Andy Williams Show

February 20 1965
Burgess Meredith and
James Franciscus of
Mr. Novak

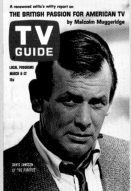

February 27 1965
Donna Douglas, Irene Ryan,
and Nancy Kulp of
The Beverly Hillbillies

March 06 1965
David Janssen of
The Fugitive

March 13 1965
Michael Landon, Lorne Greene,
Dan Blocker, and Pernell Roberts
of *Bonanza*

March 20 1965
Dorothy Malone of
Peyton Place
with Her Daughters

March 27 1965
Mary Tyler Moore and
Dick Van Dyke of
The Dick Van Dyke Show

April 03 1965
Kathy Kersh and
Vince Edwards of
Ben Casey

April 10 1965
Janet Lake and
Walter Brennan of
The Tycoon

April 17 1965
Robert Vaughn and
David McCallum of
The Man From U.N.C.L.E.

April 24 1965
Andy Griffith of
The Andy Griffith Show

May 01 1965
Connie Stevens of
Wendy and Me

May 08 1965
Bob Denver and
Tina Louise of
Gilligan's Island

May 15 1965
Robert Lansing of
12 O'Clock High

May 22 1965
Julie Andrews – Watch Julie
Andrews Rehearse a
TV Special

May 29 1965
Elizabeth Montgomery and
Dick York of
Bewitched

June 05 1965
Flipper and Brian Kelly of
Flipper

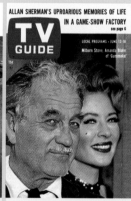

June 12 1965
Milburn Stone and
Amanda Blake of
Gunsmoke

June 19 1965
Richard Basehart and
David Hedison of
Voyage to the Bottom of the Sea

June 26 1965
Donna McKechnie, Barbara Monte,
and Lada Edmund Jr. of *Hullabaloo*

July 03 1965
Jimmy Dean of
The Jimmy Dean Show

July 10 1965
Yvonne Decarlo and
Fred Gwynne of
The Munsters

July 17 1965
The Cast of
McHale's Navy

July 24 1965
Raymond Burr of
Perry Mason

July 31 1965
Stanley Livingston, Fred
MacMurray, and Barry Livingston
of *My Three Sons*

August 07 1965
Gene Barry of
Burke's Law

August 14 1965
Robert Bray and Friend –
How Lassie Picked Her
New Master

August 21 1965
Fess Parker and
Patricia Blair of
Daniel Boone

August 28 1965
Aquatic Stars: Lucille Ball
and Splash

September 04 1965
Dan Blocker, Lorne Greene,
and Michael Landon of
Bonanza

September 11 1965
Fall Preview:
1965-1966 Shows

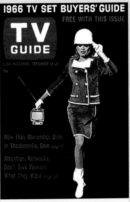

September 18 1965
Adrianne – 1966 TV Set
Buyers' Guide

September 25 1965
Jackie Gleason – Rollicking
Along on Gleason's Express
To Miami

October 02 1965
Don Adams and
Barbara Feldon of
Get Smart

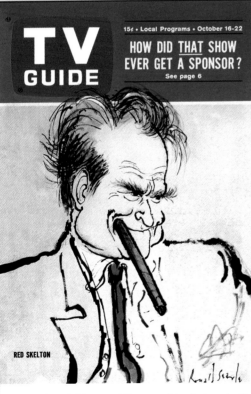

Red Skelton left home at the age of ten to travel with
a medicine show. He became a vaudeville regular
at the age of fifteen. His Broadway debut was in 1937
and his first film appearance in 1938. *The Red Skelton
Show* ran from 1951 to 1971 and was consistently in
the Top 20 rated shows. He died on 9/17/1997.

October 09 1965
Anne Francis of
Honey West

October 16 1965
Red Skelton of
The Red Skelton Show

October 23 1965
Chuck Connors of
Branded

October 30 1965
John Astin and
Carolyn Jones of
The Addams Family

November 06 1965
June Lockhart and
Guy Williams of
Lost in Space

November 13 1965
Joey Heatherton: Swinging
Girl – Swinging Fashions

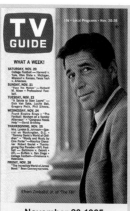

November 20 1965
Efrem Zimbalist Jr. of
The FBI

November 27 1965
Cynthia Lynn and
Bob Crane of
Hogan's Heroes

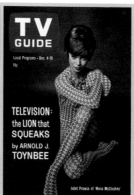

December 04 1965
Juliet Prowse of
Mona McCluskey

December 11 1965
Larry Storch, Forrest Tucker,
Melody Patterson, and Ken
Berry of *F Troop*

December 18 1965
Jim Nabors of
Gomer Pyle, USMC

Peyton Place was the first prime-time soap, airing twice a week with a continuous storyline, but producer **Paul Monash** chose to call it a "television novel." The series had no repeats and no summer hiatus which was unheard of in prime time programming. The show was promoted as scandalous and originally received more attention for its content than its scheduling.

December 25 1965
Merry Christmas

1966

January 01 1966
Carol Channing: Dolled Up For
a TV Special

January 08 1966
Eva Gabor and
Eddie Albert of
Green Acres

January 15 1966
Robert Culp and
Bill Cosby of
I Spy

January 22 1966
David Janssen of
The Fugitive

January 29 1966
The Cast of
Please Don't Eat The Daisies

February 05 1966
Barbara Eden and
Larry Hagman of
I Dream of Jeannie

February 12 1966
Ryan O'Neal and
Barbara Parkin of
Peyton Place

February 19 1966
Ben Gazzara of
Run for Your Life

February 26 1966
Charles Briles, Linda Evans,
and Barbara Stanwyck of
The Big Valley

March 05 1966
Barbara Feldon of
Get Smart

March 12 1966
Donna Douglas, Irene Ryan, Buddy
Ebsen, and Max Baer Jr. of
The Beverly Hillbillies

March 19 1966
David McCallum and
Robert Vaughn of
The Man from U.N.C.L.E.

March 26 1966
Adam West of
Batman

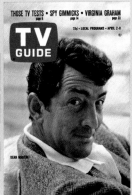

April 02 1966
Dean Martin of
The Dean Martin Show

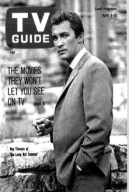

April 09 1966
Roy Thinnes of
The Long Hot Summer

April 16 1966
Lori Saunders, Linda Kaye,
and Gunilla Hutton of
Petticoat Junction

April 23 1966
Andy Williams and Dancers of
The Andy Williams Show

April 30 1966
Lucille Ball of
The Lucy Show

May 07 1966
Ray Scherer with President
Lyndon B. Johnson

May 14 1966
Frank Sinatra in a Special
This Week

May 21 1966
Robert Conrad and
Ross Martin of
The Wild, Wild West

May 28 1966
Sally Field of
Gidget

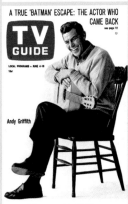

June 04 1966
Andy Griffith of
The Andy Griffith Show

June 11 1966
Alan Hale, Tina Louise,
and Bob Denver of
Gilligan's Island

June 18 1966
Agnes Moorehead and
Elizabeth Montgomery of
Bewitched

June 25 1966
William Smith, Peter Brown, Phillip
Carey, and Neville Brand of
Laredo

July 02 1966
Walter Cronkite of
CBS Evening News

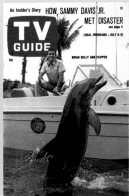

July 09 1966
Brian Kelly and Flipper of
Flipper

July 16 1966
Fred MacMurray and
William Demarest of
My Three Sons

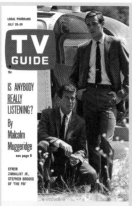

July 23 1966
Efrem Zimbalist Jr. and
Stephen Brooks of
The FBI

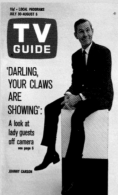

July 30 1966
Johnny Carson of
The Tonight Show

August 06 1966
Marshall Thompson of
Daktari
with Clarence

August 13 1966
Melody Patterson and
Larry Storch of
F Troop

August 20 1966
Red Skelton of
The Red Skelton Show

August 27 1966
Barbara Feldon and
Don Adams of
Get Smart

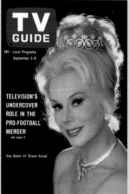

September 03 1966
Eva Gabor of
Green Acres

September 10 1966
Fall Preview:
1966-1967 Shows

September 17 1966
Joey Heatherton

September 24 1966
Barbara Eden of
I Dream Of Jeannie

October 01 1966
The Vietnam War: Is TV Giving
Us The Picture?

October 08 1966
Jim Nabors of
Gomer Pyle, USMC

October 15 1966
Peter Deuel and
Judy Carne of
Love On A Rooftop

October 22 1966
Lucille Ball in
Lucy in London

October 29 1966
Van Williams and
Bruce Lee of
The Green Hornet

November 05 1966
Robert Vaughn and
David McCallum of
The Man From U.N.C.L.E.

November 12 1966
Marlo Thomas of
That Girl

November 19 1966
Bob Crane and
Robert Clary of
Hogan's Heroes

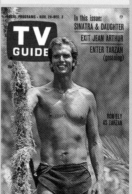

November 26 1966
Ron Ely of
Tarzan

December 03 1966
Larry Casey, Justin Tarr,
and Chris George of
Rat Patrol

1967

December 10 1966
James Arness of
Gunsmoke

December 17 1966
Michael Callan and
Patricia Harty of
Occasional Wife

December 24 1966
Merry Christmas

December 31 1966
Stefanie Powers of
The Girl from U.N.C.L.E.

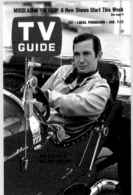

January 07 1967
Ben Gazzara of
Run For Your Life

January 14 1967
Art Carney of
The Jackie Gleason Show

January 21 1967
Diana Rigg and
Patrick Macnee of
The Avengers

January 28 1967
Mike Nesmith, Mickey Dolenz,
Peter Tork, and Davey Jones of
The Monkees

February 04 1967
Dale Robertson of
Iron Horse

February 11 1967
Steve Hill, Barbara Bain,
and Martin Landau of
Mission: Impossible

February 18 1967
Dean Martin of
The Dean Martin Show

February 25 1967
Phyllis Diller in
The Pruitts of Southampton

March 04 1967
William Shatner and
Leonard Nimoy of
Star Trek

March 11 1967
Dorothy Malone of
Peyton Place

March 18 1967
Jackie Gleason of
The Jackie Gleason Show

March 25 1967
Robert Culp and
Bill Cosby of
I Spy

April 01 1967
Cheryl Miller of
Daktari
with Judy

April 08 1967
Dick Van Dyke: He's Back
with a Special

April 15 1967
Karen Jensen – The Starlet,
1967: Revealing Study of
a New Species

April 22 1967
Anissa Jones, Sebastian
Cabot, and Brian Keith of
Family Affair

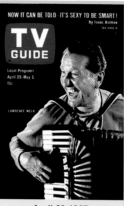

April 29 1967
Lawrence Welk of
The Lawrence Welk Show

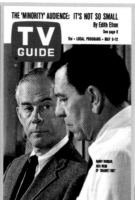

May 06 1967
Harry Morgan and
Jack Webb of
Dragnet 1967

May 13 1967
Elizabeth Montgomery of
Bewitched

May 20 1967
Andy Griffith and
Aneta Corsaut of
The Andy Griffith Show

May 27 1967
Ken Berry, Forrest Tucker,
and Larry Storch of
F Troop

June 03 1967
Dennis Cole and
Howard Duff of
The Felony Squad

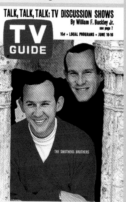

June 10 1967
Dick Smothers and
Tom Smothers of
The Smothers Brothers

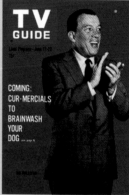

June 17 1967
Ed Sullivan of
The Ed Sullivan Show

June 24 1967
Barbara Feldon and
Don Adams of
Get Smart

July 01 1967
Chet Huntley and
David Brinkley

July 08 1967
Efrem Zimbalist Jr., of
The FBI with J. Edgar
Hoover of The FBI

July 15 1967
Lucille Ball: Redhead With
a Golden Touch

July 22 1967
Michael Landon, Dan Blocker,
and Lorne Greene of
Bonanza

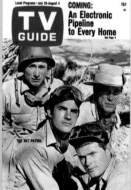

July 29 1967
Justin Tarr, Gary Raymond,
Christopher George, and Larry
Casey of *The Rat Patrol*

August 05 1967
Hugh Downs and
Barbara Walters of
Today

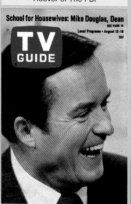

August 12 1967
Mike Douglas of
The Mike Douglas Show

August 19 1967
Barry Morse and
David Janssen of
The Fugitive

August 26 1967
Jim Nabors of
Gomer Pyle, U.S.M.C.

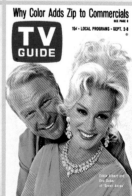

September 02 1967
Eddie Albert and
Eva Gabor of
Green Acres

September 09 1967
Fall Preview:
1967-1968 Shows

September 16 1967
Raymond Burr of
Ironside

September 23 1967
Peter Tork, Mickey Dolenz, Mike
Nesmith, and Davey Jones of
The Monkees

September 30 1967
Sally Field of
The Flying Nun

October 07 1967
Richard Benjamin, Jack Cassidy,
and Paula Prentiss of
He & She

October 14 1967
Johnny Carson of
The Tonight Show

October 21 1967
Mia Farrow in
Johnny Belinda

October 28 1967
Who Killed Hollywood Society?

November 04 1967
Stuart Whitman of
Cimarron Strip

November 11 1967
Yvette Mimieux

November 18 1967
William Shatner and
Leonard Nimoy of
Star Trek

November 25 1967
The Cast of
Garrison's Gorillas

December 02 1967
Danny and Marlo Thomas

December 09 1967
Kaye Ballard and
Eve Arden of
The Mothers-in-Law

December 16 1967
Sebastian Cabot of
Family Affair

December 23 1967
Christmas

December 30 1967
Carol Burnett of
The Carol Burnett Show

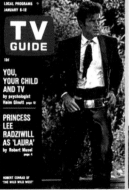

January 06 1968
Robert Conrad of
The Wild, Wild West

January 13 1968
Bob Hope

71

January 20 1968
Leif Erickson, Linda Cristal, and Cameron Mitchell of *The High Chaparral*

January 27 1968
Elizabeth Montgomery of *Bewitched*

February 03 1968
Ben Gazzara of *Run For Your Life*

February 10 1968
Dick Smothers and Tom Smothers of *The Smothers Brothers*

February 17 1968
Efrem Zimbalist Jr. and William Reynolds of *The FBI*

February 24 1968
Joey Bishop of *The Joey Bishop Show*

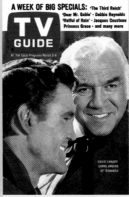

March 02 1968
David Canary and Lorne Greene of *Bonanza*

March 09 1968
Jackie Gleason of *The Jackie Gleason Show*

March 16 1968
Sally Field and Alejandro Rey of *The Flying Nun*

March 23 1968
Bill Cosby and Robert Culp of *I Spy*

March 30 1968
Lucille Ball of *The Lucy Show*

April 06 1968
Raymond Burr and Barbara Anderson of *Ironside*

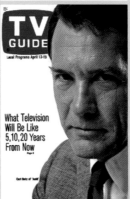

April 13 1968
Carl Betz of *Judd*

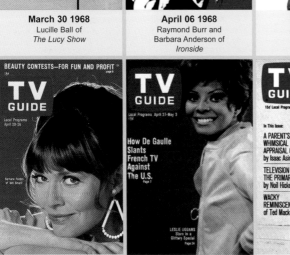

April 20 1968
Barbara Feldon of *Get Smart*

April 27 1968
Leslie Uggams Stars in a Glittery Special

May 04 1968
Greg Morris, Peter Graves, Barbara Bain, and Martin Landau of *Mission: Impossible*

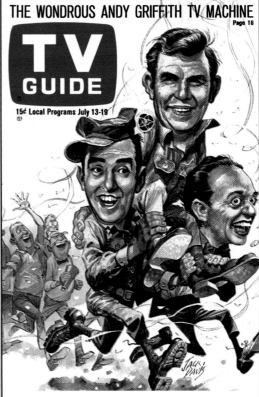

Andy Griffith was nominated for a Tony award in 1956 for his featured role in the Broadway play, *No Time for Sergeants*, and in 1958 reprised the role in a filmed version. He is best known for his classic TV shows, *The Andy Griffith Show* and *Matlock*. He has also recorded comedic and music albums.

May 11 1968
Fess Parker, Darby Hinton,
and Patricia Blair of
Daniel Boone

May 18 1968
Mike Connors of
Mannix

May 25 1968
Diana Hyland of
Peyton Place

June 01 1968
Ed Sullivan of
The Ed Sullivan Show

June 08 1968
Salvador Dali's View of
Television

June 15 1968
Linda Cristal and
Leif Erickson of
The High Chaparral

June 22 1968
Toni Helfer – How They Make
Hams Out of Tigers

June 29 1968
Robert Wagner of
It Takes a Thief

July 06 1968
Barbara Eden of
I Dream of Jeannie

July 13 1968
Jim Nabors, Andy Griffith,
and Don Knotts of
The Andy Griffith Show

July 20 1968
Barbara Stanwyck, Richard
Long, and Linda Evans of
The Big Valley

July 27 1968
Joey Heatherton and Frank
Sinatra Jr. of *Dean Martin
Presents The Golddiggers*

August 03 1968
David Brinkley, Chet Huntley, Walter
Cronkite, and Howard K. Smith –
The Network Anchormen

August 10 1968
Dennis Weaver, Ben, Beth
Brickell, and Clint Howard of
Gentle Ben

August 17 1968
Milburn Stone, James Arness,
and Amanda Blake of
Gunsmoke

August 24 1968
DeForest Kelley, William Shatner,
and Leonard Nimoy of
Star Trek

August 31 1968
Johnny Carson of
The Tonight Show

September 07 1968
Anissa Jones, Johnnie Whitaker,
Kathy Garver, and Sebastian Cabot
of *Family Affair*

September 14 1968
Fall Preview:
Special Issue

September 21 1968
Dan Rowan and
Dick Martin of
Laugh-In

CHICAGO:
A Network
News Chief's
Defense
Page 32

Diahann Carroll
of 'Julia'

At age 19, **Diahann Carroll** made her first film appearance in *Carmen Jones*. She was the first black American women to have her own sitcom, *Julia*, which aired from 1968 to 1971. In 1969, she won a Golden Globe for Best Female TV Star for the role. And on *Dynasty* from 1984 to 1987, she had the first prominent African-American role on a prime time soap.

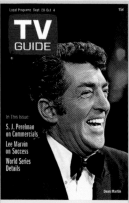

September 28 1968
Dean Martin of
The Dean Martin Show

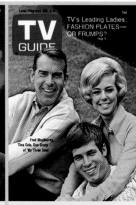

October 05 1968
Fred MacMurray, Tina Cole,
and Don Grady of
My Three Sons

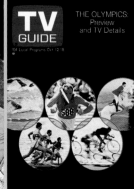

October 12 1968
The Olympics: Preview
and TV Details

October 19 1968
Jim Nabors in a Special
This Week

October 26 1968
Hope Lange of
The Ghost and Mrs. Muir

November 02 1968
Peggy Lipton, Clarence Williams III,
and Michael Cole of
The Mod Squad

November 09 1968
Barbara Feldon of
Get Smart

November 16 1968
Bob Denver and
Herb Edelman of
The Good Guys

November 23 1968
Frank Sinatra in
*Francis Albert Sinatra Does
His Thing*

November 30 1968
Ann-Margret

December 07 1968
E.J. Peaker and
Robert Morse of
That's Life

December 14 1968
Diahann Carroll of
Julia

December 21 1968
Christmas

December 28 1968
Doris Day of
The Doris Day Show

1969

January 04 1969
David Soul, Bridget Hanley, Bobby
Sherman, and Robert Brown of
Here Come The Brides

January 11 1969
No Laughing Matter:
Bob Hope's
$150,000,000 Bankroll

January 18 1969
Darren McGavin of
The Outsider

January 25 1969
Deanna Lund and
Gary Conway of
Land of the Giants

February 01 1969
The Men of
The High Chaparral

February 08 1969
The Agents of
Mission: Impossible

February 15 1969
Raymond Burr of
Ironside

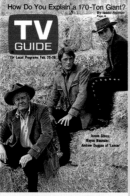

February 22 1969
James Stacy, Wayne Maunder,
and Andrew Duggan of
Lancer

March 01 1969
Lucie Arnaz, Desi Arnaz Jr.,
and Lucille Ball

March 08 1969
A Week With *Laugh-In*'s
Dingalings

March 15 1969
Buddy Foster and
Ken Berry of
Mayberry R.F.D.

March 22 1969
Elizabeth Montgomery of
Bewitched

March 29 1969
Tony Franciosa, Gene Barry,
and Robert Stack of
The Name of the Game

April 05 1969
Tom Smothers and Dick Smothers
of *The Smothers Brothers
Comedy Hour*

April 12 1969
Mary Tyler Moore and Dick
Van Dyke in *Dick Van Dyke
and the Other Woman*

April 19 1969
Lawrence Welk of
The Lawrence Welk Show

April 26 1969
Jack Paar

May 03 1969
Madeleine Sherwood and
Sally Field of
The Flying Nun

May 10 1969
The Raging Controversy over
TV's Role in Space Shoots

May 17 1969
Marlo Thomas of
That Girl

May 24 1969
Frank Blair, Barbara Walters, Joe
Garagiola, and Hugh Downs of
Today

May 31 1969
Anissa Jones, Sebastian Cabot,
and Johnnie Whitaker of
Family Affair

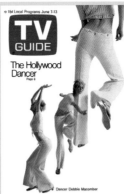

June 07 1969
Debbie Macomber of
Turn-On

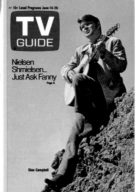

June 14 1969
Glen Campbell of
*The Glen Campbell
Goodtime Hour*

In 1968, astronauts **Walter Schirra**, **Donn Eisele**,
and **Walter Cunningham** of Apollo 7 were the
first Americans to give us TV transmissions from
space while still in Earth's orbit. In 1969, Apollo 11
astronauts **Neil Armstrong** and **Edwin "Buzz"
Aldrin** were the first to telecast from the moon.

June 21 1969
Jackie Gleason of
The Jackie Gleason Show

June 28 1969
Marc Copage and
Diahann Carroll of
Julia

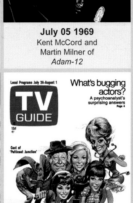

July 05 1969
Kent McCord and
Martin Milner of
Adam-12

July 12 1969
Peggy Lipton, Clarence Williams III,
and Michael Cole of
The Mod Squad

July 19 1969
The First Live Telecast
From the Moon

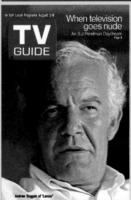

July 26 1969
The Cast of
Petticoat Junction

August 02 1969
Andrew Duggan of
Lancer

August 09 1969
Will Soaring Costs Knock
Sports Off TV?

August 16 1969
Merv Griffin of
The Merv Griffin Show

August 23 1969
Linda Cristal and
Leif Erickson of
The High Chaparral

August 30 1969
Johnny Cash of
The Johnny Cash Show

September 06 1969
Eddie Albert and
Eva Gabor of
Green Acres

September 13 1969
Fall Preview:
Special Issue

September 20 1969
Jim Nabors of
The Jim Nabors Show

September 27 1969
Robert Young and
James Brolin of
Marcus Welby, M.D.

October 04 1969
Bill Cosby of
I Spy

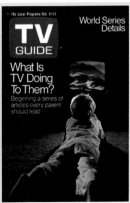

October 11 1969
Kids: What is TV Doing
to Them?

October 18 1969
Peter Lupus, Greg Morris, Leonard
Nimoy, and Peter Graves of
Mission: Impossible

October 25 1969
Joan Hotchkis, Lisa Gerritsen,
and William Windom of
My World And Welcome To It

November 01 1969
Michael Constantine, Denise
Nicholas, and Lloyd Hanes of
Room 222

November 08 1969
Andy Williams of
The Andy Williams Show

November 15 1969
Julie Sommars and
Dan Dailey of
The Governor and J.J.

November 22 1969
Barbara Eden of
I Dream of Jeannie

November 29 1969
Michael Landon, Lorne Greene,
Dan Blocker, and Pernell Roberts
of *Bonanza*

December 06 1969
Doris Day of
The Doris Day Show

December 13 1969
Michael Parks of
...Then Came Bronson

December 20 1969
Merry Christmas

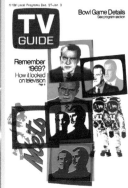

December 27 1969
Remember 1969?
How It Looked on Television

Memorable TV Show Quotes from the 1960s

"As always, should you or any of your IM force be caught or killed, the Secretary will disavow any knowledge of your actions. This tape will self-destruct in five seconds. Good luck, Jim."
Voice on Tape, *Mission Impossible*

"You just have to know how to arrest them and still make them like you. We call it technique."
Jim Reed, *Adam-12*

"There are no holidays in the fight against evil." Maxwell Smart, *Get Smart*

"I fail to comprehend your indignation, sir. I have simply made the logical deduction that you are a liar." Mr. Spock, *Star Trek*

"The way some of the younger generation carries on, some people wish that they'd develop a birth control pill that was retroactive." Milton Berle, *Rowan & Martin's Laugh-In*

TV GUIDE

The Seventies

"THE AUDIENCE WILL ALWAYS FORGIVE YOU FOR BEING WRONG AND EXCITING, BUT NEVER FOR BEING RIGHT AND DULL."
BURT REYNOLDS
OCTOBER 17, 1970

"Success has robbed me of uncertainty. I find uncertainty exciting."
Kojak's Telly Savalas
February 22, 1975

"The adulation, the money, the power can make you believe you're somebody you're not."
Happy Days' Henry Winkler
June 25, 1977

"In the education of the American people, I am Recess."
Laverne & Shirley producer Garry Marshall
May 19, 1979

"It's so weird to go on TV and do what you want!"
Saturday Night Live's John Belushi
May 29, 1976

1970

January 03 1970
Here Come the '70s!
How They Will Change the
Way You Live

January 10 1970
Fred MacMurray and
Beverly Garland of
My Three Sons

January 17 1970
Don Mitchell, Barbara Anderson,
Don Galloway, and Raymond Burr
of *Ironside*

January 24 1970
Tom Jones in
This Is Tom Jones

January 31 1970
Debbie Reynolds of
The Debbie Reynolds Show

February 07 1970
Elizabeth Montgomery and
Dick Sargent of
Bewitched

February 14 1970
Linda Harrison, Laraine Stephens,
and Karen Jensen of
Bracken's World

February 21 1970
James Daly and
Chad Everett of
Medical Center

February 28 1970
Clarence Williams III, Michael
Cole, and Peggy Lipton of
The Mod Squad

March 07 1970
The *Hee Haw* Group:
They Have Last Laugh

March 14 1970
Diahann Carroll of
Julia

March 21 1970
Jackie Gleason of
The Jackie Gleason Show

March 28 1970
Dan Rowan and
Dick Martin of
Rowan and Martin's Laugh-In

April 04 1970
The Cast of
The Brady Bunch

April 11 1970
Carol Burnett of
The Carol Burnett Show

April 18 1970
Burl Ives, James Farentino,
and Joseph Campanella of
The Bold Ones

April 25 1970
Raquel Welch and
John Wayne in
Raquel!

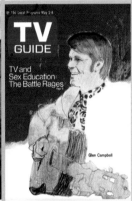

May 02 1970
Glen Campbell of
*The Glen Campbell
Goodtime Hour*

May 09 1970
David Frost of
The David Frost Show

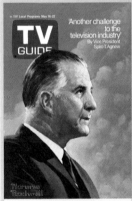

May 16 1970
Vice President Spiro Agnew –
Another Challenge to the
Television Industry

May 23 1970
Tricia Nixon with Mike
Wallace and Harry Reasoner

May 30 1970
Julie Sommars of
The Governor and J.J.

June 06 1970
Robert Young of
Marcus Welby, M.D.

June 13 1970
Johnny Cash of
The Johnny Cash Show

June 20 1970
Susan Neher, Joyce Menges, John
Forsythe, and Melanie Fullerton of
To Rome With Love

June 27 1970
Liza Minnelli Does a Special

July 04 1970
Miyoshi Umeki, Brandon Cruz,
and Bill Bixby of
The Courtship of Eddie's Father

July 11 1970
The Cast of
The Beverly Hillbillies

July 18 1970
The Golddiggers
in London

July 25 1970
The Cast of
Mayberry R.F.D.

August 01 1970
Chet Huntley of
The Huntley-Brinkley Report

August 08 1970
Ted Bessel and
Marlo Thomas of
That Girl

August 15 1970
Johnny Carson of
The Tonight Show

August 22 1970
Ken Curtis, Milburn Stone, James
Arness, and Amanda Blake of
Gunsmoke

August 29 1970
Eddie Albert of
Green Acres

September 05 1970
Richard Burton, Lucille Ball
and Elizabeth Taylor

September 12 1970
Fall Preview:
Special Issue

September 19 1970
Mary Tyler Moore of
The Mary Tyler Moore Show

September 26 1970
Lloyd Haines, Denise Nicholad,
Karen Valentine, and Michael
Constantine of *Room 222*

October 03 1970
Red Skelton of
The Red Skelton Show

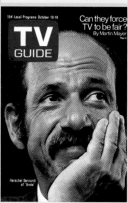

October 10 1970
Herschel Bernardi of
Arnie

October 17 1970
The Cast of
The Partridge Family

October 24 1970
Don Knotts of
The Don Knotts Show

October 31 1970
Mike Connors of
Mannix

November 07 1970
Renne Jarrett, John Fink,
and Celeste Holm of
Nancy

November 14 1970
Christopher George of
The Immortal

November 21 1970
Sally Marr – What It Takes To
Be a Starlet in the '70s

November 28 1970
John Wayne's $2,000,000
Special

December 05 1970
Dick Cavett of
The Dick Cavett Show

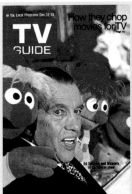

December 12 1970
Ed Sullivan and The Muppets in
Christmas Show

December 19 1970
Holiday Preview

December 26 1970
Diahann Carroll and
Fred Williamson of
Julia

1971

January 02 1971
Remember 1970?

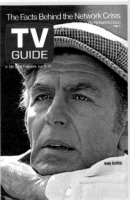

January 09 1971
Andy Griffith of
Headmaster

January 16 1971
June Carter and
Johnny Cash of
The Johnny Cash Show

January 23 1971
Flip Wilson of
The Flip Wilson Show

January 30 1971
James Arness of
Gunsmoke

February 06 1971
Tony Randall and
Jack Klugman of
The Odd Couple

February 13 1971
Goldie Hawn in
Pure Goldie

February 20 1971
Doris Day of
The Doris Day Show

February 27 1971
Sharon Acker and
Hal Holbrook of
The Senator

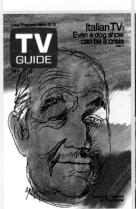

March 06 1971
Broderick Crawford of
The Interns

March 13 1971
Gene Barry and
Robert Stack of
The Name of the Game

March 20 1971
Harry Reasoner of
The ABC Evening News

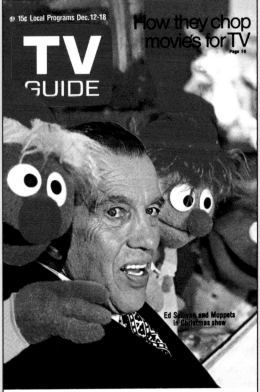

Ed Sullivan began his career as a newspaper writer
and radio broadcaster. By the 30's, he was writing and
appearing as himself in plays on Broadway. *The Ed
Sullivan Show* ran from 1948 to 1971 and helped
launch many future stars such as **Elvis Presley** and
Martin & Lewis. He died on 10/13/1974 of cancer.

81

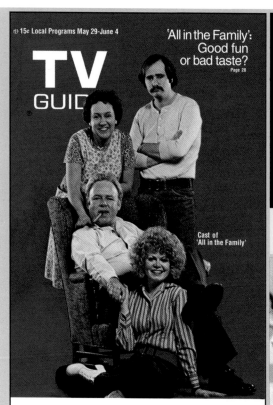

Cast of 'All in the Family'

Based on the BBC series *Till Death Us Do Part*, *All in the Family* was an influential sitcom providing satire based on real life instead of escapism. The show aired from 1971 to 1979 and introduced us to *The Jeffersons*, who went on to have their own series in 1975.

March 27 1971
Michael Landon, Lorne Greene, Dan Blocker, and Mitch Vogel of *Bonanza*

April 03 1971
Cable TV: What's All the Talk About?

April 10 1971
Bob Hope Looks Back on His 30 Years With Oscar

April 17 1971
Paul Newman in an Auto Racing Special

April 24 1971
Elena Verdugo and Robert Young of *Marcus Welby, M.D.*

May 01 1971
Lisa Gerritsen and Mary Tyler Moore of *The Mary Tyler Moore Show*

May 08 1971
Henry Fonda of *The Smith Family*

May 15 1971
Television Journalism – An Inside Story

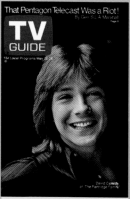

May 22 1971
David Cassidy of *The Partridge Family*

May 29 1971
Jean Stapleton, Carroll O'Connor, Rob Reiner, and Sally Struthers of *All in the Family*

June 05 1971
Dan Rowan and Dick Martin of *Laugh-In*

June 12 1971
Lucille Ball of *Here's Lucy*

June 19 1971
Brandon Cruz and Bill Bixby of *The Courtship of Eddie's Father*

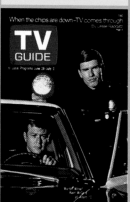

June 26 1971
Martin Milner and Kent McCord of *Adam-12*

July 03 1971
Michael Cole, Peggy Lipton, and Clarence Williams III of *The Mod Squad*

July 10 1971
Cookie Monster of *Sesame Street*

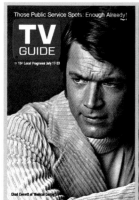

July 17 1971
Chad Everett of
Medical Center

July 24 1971
Lefty, the star of Disney's
Ding-a-Ling Lynx

July 31 1971
Henry VIII and His Six Wives
Come to Television

August 07 1971
The Cast of
As the World Turns

August 14 1971
Mitch Vogel, Lorne Greene, Dan
Blocker, and Michael Landon of
Bonanza

August 21 1971
Public Television:
Is Anybody Watching?

August 28 1971
Howard Cosell, Don Meredith,
and Frank Gifford of
Monday Night Football

September 04 1971
Jack Lord of
Hawaii Five-O

September 11 1971
Fall Preview:
Special Issue

September 18 1971
Sandy Duncan of
Funny Face

September 25 1971
Shirley MacLaine of
Shirley's World

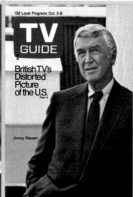

October 02 1971
Jimmy Stewart of
The Jimmy Stewart Show

October 09 1971
Hope Lange and
Dick Van Dyke of
The New Dick Van Dyke Show

October 16 1971
Mia Farrow of
Peyton Place and in
Goodbye, Raggedy Ann

October 23 1971
James Franciscus of
Longstreet

October 30 1971
Larry Hagman and
Donna Mills of
The Good Life

November 06 1971
William Conrad of
Cannon

November 13 1971
Rupert Crosse and
Don Adams of
The Partners

November 20 1971
Sally Struthers, Jean Stapleton,
Carroll O'Connor, and Rob Reiner
of *All in the Family*

November 27 1971
Joanne Woodward in
All The Way Home

December 04 1971
Julie Andrews and
Carol Burnett in
Julie and Carol at Lincoln Center

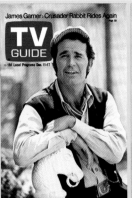

December 11 1971
James Garner of
Nichols

December 18 1971
The Cast of
The Partridge Family

December 25 1971
Christmas

1972

January 01 1972
Remember 1971?

January 06 1972
Flip Wilson of
The Flip Wilson Show

January 15 1972
America Out of Focus

January 22 1972
Greg Morris, Peter Graves, Peter
Lupus, and Lynda Day George of
Mission: Impossible

January 29 1972
David Janssen of
O'Hara, U.S. Treasury

February 05 1972
Raymond Burr and
Elizabeth Baur of
Ironside

February 12 1972
Arthur Hill of
Owen Marshall, Counselor at Law

February 19 1972
President Nixon
and En-lai Chou

February 26 1972
Mary Tyler Moore of
The Mary Tyler Moore Show

March 04 1972
Johnny Carson of
The Tonight Show

March 11 1972
James Brolin and
Robert Young of
Marcus Welby, M.D.

March 18 1972
Sonny and Cher Bono of
The Sonny & Cher Comedy Hour

March 25 1972
Peter Falk of
Columbo

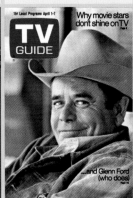

April 01 1972
Glenn Ford of
Cade's County

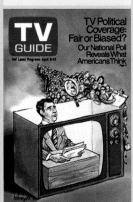

April 08 1972
TV Political Coverage:
Fair or Biased?

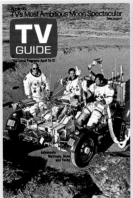

April 15 1972
Astronauts Thomas K. Mattingly,
Charles M. Duke, and
John W. Young

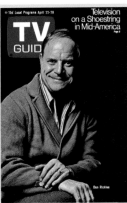

April 22 1972
Don Rickles of
The Don Rickles Show

April 29 1972
Susan Saint James and
Rock Hudson of
McMillan & Wife

May 06 1972
Sandy Duncan of
Funny Face

May 13 1972
Demond Wilson and
Redd Foxx of
Sanford and Son

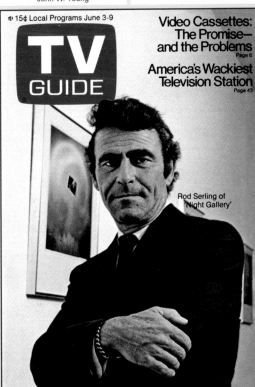

Although he is most famous for his TV programs,
Night Gallery and *The Twilight Zone*, **Rod Serling**
began as a writer for shows like *Studio One.* He wrote
Requiem for a Heavyweight which aired on the
Hallmark Hall of Fame in 1956. In the August 1, 2004
issue, **TV Guide** voted him the #1 Greatest Sci-Fi
Legend. He entered the twilight zone on 6/28/1975.

May 20 1972
Efrem Zimbalist Jr. of *The FBI*
and J. Edgar Hoover of The FBI

May 27 1972
Carroll O'Connor and
Jean Stapleton of
All in the Family

June 03 1972
Rod Serling of
Night Gallery

June 10 1972
Doris Day of
The Doris Day Show

June 17 1972
Julie London of
Emergency!

June 24 1972
Mike Connors of
Mannix

July 01 1972
Carol Burnett of
The Carol Burnett Show

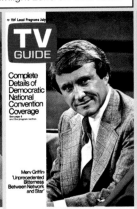

July 08 1972
Merv Griffin of
The Merv Griffin Show

July 15 1972
David Cassidy of
The Partridge Family

July 22 1972
Producer Jack Webb, Martin
Milner, and Kent McCord of
Adam-12

July 29 1972
All About
Love, American Style

August 05 1972
War and Peace
Comes To Television

August 12 1972
Leonardo Da Vinci:
Unusual Drama Series
Starts This Week

August 19 1972
Chad Everett of
Medical Center

August 26 1972
The Olympics

September 02 1972
Jack Klugman and
Tony Randall of
The Odd Couple

September 09 1972
Fall Preview:
Special Issue

September 16 1972
Yul Brynner and
Samantha Eggar in
Anna and the King

September 23 1972
George Peppard of
Banacek

September 30 1972
Meredith Baxter and
David Birney of
Bridget Loves Bernie

October 07 1972
The Cast of
Bonanza

October 14 1972
Robert Conrad of
Assignment: Vienna

October 21 1972
Carroll O'Connor and
Cloris Leachman star in
Of Thee I Sing

October 28 1972
Snoopy, Charlie Brown, and
Woodstock

November 04 1972
John Wayne: He Learned
to Love TV

November 11 1972
Allistair Cooke's
America

November 18 1972
Beatrice Arthur of
Maude

November 25 1972
Doug McClure, Tony Franciosa,
and Hugh O'Brian of
Search

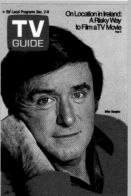

December 02 1972
Mike Douglas of
The Mike Douglas Show

December 09 1972
Julie Andrews of
The Julie Andrews Hour

December 16 1972
The Duke and Duchess of
Windsor – Television Recalls the
Love Affair of the Century

December 23 1972
Christmas

December 30 1972
Barbara Walters of
Today

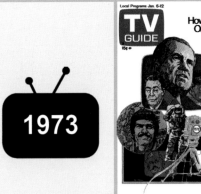
1973

January 06 1973
Richard Nixon, Leonid Brezhnev,
Chou En-Lai, and Mark Spitz

January 13 1973
China – Inside The
Forbidden City

January 20 1973
Bob Newhart and
Suzanne Pleshette of
The Bob Newhart Show

January 27 1973
Sam Melville, Georg Stanford
Brown, and Michael Ontkean of
The Rookies

February 03 1973
Bill Cosby of
The New Bill Cosby Show

February 10 1973
John Calvin, Paul Lynde,
and Jane Actman of
The Paul Lynde Show

February 17 1973
Susan Saint James and
Rock Hudson of
McMillan & Wife

February 24 1973
The Cast of
*M*A*S*H*

March 03 1973
William Conrad of
Cannon

March 10 1973
Marlo Thomas Returns in a
Special This Week

March 24 1973
Ann-Margret: Coming Up
in a Special

March 31 1973
Lucille Ball and
Desi Arnaz Jr.

March 17 1973
Redd Foxx and
Demond Wilson of
Sanford and Son

Bill Cosby is one of the most well known entertainers. Despite his comedic background, his big break came in 1965 when he landed a role on *I Spy* for which he won 3 Emmys during its 4 year run. He is now a television fixture and his 70's cartoon show, *Fat Albert and the Cosby Kids*, was made into a live-action film in 2004.

When Is Children's TV Going to Grow Up?
A new series by Edith Efron

April 07 1973
The Flintstones, Sesame Street, H.R. Pufnstuf, Sabrina The Teenage Witch, The Jackson Five

Fight of the Week for Thinkers: 'The Advocates'

April 14 1973
Shelly Fabares and Brian Keith of *The Little People*

Permissive TV: The FCC Chairman's Opinions

Easter Special: Raymond Burr As the Man Who Became Pope John

April 21 1973
Raymond Burr in *Portrait: A Man Whose Name Was John*

The Waltons – A Surprising Success

April 28 1973
The Waltons – A Surprising Success

How Censors Cut the Bleep Out of TV

May 05 1973
Peter Falk of *Columbo*

Previewing TV's Longest Space Spectacular

May 12 1973
Shirley Booth of *A Touch of Grace*

Did TV Victimize the Loud Family?

May 19 1973
Mary Tyler Moore of *The Mary Tyler Moore Show*

Who's That Fat Bum On Television? Me! By Jimmy Breslin

May 26 1973
Karl Malden and Michael Douglas of *The Streets of San Francisco*

TV's Kid-Show Hosts: Endangered Species?

June 02 1973
Michael Evans and Carroll O'Connor of *All In The Family*

Annoying Reruns? The Facts Behind the Complaints

June 09 1973
Richard Widmark of *Madigan*

Instant Ratings: Now They Can Cancel Your Favorites Faster

June 16 1973
Bea Arthur and Bill Macy of *Maude*

'Kung Fu': An Eastern Western—And A Hit

June 23 1973
David Carradine of *Kung Fu*

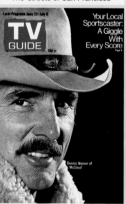

Your Local Sportscaster: A Giggle With Every Score

June 30 1973
Dennis Weaver of *McCloud*

Jacqueline Susann: Some Talk Shows Bite

July 07 1973
Dick Cavett of *The Dick Cavett Show*

A New Survey: Viewer Attitudes On Adult Themes, News Bias, TV Quality

Sonny and Cher: In Public and In Private

July 14 1973
Sonny and Cher of *The Sonny & Cher Show*

TV Medical Shows: They Really Do Save Lives

July 21 1973
Robert Young of *Marcus Welby, M.D.* and Chad Everett of *Medical Center*

THE LIE THAT WOULDN'T DIE
TV'S GREAT SEX MOVIE SCARE

July 28 1973
TV's Great Sex Movie Scare

Here Come (Yawn) More Late, Late Shows

August 04 1973
Martin Milner and Kent McCord of *Adam-12*

What Has Television Got Against Women?

Country Music Booms

August 11 1973
Roy Clark of *Hee Haw*

Camera At 60 Fathoms: How Underwater TV Saved The Minisub Sea-Link

August 18 1973
Robert Fuller of *Emergency!*

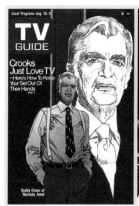

August 25 1973
Buddy Ebsen of
Barnaby Jones

September 01 1973
The Miss Americas Bert
Parks Never Met

September 08 1973
Fall Preview

September 15 1973
Pro Football '73

September 22 1973
Jack Lord and
James MacArthur in
Hawaii Five-O

September 29 1973
The War in Vietnam: What
Happened vs. What We Saw

October 06 1973
Diana Rigg of
Diana

October 13 1973
Does TV Go Too Far?

The first Miss America Pageant, known as the
National Beauty Tournament, was held in 1921 as
part of Atlantic City's Fall Frolic festivities. The
first one to be broadcast nationally was in 1954,
and **Lee Meriwether** won the crown. It has been
held annually since 1935 and inspired a host
of other beauty pageants.

October 20 1973
Telly Savalas of
Kojak

October 27 1973
Blythe Danner and
Ken Howard of
Adam's Rib

November 03 1973
Deidre Lanihan of
Needles and Pins

November 10 1973
A Very Special Week

November 17 1973
Frank Sinatra Returns to TV
in a Special

November 24 1973
Cousteau Explores Antartica

December 01 1973
Bill Bixby of
The Magician

December 08 1973
Georgia Engel, Mary Tyler Moore,
and Valerie Harper of
The Mary Tyler Moore Show

December 15 1973
Katharine Hepburn in
The Glass Menagerie

December 22 1973
Christmas

December 29 1973
Mason Reese: 7 Year Old
Huckster

1974

January 05 1974
How You Saw the World on
Television in 1973

January 12 1974
Beatrice Arthur, Bill Macy,
and Conrad Bain of
Maude

January 19 1974
Bob Hope: The Comedian
Turns Serious

January 26 1974
David Carradine of
Kung Fu

February 02 1974
Dom DeLuise of
Lotsa Luck

February 09 1974
The Cast of
M*A*S*H

February 16 1974
Michael Douglas and
Karl Malden of
The Streets of San Francisco

February 23 1974
Richard Boone of
Hec Ramsey

March 02 1974
Jimmy Stewart of
Hawkins

Based on the 1970 movie, *M*A*S*H* debuted in
September of 1972 and by the end of the first season
was in danger of cancellation. It survived and in its
second season entered the Top 20 and never left.
The series ended on February 28, 1983 with a two
and a half-hour finale which drew the largest
audience ever for a TV show episode.

March 09 1974
How Show Biz Takes Over
Local News

March 16 1974
Carol Burnett and
Vicki Lawrence of
The Carol Burnett Show

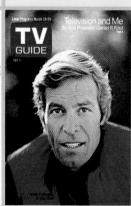

March 23 1974
James Franciscus of
Doc Elliot

March 30 1974
Susan Strasberg and
Tony Musante of
Toma

April 06 1974
Carroll O'Connor, Bill Macy,
Redd Foxx, and Producer
Norman Lear

April 13 1974
Richard Thomas, Michael
Learned, and Ralph Waite of
The Waltons

April 20 1974
Peter Falk of
Columbo

April 27 1974
A Best-Selling Novel,
QB-VII, Comes to TV

May 04 1974
Sam Melville, Georg Stanford
Brown, and Michael Ontkean of
The Rookies

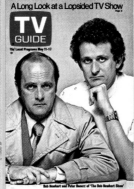

May 11 1974
Bob Newhart and
Peter Bonerz of
The Bob Newhart Show

May 18 1974
Lee Majors of
The Six Million Dollar Man

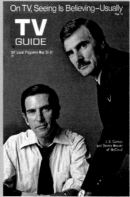

May 25 1974
J.D. Cannon and
Dennis Weaver of
McCloud

June 01 1974
The Day it all Ended for
Sonny and Cher

June 08 1974
Marilyn Baker of KQED-TV
San Francisco

June 15 1974
Kathy O'Dare and
Ron Howard of
Happy Days

June 22 1974
John Chancellor of
NBC Nightly News

June 29 1974
Esther Rolle and
John Amos of
Good Times

July 06 1974
Lucille Ball – End of an
Era: Lucy Bows Out
After 23 years

July 13 1974
Johnny Carson of
The Tonight Show

July 20 1974
The Boom in Made-for-TV Films

July 27 1974
Lee McCain and
Ronny Cox of
Apple's Way

August 03 1974
Kevin Tighe and
Randolph Mantooth of
Emergency!

August 10 1974
Games Viewers Play

August 17 1974
Police Story

August 24 1974
Model Susie Blakely: From Texas to TV Commercials – and $100,000 a Year

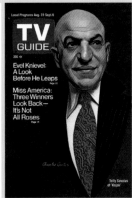

August 31 1974
Telly Savalas of *Kojak*

September 07 1974
Fall Preview

September 14 1974
They're Off and Running!

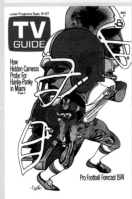

September 21 1974
Pro Football Forecast 1974

September 28 1974
Paul Sand of *Friends and Lovers*

October 05 1974
Redd Foxx, Demond Wilson, and Friend of *Sanford and Son*

October 12 1974
Valerie Harper of *Rhoda*

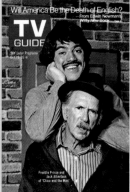

October 19 1974
Freddie Prinze and Jack Albertson of *Chico and the Man*

October 26 1974
Ralph Waite, Will Geer, and Richard Thomas of *The Waltons*

November 02 1974
The Cast of *M*A*S*H*

November 09 1974
Sophia Loren: An Appreciation

November 16 1974
Robert Duvall, Al Pacino, Marlon Brando, and James Caan

November 23 1974
What A Week!

November 30 1974
Teresa Graves of *Get Christie Love*

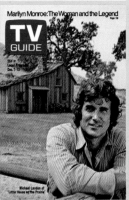

December 07 1974
Michael Landon of *Little House on the Prairie*

December 14 1974
The Cast of *Good Times*

December 21 1974
Santa Claus and Rudolph

December 28 1974
Memorable Bowl Games, Wacky Parades

Why Is Chico Crying All the Way to the Bank? Page 18

TV GUIDE

Local Programs March 1-8
25¢

Jack Albertson and Freddie Prinze of 'Chico and the Man'

Chico and the Man premiered on September 1, 1974 starring comedian **Freddie Prinze** and seasoned actors **Jack Albertson** and **Scatman Crothers**. It became an instant hit and featured many guest stars. After Prinze's death on 1/29/1977, the show struggled through another season but just wasn't the same.

1975

January 04 1975
Angie Dickinson of
Police Woman

January 11 1975
David Janssen of
Harry O

January 18 1975
Clifton Davis and
Theresa Merritt of
That's My Mama

January 25 1975
Gene Shalit, Jim Hartz, and
Barbara Walters of
Today

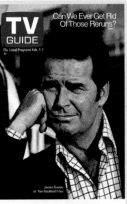

February 01 1975
James Garner of
The Rockford Files

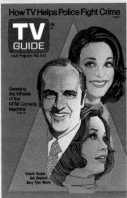

February 08 1975
Valerie Harper, Bob Newhart,
and Mary Tyler Moore

February 15 1975
Georg Stanford Brown, Bruce
Fairbairn, Sam Melville, and Gerald
S. O'Loughlin of *The Rookies*

February 22 1975
Telly Savalas of
Kojak

March 01 1975
Jack Albertson and
Freddie Prinze of
Chico and the Man

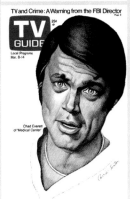

March 08 1975
Chad Everett of
Medical Center

March 15 1975
Karen Valentine of
Karen

March 22 1975
Karl Malden and
Michael Douglas of
The Streets of San Francisco

March 29 1975
Beatrice Arthur and
Hermione Baddeley of
Maude

April 05 1975
Baseball: This Year's Winners

April 12 1975
Cher – Without Sonny

April 19 1975
Frank Converse and
Claude Atkins of
Movin' On

April 26 1975
Dennis Weaver, J.D. Cannon,
and Terry Carter of
McCloud

May 03 1975
Valerie Harper and
David Groh of
Rhoda

May 10 1975
Muhammad Ali Defends His
Title on Home TV This Week

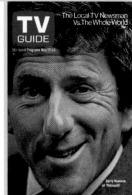

May 17 1975
Barry Newman of
Petrocelli

May 24 1975
Jason Robards and Colleen
Dewhurst in O'Neill's
A Moon for the Misbegotten

May 31 1975
The Cast of
The Bob Newhart Show

June 07 1975
The Cast of
Little House on the Prairie

June 14 1975
Violence on TV – Does It Affect
Our Society?

June 21 1975
Sherman Hemsley, Isabel
Sanford, and Mike Evans of
The Jeffersons

June 28 1975
Special Bicentennial Issue

July 05 1975
Telma Hopkins, Tony Orlando,
and Joyce Vincent Wilson of
Tony Orlando and Dawn

July 12 1975
Apollo/Soyuz Mission
on Television

July 19 1975
The Cast of
Barney Miller

July 26 1975
Howard K. Smith and
Harry Reasoner of
ABC Evening News

August 02 1975
Mike Douglas of
The Mike Douglas Show

August 09 1975
Buddy Ebsen Hits the Road

August 16 1975
The Cast of
Emergency!

August 23 1975
Ralph Waite, Richard Thomas,
and Michael Learned of
The Waltons

August 30 1975
Carroll O'Connor of
All in the Family

September 06 1975
Fall Preview:
Special Issue

September 13 1975
NFL Winners

September 20 1975
Barbara Walters Visits
European Royalty

September 27 1975
Howard Cosell of
*Saturday Night Live with
Howard Cosell*

October 04 1975
Lee Remick in
Jennie

October 11 1975
Glenn Ford, Julie Harris, Elizabeth
Cheshire, and Lance Kerwin of
The Family Holvak

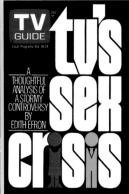

October 18 1975
TV's Sex Crisis

October 25 1975
Cloris Leachman of
Phyllis

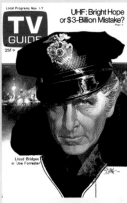

November 01 1975
Lloyd Bridges of
Joe Forrester

November 08 1975
Julie Kavner and
Valerie Harper of
Rhoda

November 15 1975
David Soul and
Paul Michael Glaser of
Starsky and Hutch

November 22 1975
A Banner Week!

November 29 1975
Tony Curtis of
McCoy

December 06 1975
Does America Want Family
Viewing Time?

December 13 1975
Robert Wagner and
Eddie Albert of
Switch

December 20 1975
Christmas

December 27 1975
Fred and Robert Blake of
Baretta

January 03 1976
Telly Savalas of
Kojak

January 10 1976
Ron Howard and
Henry Winkler of
Happy Days

January 17 1976
Angie Dickinson and
Earl Holliman of
Police Woman

January 24 1976
Mike Farrell, Alan Alda,
and Harry Morgan of
*M*A*S*H*

January 31 1976
Steve Forrest of
S.W.A.T.

February 07 1976
The Cast of
Barney Miller

February 14 1976
Redd Foxx of
Sanford and Son

In 1935, at age thirteen, **Redd Foxx** started his career
by playing washboard in a street band. In the 40's he
began doing stand-up comedy. He landed his most
famous role, Fred Sanford of *Sanford & Son* in 1972.
The series aired until 1977 and was revived for a year
in 1980 under the name *Sanford* without **Demond
Wilson** playing "son." Redd Foxx died on 10/11/1991.

February 21 1976
William Conrad of
Cannon

February 28 1976
Bob Hope Tries
Something Different

March 06 1976
Noah Beery and
James Garner of
The Rockford Files

March 13 1976
Jack Albertson, Freddie Prinze,
and Scatman Crothers of
Chico and the Man

March 20 1976
Danny Thomas of
The Practice

March 27 1976
Jack Palance of
Bronk

April 03 1976
Baseball Faces an Explosive Year

April 10 1976
Police Story

April 17 1976
Gabriel Kaplan and
Marcia Strassman of
Welcome Back, Kotter

April 24 1976
Beatrice Arthur of
Maude

May 01 1976
George Kennedy of
The Blue Knight

May 08 1976
Lindsay Wagner of
The Bionic Woman

May 15 1976
Hal Williams, Jose Perez, Bobby
Sandler, and Rick Hurst of
On the Rocks

May 22 1976
Cindy Williams and
Penny Marshall of
Laverne & Shirley

May 29 1976
Michael Landon and His
Little House on the Prairie
Daughters

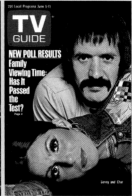

June 05 1976
Sonny and Cher of
The Sonny & Cher Show

June 12 1976
David Janssen and
Anthony Zerbe of
Harry O

June 19 1976
Louise Lasser of
Mary Hartman, Mary Hartman

June 26 1976
Mary Tyler Moore
in Red Square:
Mission to Moscow

July 03 1976
Special Issue: Television
Celebrates the Big Day

July 10 1976
Convention Coverage:
Complete Details

July 17 1976
The Olympics

July 24 1976
Bonnie Franklin of
One Day at a Time

July 31 1976
Terrorism and Television – The
Medium in the Middle

August 07 1976
Marie Osmond and
Donny Osmond of
Donny & Marie

August 14 1976
Peter Falk of
Columbo

August 21 1976
Richard Thomas, Will Geer,
and Ellen Corby of
The Waltons

August 28 1976
Lee Majors of
The Bionic Man

September 04 1976
Annual (Gulp!) Pro-Football
Predictions

September 11 1976
Bob Dylan Today:
TV Special This Week

September 18 1976
Fall Preview:
Special Issue

September 25 1976
Farrah Fawcett, Kate Jackson, and Jaclyn Smith of *Charlie's Angels*

October 02 1976
David Birney of *Serpico*

October 09 1976
Bernadette Peters and Richard Crenna of *All's Fair*

October 16 1976
How World Series Jitters Turn Heroes Into Bums

October 23 1976
Linda Lavin of *Alice*

October 30 1976
Jimmy Carter and Gerald Ford – Day of Decision: How Television Will Count The Votes

November 06 1976
Vivien Leigh and Clark Gable in *Gone With The Wind*

November 13 1976
Dorothy Hamill Skates into Television

November 20 1976
NBC Throws an All-Star 50th Birthday Party

November 27 1976
Paul Michael Glaser and David Soul of *Starsky and Hutch*

December 04 1976
Tony Randall of *The Tony Randall Show*

December 11 1976
Valerie Harper of *Rhoda*

December 18 1976
John Chancellor and David Brinkley: The Race to Catch Conkrite

December 25 1976
Santa Claus

1977

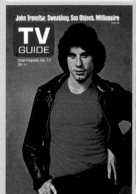

January 01 1977
John Travolta of *Welcome Back, Kotter*

January 08 1977
Super Bowl

January 15 1977
Presidential Inauguration of Jimmy Carter

January 22 1977
Roots: The Story Behind the Search

January 29 1977
Lynda Carter of *Wonder Woman*

February 05 1977
Barbara Walters and ABC:
Is the Marriage Working?

February 12 1977
Telly Savalas and
George Savalas of
Kojak

February 19 1977
Nancy Walker of
Blansky's Beauties

February 26 1977
Martha Raye and
Rock Hudson of
McMillan

March 05 1977
Liv Ullman in
Scenes from a Marriage

March 12 1977
Lauren Hutton in
The Rhinemann Exchange

March 19 1977
Mary Tyler Moore of
The Mary Tyler Moore Show

March 26 1977
Jack Klugman of
Quincy

April 02 1977
Dinah Shore with Golf Champs
Judy Rankin, Jane Blalock,
and Joanne Garner

April 09 1977
Baseball '77: The Winners Are...

Roots, airing January 23 to 30 in 1977 was a ground-breaking event in television. Based on **Alex Haley**'s novel, it defied customary programming by portraying whites as bad guys and blacks as heroes. It employed an impressive list of actors, and the 8th night finale ranks 3rd in the highest single-episode ratings ever.

April 16 1977
Frank Sinatra: An
Exclusive Interview

April 23 1977
Mike Wallace, Morley Safer,
and Dan Rather of
60 Minutes

April 30 1977
David Frost with
Richard Nixon

May 07 1977
Valerie Bertinelli, Bonnie Franklin,
and Mackenzie Phillips of
One Day at a Time

May 14 1977
Tom Brokaw of
Today

May 21 1977
Farrah Fawcett-Majors of
Charlie's Angels

How Well Do Networks Cover Real Crime? Page 4

TV GUIDE

Local Programs Aug. 20-26 25¢

James Garner and Joe Santos of 'The Rockford Files'

James Garner started his career in 1956 with a variety of supporting television and film roles. In 1957 he landed a co-starring role on the series *Maverick* and quickly stole the show. He has since starred in numerous films and TV shows. *The Rockford Files* is a 70's classic which spawned many TV movies in the 90's.

May 28 1977
Robert Blake of
Baretta

June 04 1977
Alan Alda of
*M*A*S*H*

June 11 1977
Dan Haggerty and Bozo of
*The Life and Times of
Grizzly Adams*

June 18 1977
Cindy Williams and
Penny Marshall of
Laverne & Shirley

June 25 1977
The Cast of
The Waltons

July 02 1977
Linda Lavin and
Polly Holliday of
Alice

July 09 1977
Peter Isacksen and
Don Rickles of
C.P.O. Sharkey

July 16 1977
The Cast of
Barney Miller

July 23 1977
Public TV in Turmoil

July 30 1977
Johnny Carson of
The Tonight Show

August 06 1977
Fozzie Bear and
Kermit the Frog of
The Muppets

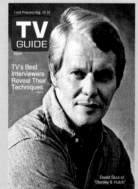

August 13 1977
David Soul of
Starsky & Hutch

August 20 1977
James Garner and
Joe Santos of
The Rockford Files

August 27 1977
Sex and Violence: Hollywood
Fights Back

September 03 1977
Andy Griffith, Jason Robards,
Robert Vaughn, & Cliff Robertson in
Washington: Behind Closed Doors

September 10 1977
Fall Preview:
Special Issue

September 17 1977
Pro Football Winners

September 24 1977
Betty White and
John Hillerman of
The Betty White Show

October 01 1977
Squire Frickell and
Tony Roberts of
Rosetti and Ryan

October 08 1977
Marie Osmond and
Donny Osmond of
Donny & Marie

October 15 1977
Ed Asner of
Lou Grant

October 22 1977
The Cast of
Welcome Back, Kotter

October 29 1977
Beverly Archer of
We've Got Each Other

November 05 1977
Parker Stevenson and
Shaun Cassidy of
The Hardy Boys

November 12 1977
Al Pacino, Marlon Brando,
and Robert DeNiro in
The Godfather

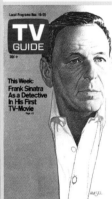

November 19 1977
Frank Sinatra in
Contract on Cherry Street

November 26 1977
The Cast of
Soap

December 03 1977
Patrick Duffy of
The Man From Atlantis

December 10 1977
What the Censors Cut….
And Why

December 17 1977
Bonnie Franklin, Mackenzie Phillips,
Valerie Bertinelli, and Pat
Harrington of *One Day at a Time*

December 24 1977
Santa Claus

December 31 1977
Kevin Dobson and
Telly Savalas of
Kojak

1978

January 07 1978
Henry Winkler, Ron Howard,
Donny Most, and Anson Williams
of *Happy Days*

January 14 1978
The First Nighttime Superbowl

January 21 1978
The Cast of
Family

January 28 1978
Dan Haggerty and Bozo of
*The Life and Times of
Grizzly Adams*

February 04 1978
The Cast of
The Love Boat

February 11 1978
Jack Klugman and
Garry Walberg of
Quincy

February 18 1978
Jaclyn Smith, Kate Jackson,
and Cheryl Ladd of
Charlie's Angels

February 25 1978
The Cast of
*M*A*S*H*

March 04 1978
Lynnie Greene and
Bess Armstrong of
On Our Own

March 11 1978
Kene Holliday and
Victor French of
Carter Country

March 18 1978
Lindsay Wagner of
The Bionic Woman

March 25 1978
Walter Cronkite and
Mary Tyler Moore

April 01 1978
Baseball 1978

April 08 1978
Polly Holliday, Linda Lavin, Beth
Howland, and Vic Tayback of
Alice

April 15 1978
Holocaust Miniseries

April 22 1978
Changing the Shape of
Television

April 29 1978
Cindy Williams, Penny Marshall,
Michael McKean, and David L.
Landers of *Laverne & Shirley*

May 06 1978
Buddy Ebsen of
Barnaby Jones

May 13 1978
The Cast of
Little House on the Prairie

May 20 1978
Suzanne Somers, Joyce DeWitt
and John Ritter of
Three's Company

May 27 1978
The Phil Donahue Talk Show
Phenomenon

June 03 1978
Paul Michael Glaser and
David Soul of
Starsky & Hutch

June 10 1978
UFOs on TV: Flying in the
Face of Logic

June 17 1978
Valerie Harper of
Rhoda

June 24 1978
Can You Believe the Ratings?

July 01 1978
Ricardo Montalban and
Herve Villechaize of
Fantasy Island

July 08 1978
Cast Members of
The Young and The Restless

July 15 1978
Robert Conrad of
The Black Sheep Squadron

July 22 1978
Gavin MacLeod of
The Love Boat

July 29 1978
The Cast of
Saturday Night Live

August 05 1978
Sherman Hemsley, Paul Benedict,
and Isabel Sanford of
The Jeffersons

The Cast of 'Saturday Night Live

Saturday Night Live debuted on October 11, 1975 and was originally named *Saturday Night* to avoid confusion with another show airing on Saturdays. It is one of the longest running variety programs and many members of the cast have gone on to films or their own television shows.

August 12 1978
David Hartman of
Good Morning America

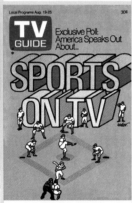

August 19 1978
Sports on TV

August 26 1978
Cheryl Ladd of
Charlie's Angels

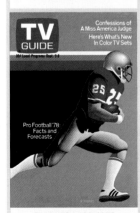

September 02 1978
Pro Football '78:
Facts and Forecasts

September 09 1978
Fall Preview:
Special Issue

September 16 1978
Dirk Benedict, Lorne Greene,
and Richard Hatch of
Battlestar Galactica

September 23 1978
Mary Tyler Moore of
Mary

September 30 1978
Richard Chamberlain, Robert
Conrad, and Barbara Carrera in
Centennial

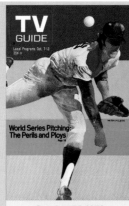

October 07 1978
World Series Pitching: The
Perils and Ploys

October 14 1978
Robert Urich of
Vegas

October 21 1978
Gordon Jones, Tim Reid, Gary
Sandy, and Howard Hesseman of
WKRP in Cincinnati

October 28 1978
Pam Dawber and
Robin Williams of
Mork & Mindy

November 04 1978
John Travolta of
Welcome Back, Kotter

November 11 1978
Ron Leibman of
Kaz

November 18 1978
Foreign Lobbyists: How They
Try To Manipulate Television

November 25 1978
Suzanne Somers of
Three's Company

December 02 1978
Benji's Very Own Christmas Story

December 09 1978
Linda Kelsey and
Ed Asner of
Lou Grant

December 16 1978
The Cast of
Eight is Enough

December 23 1978
Santa Claus

December 30 1978
Dick Clark of
Dick Clark's Live Wednesday

January 06 1979
Carroll O'Connor and
Jean Stapleton of
All in the Family

January 13 1979
Roone Arledge, Richard Salent, and
Les Crystal – The Hottest Television
News Controversies

January 20 1979
Super Bowl XIII

January 27 1979
Katharine Hepburn: The Making
of a TV Movie

February 03 1979
Larry Wilcox and
Erik Estrada of
CHiPS

February 10 1979
Shakespeare: TV Tackles All
37 Plays

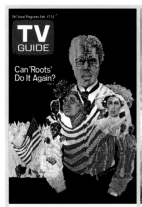

February 17 1979
Can *Roots* Do It Again?

February 24 1979
James Arness of
How the West Was Won

March 03 1979
Gary Coleman of
Diff'rent Strokes

March 10 1979
Harry Reasoner, Dan Rather,
Morley Safer, and Mike Wallace
of *60 Minutes*

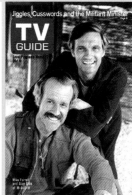

March 17 1979
Alan Alda and
Mike Farrell of
*M*A*S*H*

March 24 1979
Ricardo Montalban of
Fantasy Island

March 31 1979
Baseball, '79: Picking
the Winners

April 07 1979
Maren Jensen of
Battlestar Galactica

April 14 1979
John S. Ragin and
Jack Klugman of
Quincy

April 21 1979
Walter Cronkite of
CBS News

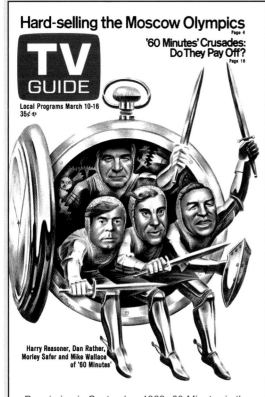

Premiering in September 1968, *60 Minutes* is the oldest news magazine TV show and set the standard for all those that followed. With a wide range of stories, (breaking news, investigative pieces, interviews, and satirical commentary) *60 Minutes* remains the most watched news magazine on television.

April 28 1979
Danny Devito and
Judd Hirsch of
Taxi

May 05 1979
James Stephen and
John Houseman of
The Paper Chase

May 12 1979
What Viewers Love/Hate
About Television

May 19 1979
Penny Marshall and
Cindy Williams of
Laverne & Shirley

May 26 1979
Ken Howard of
The White Shadow

June 02 1979
James Garner of
The Rockford Files

105

June 09 1979
Donna Pescow of
Angie

June 16 1979
Patrick Duffy, Victoria Principal,
and Jim Davis of
Dallas

June 23 1979
Johnny Carson of
The Tonight Show

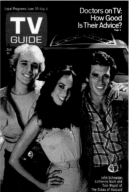

June 30 1979
John Schneider, Catherine Bach,
and Tom Wopat of
The Dukes of Hazzard

July 07 1979
The Cast of
Barney Miller

July 14 1979
Michael Landon, Melissa Sue
Anderson, and Linwood Boomer
of *Little House on the Prairie*

July 21 1979
Greg Evigan and Sam of
B.J. and the Bear

July 28 1979
Lou Ferrigno and
Bill Bixby of
The Incredible Hulk

August 04 1979
Joyce DeWitt of
Three's Company

August 11 1979
Rod Arrants of
Search For Tomorrow

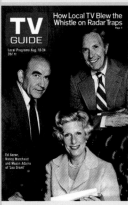

August 18 1979
Ed Asner, Nancy Marchand,
and Mason Adams of
Lou Grant

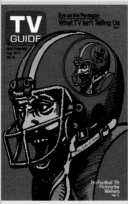

August 25 1979
Pro Football '79: Picking
the Winners

September 01 1979
Do Miss Americas Really Live
Happily Ever After?

September 08 1979
Fall Preview:
Special Issue

September 15 1979
Robert Guillaume of
Benson

September 22 1979
Carroll O'Connor: Stormy Years
with Archie

September 29 1979
Pope John Paul II and Television:
A Perfect Match

October 06 1979
The World Series: How to Win
with Craft and Cunning

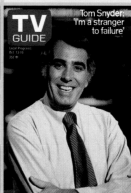

October 13 1979
Tom Snyder of
Tomorrow

October 20 1979
Loni Anderson, Gary Sandy,
and Howard Hessman of
WKRP in Cincinnati

October 27 1979
Muhammad Ali in
Freedom Road

November 03 1979
Stefanie Powers and
Robert Wagner of
Hart to Hart

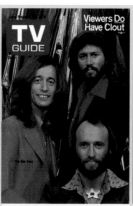

November 10 1979
Robin Gibb, Barry Gibb,
and Maurice Gibb of
The Bee Gees

November 17 1979
Wilfrid Hyde-White and
Shelley Smith of
The Associates

November 24 1979
Pernell Roberts of
Trapper John, M.D.

December 01 1979
Barbara Walters: My Most
Revealing Interviews

December 08 1979
Talk Show Hosts: Who Are
TV's Best – and Why?

December 15 1979
Henry Winkler: My Life – From
Fonzie to Scrooge

December 22 1979
Santa Claus

December 29 1979
Jaclyn Smith, Cheryl Ladd
and Shelley Hack of
Charlie's Angels

Memorable TV Show Quotes from the 1970s

"Barnes just broke the cardinal rule in politics: never get caught in bed with a dead woman or a live man." J.R. Ewing, *Dallas*

"Man, you're like school during the summer. No class." Rudy, *Fat Albert and the Cosby Kids*

"What'd you say that I said that you said?" Roy DeSoto, *Emergency!*

"I just thank God I'm an atheist." Mike Stivic, *All in the Family*

"Ah...you 'assumed'. My dear, you should never assume. You see, when you 'assume' you make an ass...out of you...and me." Felix Unger, *The Odd Couple*

"Don't make me angry. You wouldn't like me when I'm angry."
David Banner, *The Incredible Hulk*

Colonel Sherman Potter: "By the way, what war is this?"
Benjamin Franklin "Hawkeye" Pierce: "The latest war to end all wars."
*M*A*S*H*

"You can't corrupt it. And you know why? Because to corrupt it, you've got to show how corrupt you really are." Theo Kojak, *Kojak*

"I'm an experienced woman. I've been around...Well, alright, I might not've been around, but I've been...nearby." Mary Richards, *Mary Tyler Moore*

Richie Cunningham: "All we had was beer in teeny-weeny little glasses."
Howard Cunningham: "How many teeny-weeny little glasses did you have?"
Richie Cunningham: "Seventy-two."
Happy Days

TV GUIDE

The Eighties

"Could Bruce Willis be the next TV leading man to parlay his small-screen success into big-screen stardom?"
TV Guide
May 24, 1986

"Take Howdy Doody. I believed Howdy was in a little world inside that glowing box. I was hypnotized, and I wanted to go away, to be with him in there."
Taxi's Andy Kaufman
June 6, 1981

"It's the pressure. Can you imagine me — or anybody — replacing Carson?"
David Letterman
October 2, 1982

"Cheers to any sports telecast that does not show the crowd doing The Wave."
TV Guide
February 2, 1985

"I think there are altogether too many action shows where the best parts are given to automobiles."
Miss Piggy
August 1, 1981

1980

January 05 1980
Jamie Farr, Alan Alda, and Loretta Swit of
*M*A*S*H*

January 12 1980
Erik Estrada and Larry Wilcox of
CHiPs

January 19 1980
Super Bowl '80

January 26 1980
Richard Mulligan and Cathryn Damon of
Soap

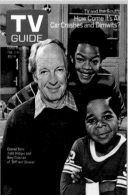

February 02 1980
Conrad Bain, Todd Bridges, and Gary Coleman of
Diff'rent Strokes

February 09 1980
Olympics Preview

February 16 1980
Buddy Ebsen and Lee Meriwether of
Barnaby Jones

February 23 1980
Selecting Our Leaders: The TV Drama Begins

March 01 1980
Herve Villechaize and Ricardo Montalban of
Fantasy Island

March 08 1980
Mary Crosby, Larry Hagman,
and Linda Gray of
Dallas

March 15 1980
The Cast of
Family

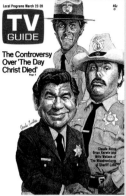

March 22 1980
Claude Atkins, Brian Kerwin,
and Mills Watson of
The Misadventures of Sherrif Lobo

March 29 1980
Martin Balsam and
Carroll O'Connor of
Archie Bunker's Place

April 05 1980
1980 Baseball: Picking Winners

April 12 1980
Olivia Newton-John – In an
ABC Special This Week

The first Super Bowl was played in 1967. The name originated when Chiefs' owner **Lamar Hunt** referred to it as the Super Bowl after seeing his daughter play with a "super ball." It airs the last Sunday in January (or the first in February) and four of them currently hold slots in Nielsen's All-Time Top 10 rated programs.

April 19 1980
Linda Lavin, Vic Tayback, Beth
Howland, and Diane Ladd of
Alice

April 26 1980
Beau Bridges and
Helen Shaver of
United States

May 03 1980
Robin Williams and
Pam Dawber of
Mork & Mindy

May 10 1980
Mackenzie Phillips, Bonnie Franklin,
and Valerie Bertinelli of
One Day at a Time

May 17 1980
Franklin Cover, Isabel Sanford,
Roxie Roker, and Sherman
Hemsley of *The Jeffersons*

May 24 1980
Situation Comedies: Are They
Getting Better – or Worse?

May 31 1980
Phyllis Davis, Bart Braverman,
Greg Morris, and Robert Urich
of *Vegas*

June 07 1980
Joan Van Ark and
Ted Shackelford of
Knots Landing

June 14 1980
Lynn Redgrave of
House Calls

June 21 1980
Robert Wagner and
Stefanie Powers of
Hart to Hart

June 28 1980
Gregory Harrison and
Pernell Roberts of
Trapper John, M.D.

July 05 1980
The Cast of
Little House on the Prairie

July 12 1980
John Schneider, Catherine Bach,
and Tom Wopat of
The Dukes of Hazzard

July 19 1980
Lauren Tewes, Gavin MacLeod,
and Ted Lange of
The Love Boat

July 26 1980
Judd Hirsch, Marilu Henner,
and Tony Danza of
Taxi

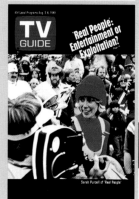

August 02 1980
Sarah Purcell of
Real People

August 09 1980
Children's Television: Experts Pick
the Best – and Worst – Shows

August 16 1980
Tom Wopat, Erik Estrada,
and Greg Evigan –
TV's Incredible Hunks

August 23 1980
Genie Francis of
General Hospital

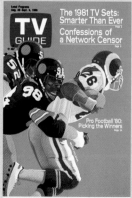

August 30 1980
Pro Football '80: Picking the
Winners

September 06 1980
Richard Chamberlain in
Shogun

September 13 1980
Fall Preview:
Special Issue

September 20 1980
Priscilla Presley of
Those Amazing Animals

September 27 1980
Cosmos: A New Series Explores
the Universe

October 04 1980
Ed Aner and
Mason Adams of
Lou Grant

October 11 1980
World Series

October 18 1980
Sophia Loren of
Sophia

October 25 1980
James Gregory and
Hal Linden of
Barney Miller

November 01 1980
John Anderson, Jimmy Carter, and
Ronald Reagan – How You Can
Pick The Winner

November 08 1980
Polly Holliday of
Flo

November 15 1980
Larry Hagman of
Dallas

November 22 1980
Pam Dawber of
Mork & Mindy

November 29 1980
Frank Gifford, Howard Cosell, Fran
Tarkenton, and Don Meredith of
ABC Monday Night Football

December 06 1980
Todd Bridges and
Gary Coleman of
Diff'rent Strokes

December 13 1980
Diana Canova of
I'm A Big Girl Now

December 20 1980
Christmas

December 27 1980
Tom Selleck of
Magnum, P.I.

1981

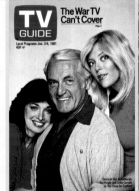

January 03 1981
Deborah Van Valkenburgh, Ted
Knight, and Lydia Cornell of
Too Close for Comfort

January 10 1981
David Hartman of
Good Morning America

January 17 1981
Ronald Reagan –
Inauguration Day

January 24 1981
Super Bowl '81:
The Inside Story

January 31 1981
Bob Hope, Johnny Carson,
and George Burns –
Tribute to Jack Benny

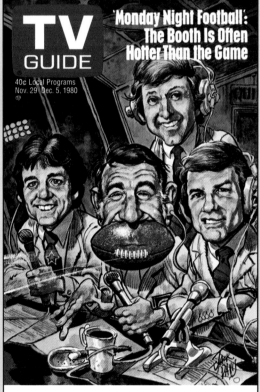

February 07 1981
Jane Seymour in
East of Eden

February 14 1981
The Cast of
WKRP in Cincinnati

February 21 1981
Faye Dunaway in
Evita Peron

ABC began broadcasting football on Monday nights
in 1970. It is the longest running prime time sports
program and often features former NFL stars as
announcers. Beginning with the 2006 season,
Monday Night Football will make its home on ESPN.

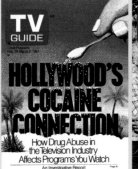

February 28 1981
Hollywood's Cocaine Connection

March 07 1981
Tom Wopat, Catherine Bach, John Schneider, and Sorrell Booke of
The Dukes of Hazzard

March 14 1981
Suzanne Somers of
Three's Company

March 21 1981
Wayne Rogers and Lynn Redgrave of
House Calls

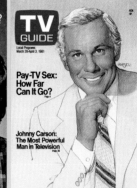

March 28 1981
Johnny Carson: The Most Powerful Man in Television

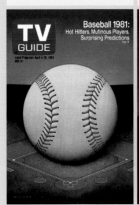

April 04 1981
Baseball 1981

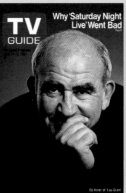

April 11 1981
Ed Asner of
Lou Grant

April 18 1981
Ted Koppel of
ABC News

April 25 1981
Alan Alda of
*M*A*S*H*

May 02 1981
John Davidson, Cathy Lee Crosby, and Fran Tarkenton of
That's Incredible!

May 09 1981
Larry Hagman and Patrick Duffy of
Dallas

May 16 1981
Robert Wagner, Lionel Stander, and Stefanie Powers of
Hart to Hart

May 23 1981
Barbara Eden of
Harper Valley P.T.A.

May 30 1981
Dan Rather of
CBS Evening News

June 06 1981
Judd Hirsch and Andy Kaufman of
Taxi

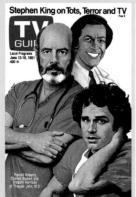

June 13 1981
Pernell Roberts, Charles Siebert, and Gregory Harrison of
Trapper John, M.D.

June 20 1981
The Hosts of
Real People

June 27 1981
Linda Evans of
Dynasty

July 04 1981
Gary Coleman and Dana Plato of
Diff'rent Strokes

July 11 1981
Donna Mills, Morgan Fairchild, and Pamela Sue Martin – Prime-time Vixens

July 18 1981
Greg Evigan, Judy Landers,
and the Chimp of
B.J. and the Bear

July 25 1981
Prince Charles and Lady Diana
Spencer – The Royal Wedding

August 01 1981
Miss Piggy of
The Muppet Show

August 08 1981
Carroll O'Connor – Why
Archie Bunker Survives

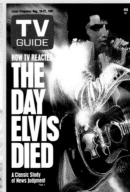

August 15 1981
Elvis Presley

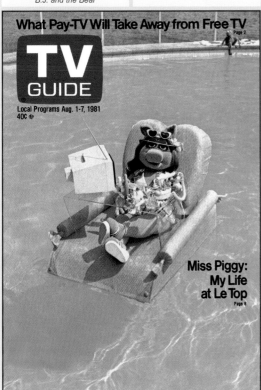

Jim Henson introduced *The Muppet Show* in 1976.
Guest stars were only allowed to appear on the show
once and were given scenes with their favorite
Muppet. **Miss Piggy** and **Animal** were asked for the
most. The program ended in 1981. Jim Henson died
on 5/16/1990 but the Muppets reunited in 1996 for
Muppets Tonight, which ran until 1998.

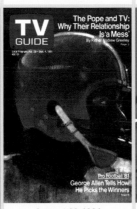

August 29 1981
Pro Football '81

September 05 1981
Backstage with Miss America

August 22 1981
Ann Jillian of
It's a Living

September 12 1981
Fall Preview:
Special Issue

September 19 1981
Kate Mulgrew in
The Manions of America

September 26 1981
The Battle for Northern Ireland:
How TV Tips the Balance

October 03 1981
Valerie Bertinelli of
One Day at a Time

October 10 1981
Jaclyn Smith as
Jacqueline Kennedy

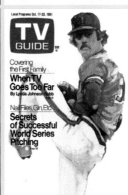

October 17 1981
Secrets of Successful World
Series Pitching

October 24 1981
Blind Spot in the Middle East

October 31 1981
Bruce Weitz, Daniel J. Travanti,
and Michael Conrad of
Hill Street Blues

November 07 1981
Mimi Kennedy and
Peter Cook of
The Two Of Us

November 14 1981
Loretta Lynn: Coal Miner's
Daughter in Her First
TV Special

November 21 1981
John Lennon

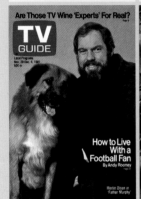

November 28 1981
Merlin Olsen of
Father Murphy

December 05 1981
Lorna Patterson of
Private Benjamin

December 12 1981
A Shopper's Guide to 1981's
Best Video Games

Michael Landon was headed for an athletic career until an injury sent him to acting. His first big role was in *I Was a Teenage Werewolf* in 1957. He began directing as early as *Bonanza* and started producing in the 70's with the TV movie, *The Jackie Robinson Story*. Michael Landon died on 7/1/1991 from cancer.

December 19 1981
Christmas

December 26 1981
Henry Fonda –
By Katharine Hepburn

1982

January 02 1982
John Hillerman and
Tom Selleck of
Magnum, P.I.

January 09 1982
Michael Landon of
Little House on the Prairie

January 16 1982
Bending the Rules in Hollywood

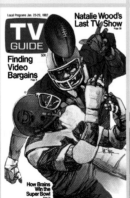

January 23 1982
How Brains Win the Super Bowl

January 30 1982
Robert Pine, Larry Wilcox,
and Erik Estrada of
CHiPS

February 06 1982
Sherman Hemsley of
The Jeffersons

February 13 1982
A Noted Historian Judges TV's
Holocaust Films

February 20 1982
Ed Bradley, Morley Safer, Mike
Wallace, and Harry Reasoner of
60 Minutes

February 27 1982
Pamela Sue Martin, John Forsythe,
and Linda Evans of
Dynasty

March 06 1982
Swoosie Kurtz, Tony Randall,
and Kaleena Kiff of
Love, Sidney

March 13 1982
Priscilla Barnes, John Ritter,
and Joyce DeWitt of
Three's Company

March 20 1982
President Ronald Reagan

March 27 1982
Larry Hagman of
Dallas

April 03 1982
Baseball 82: Our Expert
Predictions

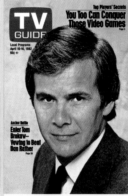

April 10 1982
Tom Brokaw of
NBC Nightly News

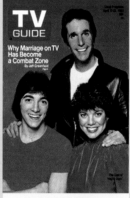

April 17 1982
Henry Winkler, Scott Baio,
and Erin Moran of
Happy Days

April 24 1982
Ingrid Bergman in
A Woman Called Golda

May 01 1982
John Schneider, Catherine Bach,
and Tom Wopat of
The Dukes of Hazzard

May 08 1982
Goldie Hawn – This Week:
A Goldie Hawn Special

May 15 1982
Ken Marshall of
Marco Polo

May 22 1982
Billy Moses, Lorenzo Lamas,
and Jane Wyman of
Falcon Crest

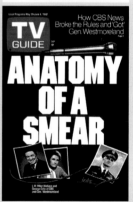

May 29 1982
Mike Wallace, George Crile,
and General William
Westmoreland

June 05 1982
Lauren Tewes and
Gavin MacLeod of
The Love Boat

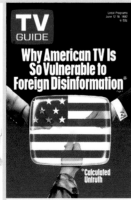

June 12 1982
Why American TV Is So
Vulnerable to Foreign
Disinformation

June 19 1982
Daniel J. Travanti and
Veronica Hamel of
Hill Street Blues

June 26 1982
Michele Lee of
Knot's Landing

July 03 1982
Deborah Van Valkenburgh, Lydia
Cornell, and Ted Knight of
Too Close for Comfort

115

TV GUIDE

Local Programs
Sept. 18–24, 1982
50¢

Dateline 'Dallas'
If You Think J.R. Is Tough, Meet Victoria Principal
Page 14

Pro Football's
Best– and
Worst–
Sportscasters
Page 4

Victoria Principal was born in Japan and was in a commercial at the age of five. She started modeling in high school and was Miss Miami in 1969. In 1971, she moved to L.A. where she landed her first film role in *The Life and Times of Judge Roy Bean*. After *Dallas* she began her own production company, and created a line of skincare products while continuing to act.

July 10 1982
The Cast of
The Facts of Life

July 17 1982
Rick Springfield of
General Hospital

July 24 1982
William Katt of
The Greatest American Hero

July 31 1982
Katherine Cannon and
Merlin Olsen of
Father Murphy

August 07 1982
Carroll O'Connor and
Denise Miller of
Archie Bunker's Place

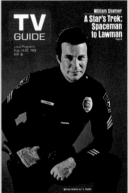

August 14 1982
William Shatner of
T.J. Hooker

August 21 1982
Nell Carter and
Dolph Sweet of
Gimme a Break!

August 28 1982
Penny Marshall and
Cindy Williams of
Laverne & Shirley

September 04 1982
Almost Miss America

September 11 1982
Fall Preview:
Special Issue

September 18 1982
Victoria Principal of
Dallas

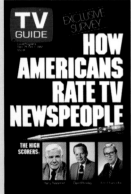

September 25 1982
Harry Reasoner, David Brinkley,
and John Chancellor –
The High Scorers

October 02 1982
Genie Francis of
General Hospital

October 09 1982
World Series

October 16 1982
Erik Estrada and
Morgan Fairchild in
Honey Boy

October 23 1982
Linda Evans and
Joan Collins of
Dynasty

October 30 1982
Pernell Roberts of
Trapper John, M.D.

November 06 1982
Gene Anthony Ray and
Erica Gimpel of
Fame

November 13 1982
The Blue and The Gray

November 20 1982
Priscilla Barnes, John Ritter, Joyce
DeWitt, and Richard Kline of
Three's Company

November 27 1982
Meredith Baxter Birney of
Family Ties

December 04 1982
A Shopper's Guide to 1982's
Best Video Games

December 11 1982
Sally Struthers of
Gloria
with Daughter, Samantha

December 18 1982
The Cast of
Too Close For Comfort

December 25 1982
Christmas

1983

January 01 1983
Bob Newhart and
Mary Frann of
Newhart

January 08 1983
John Madden's Breakthrough

January 15 1983
The Cast of
9 to 5

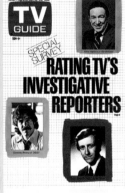

January 22 1983
Geraldo Rivera of *20/20*, Mike
Wallace of *60 Minutes*, and Brian
Ross of *NBC Nightly News*

January 29 1983
Robert Mitchum and
Ali McGraw in
The Winds of War

February 05 1983
Cheryl Ladd in
Grace Kelly

February 12 1983
The Cast of *M*A*S*H*:
(Group Photo)
David Ogden Stiers, Harry Morgan,

Fold Out
Loretta Swit, Mike Farrell,
Jamie Farr, Alan Alda, and
William Christopher

February 19 1983
Armand Assante, Jaclyn Smith,
and Ken Howard in
Rage of Angels

February 26 1983
Kim Delaney, Laurence Lau,
and Susan Lucci of
All My Children

March 05 1983
Valerie Bertinelli of
One Day At A Time

March 12 1983
Bruce Weitz of
Hill Street Blues

March 19 1983
Gary Coleman of
Diff'rent Strokes
with Nancy Reagan

March 26 1983
Richard Chamberlain
and Rachel Ward in
The Thorn Birds

April 02 1983
Donna Mills of
Knot's Landing

April 09 1983
Elvis Presley – Judging His Music

April 16 1983
Morley Safer, Ed Bradley, Harry
Reasoner, and Mike Wallace
of *60 Minutes*

April 23 1983
Linda Purl and
Henry Winkler of
Happy Days

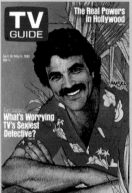

April 30 1983
Tom Selleck of
Magnum, P.I.

May 07 1983
Rick Shroder, Erin Gray, and
Joel Higgins of
Silver Spoons

May 14 1983
Kathleen Beller and
John James of
Dynasty

May 21 1983
Bob Hope – 80th Birthday Special

May 28 1983
Audrey Landers, Ken Kercheval,
and Larry Hagman of
Dallas

June 04 1983
Heather Thomas, Lee Majors,
and Doug Barr of
The Fall Guy

June 11 1983
Alan Alda; Linda Evans; Erik
Estrada; Valerie Bertinelli: They're
Stars – But Can They Act?

June 18 1983
Jameson Parker and
Gerald McRaney of
Simon & Simon

June 25 1983
David Hasselhoff of
Knight Rider

July 02 1983
*M*A*S*H*; *Dynasty*;
The Thorn Birds –
The Best and Worst We Saw

July 09 1983
Ana Alicia, Lorenzo Lamas,
and Jane Wyman of
Falcon Crest

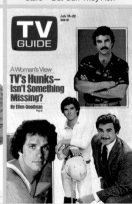

July 16 1983
Gregory Harrison; Pierce Brosnan;
Tom Selleck; Lee Horsley: TV
Hunks – Isn't Something Missing?

July 23 1983

Donna Mills, Ted Shackelford,
and Joan Van Ark of
Knots Landing

July 30 1983

Isabel Sanford and
Sherman Hemsley of
The Jeffersons

August 06 1983

Judy Woodruff of NBC,
Lesley Stahl of CBS,
and Anne Garrels of ABC

August 13 1983

Deirdre Hall and
Wayne Northrop of
Days of Our Lives

August 20 1983

Robert Wagner and
Stefanie Powers of
Hart to Hart

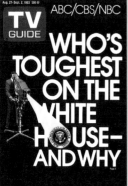

August 27 1983

Who's Toughest on the White
House – And Why

September 03 1983

Rob Reiner, Jean Stapleton, Carroll
O'Connor, and Sally Struthers of
All in the Family

September 10 1983

AfterMASH; *Mr. Smith*;
Hotel – Fall Preview

September 17 1983

Behind Our Love-Hate Affair
With Miss America

September 24 1983

Priscilla Barnes, John Ritter,
and Joyce DeWitt of
Three's Company

October 01 1983

Gregory Harrison of
Trapper John, M.D.

October 08 1983

Anne Murray and
Willie Nelson Host
Country Music Awards

October 15 1983

Larry Hagman of *Dallas*
and Joan Collins
of *Dynasty*

October 22 1983

Mr. Smith of
Mr. Smith

October 29 1983

James Brolin and
Connie Sellecca of
Hotel

November 05 1983

Merete Van Kamp in
Princess Daisy

November 12 1983

President and Mrs. John F.
Kennedy – Why The Kennedys
Aroused Such Passions

November 19 1983

Doug Scott and
John Collum in
The Day After

November 26 1983

Linda Evans and
Kenny Rogers in
Gambler II

December 03 1983

Barbara Walters Interviews
Johnny Carson

1984

December 10 1983
Tom Selleck of
Magnum, P.I.

December 17 1983
Erin Gray of
Silver Spoons

December 24 1983
The Cast of
The Love Boat

December 31 1983
Farrah Fawcett – Surprising
Portrait

January 07 1984
William Christopher, Harry Morgan,
Rosalind Chao, and Jamie Farr
of *AfterMASH*

January 14 1984
Emmanuel Lewis of
Webster

January 21 1984
TV Game Show Hosts

January 28 1984
Cybill Shepherd in
The Yellow Rose

February 04 1984
Winter Olympics '84

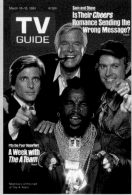

February 11 1984
Kate Jackson and
Bruce Boxleitner of
Scarecrow and Mrs. King

February 18 1984
Ted Danson, Shelley Long, and
Rhea Perlman of
Cheers

February 25 1984
Harry Reasoner, Ed Bradley,
Mike Wallace, and Morley Safer
of *60 Minutes*

March 03 1984
Ann Margaret and
Treat Williams in
A Streetcar Named Desire

March 10 1984
Dirk Benedict, George Peppard,
Mr. T, and Dwight Schultz of
The A-Team

March 17 1984
Priscilla Presley of
Dallas

March 24 1984
Veronica Hamel and
Daniel J. Travanti of
Hill Street Blues

March 31 1984
Teri Copley of
We Got It Made

April 07 1984
Mike Wallace and
Barry Bostwick as George
Washington

April 14 1984
Rebecca Holden and
David Hasselhoff of
Knight Rider

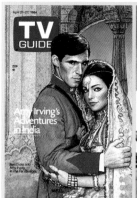

April 21 1984
Ben Cross and
Amy Irving in
The Far Pavilions

April 28 1984
The Cast of
Happy Days

May 05 1984
Lesley-Anne Down in
The Last Days of Pompeii

May 12 1984
Crystal Gayle Co-Hosts NBC's
Country Music Awards

May 19 1984
Morgan Fairchild in
*The Zany Adventures of
Robin Hood*

May 26 1984
Daniel Hugh-Kelly and
Brian Keith of
Hardcastle & McCormick

June 02 1984
Victoria Principal of
Dallas

June 09 1984
Pierce Brosnan and
Stephanie Zimbalist of
Remington Steele

June 16 1984
Larry Hagman of *Dallas*;
Joan Collins of *Dynasty*;
Stefanie Powers of *Hart to Hart*

June 23 1984
Connie Sellecca of
Hotel

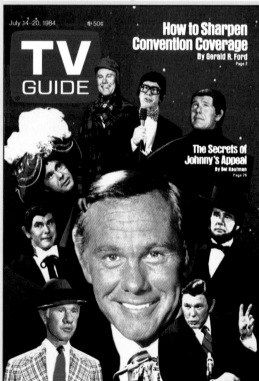

June 30 1984
Lace; *Kennedy*; Blair Brown –
The Best and Worst We Saw

July 07 1984
Valerie Bertinelli of
One Day at a Time

July 14 1984
Johnny Carson – The Secrets of
Johnny's Appeal

Johnny Carson started performing at age 14 as "The Great Carsoni" in his hometown. He took over as host of *The Tonight Show* after **Jack Paar**'s resignation in 1962, and for 30 years reigned as the "King of Late Night TV." Who can forget the late night hosts' battle to succeed him? Johnny Carson died on 1/23/2005.

July 21 1984
Ted Shackelford, Donna Mills,
and Lisa Hartman of
Knots Landing

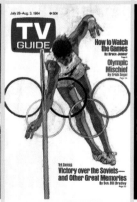

July 28 1984
'84 Summer Olympics

August 04 1984
Jameson Parker and
Gerald McRaney of
Simon & Simon

121

August 11 1984
The Cast of
Call to Glory

August 18 1984
Jane Pauley of
Today Show

August 25 1984
Lindsay Bloom and
Stacy Keach of
Mike Hammer

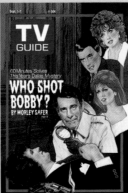

September 01 1984
60 Minutes Solves This
Year's *Dallas* Mystery:
Who Shot Bobby?

September 08 1984
Fall Preview

As a small child he sang on the street for pennies, and **George Burns** never considered being anything but a performer. He played straight man to wife, **Gracie**, on *The George Burns and Gracie Allen Show*, and did not establish himself as a comedian until after her death in 1964. He was the oldest recipient of an Oscar when he won, at the age of 80, for Best Supporting Actor for *The Sunshine Boys* in 1976. He died on 3/9/1996.

September 15 1984
Catherine Bach and
George Burns in
This Week's Special

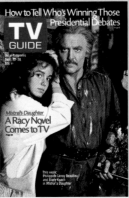

September 22 1984
Philippine Leroy Beaulieu
and Stacy Keach in
Mistral's Daughter

September 29 1984
Mary Tyler Moore and
James Garner in
Heartsounds

October 06 1984
Terry Farrell, Morgan Fairchild,
and Nicollette Sheridan of
Paper Dolls

October 13 1984
Keshia Knight Pulliam
and Bill Cosby of
The Cosby Show

October 20 1984
Daniel J. Travanti, Sophia Loren,
and Eduardo Ponti in
Aurora by Night

October 27 1984
Brooke Shields in
Wet Gold

November 03 1984
Tales of Election Night Drama

November 10 1984
Michael Nader and
Joan Collins of
Dynasty

November 17 1984
Carol Alt, Kim Alexis, and Kelly
Emberg – What It's Like to Be
a Top TV Model

November 24 1984
Jane Curtin and
Susan Saint James of
Kate & Allie

December 01 1984
Shari Belafonte-Harper of
Hotel

December 08 1984
Ana Alicia and
Billy Moses of
Falcon Crest

December 15 1984
Jaclyn Smith; Connie Selleca;
Priscilla Presley – TV's 10
Most Beautiful Women

December 22 1984
Susan Clark, Emmanuel Lewis,
and Alex Karras of
Webster

December 29 1984
Larry Hagman and
Linda Gray of
Dallas

1985

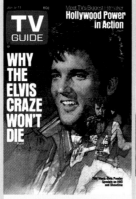

January 05 1985
Elvis Presley – Elvis Presley
Specials on HBO and Showtime

January 12 1985
Donna Mills and
William Devane of
Knots Landing

January 19 1985
Inauguration and Super Bowl

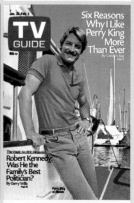

January 26 1985
Perry King of
Riptide

February 02 1985
Sharon Gless and
Tyne Daly of
Cagney & Lacey

February 09 1985
Ellen Foley and
Harry Anderson of
Night Court

February 16 1985
The Cast of
Hollywood Wives

February 23 1985
Bruce Springsteen, Prince,
and Michael Jackson –
The Grammys

March 02 1985
Michael Landon of
Highway to Heaven

March 09 1985
Angela Lansbury of
Murder, She Wrote

March 16 1985
Lauren Tewes of
The Love Boat

March 23 1985
Diahann Carroll of
Dynasty

March 30 1985
A.D. – Creating a Tale of
Corruption and Faith

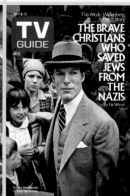

April 06 1985
Richard Chamberlain in
Wallenberg: A Hero's Story

April 13 1985

Blair Brown, Harry Hamlin, and James Garner in *Space*

April 20 1985

Deborah Shelton of *Dallas*

April 27 1985

The Cast of *Family Ties*

May 04 1985

Phoebe Cates in *Lace II*

May 11 1985

Cheryl Ladd in *A Death In California*

May 18 1985

Gabriel Byrne as Christopher Columbus

May 25 1985

Anthony Hamilton and Jennifer O'Neill of *Cover Up*

June 01 1985

The Cast of *Hill Street Blues*

June 08 1985

Jameson Parker and Gerald McRaney of *Simon & Simon*

June 15 1985

Surprise! Has TV Got a Summer for You!

June 22 1985

Nancy Reagan – Judging the Influence of America's First Ladies

June 29 1985

Bill Cosby; Farrah Fawcett; *Dynasty* – The Best and Worst We Saw

July 06 1985

Shelley Long, Ted Danson, and George Wendt of *Cheers*

July 13 1985

Heather Thomas of *The Fall Guy*

July 20 1985

TV's Hottest Soap Couples

July 27 1985

Philip Michael Thomas and Don Johnson of *Miami Vice*

August 03 1985

Catherine Hickland and David Hasselhoff – Romance on the Set

August 10 1985

Madonna in "Material Girl"

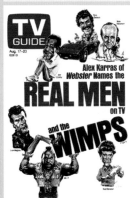

August 17 1985

Real Men and the Wimps on TV

August 24 1985

Lisa Hartman and Alec Baldwin of *Knots Landing*

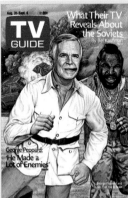

August 31 1985
George Peppard
and Mr. T of
The A-Team

September 07 1985
Phylicia Ayers-Allen and
Bill Cosby of
The Cosby Show

September 14 1985
Fall Preview:
Special Issue

Dallas started the trend that others soon followed.
With cliffhangers like *Dallas*'s 1980 "Who shot JR?"
and scenes like *Dynasty*'s 1983 catfight between
Linda Evans and **Joan Collins**, soap operas
made a home in prime time. But we all felt a
little cheated that *Dallas*'s 1985 season with
Bobby's death was only a dream.

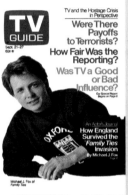

September 21 1985
Michael J. Fox of
Family Ties

September 28 1985
Howard Cosell; Frank Gifford;
Don Meredith; O.J. Simpson

October 05 1985
Cybill Shepherd and
Don Johnson in
The Long Hot Summer

October 12 1985
Victoria Principal of
Dallas

October 19 1985
Betty White, Bea Arthur, and
Rue McClanahan of
The Golden Girls

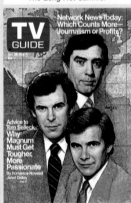

October 26 1985
Dan Rather, Peter Jennings,
and Tom Brokaw

November 02 1985
Patrick Swayze, Wendy Kilbourne,
James Read, and Lesley-Anne
Down in *North and South*

November 09 1985
Prince Charles and Princess
Diana – Does TV Go Too Far in
Covering the Royal Couple?

November 16 1985
Cast Members of
Dynasty II: The Colbys

November 23 1985
Judith Light, Katherine Helmond,
and Tony Danza of
Who's The Boss?

November 30 1985
Is *Knots Landing* Now Better
Than *Dallas* and *Dynasty*?

December 07 1985
Cybill Shepherd of
Moonlighting

December 14 1985
Robert Blake of
Hell Town

December 21 1985
Victor French and
Michael Landon of
Highway to Heaven

December 28 1985
John Rubenstein, Penny Peyser,
and Jack Warden of
Crazy Like a Fox

1986

January 04 1986
Connie Sellecca of
Hotel

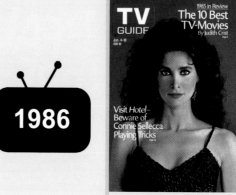

January 11 1986
Bruce Boxleitner and
Kate Jackson of
Scarecrow and Mrs. King

January 18 1986
John Larroquette, Harry Anderson,
and Markie Post of
Night Court

January 25 1986
Joan Collins in
Sins

February 01 1986
Maximilian Schell in
Peter The Great

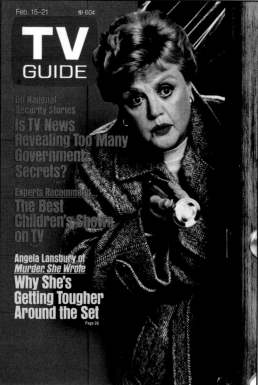

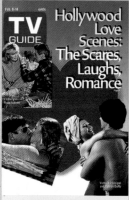

February 08 1986
Linda Evans and Rock Hudson;
Lorenzo Lamas and Laura Johnson;
Victoria Principal and Patrick Duffy

February 15 1986
Angela Lansbury of
Murder, She Wrote

February 22 1986
Jane Seymour, Lee Horsley,
and Cheryl Ladd of
Crossings

Born in London, England, **Angela Lansbury** came to
the United States in 1940. Shortly after, she began
acting in films, earning an Oscar nomination for the
1944 movie, *Gaslight*. She made her Broadway debut
in 1957 and won four Tony awards in her 16 years on
the stage. TV Viewers best know her (and love her) as
Jessica Fletcher on *Murder, She Wrote*.

March 01 1986
Linda Evans of
Dynasty

March 08 1986
Don Johnson and
Philip Michael Thomas of
Miami Vice

March 15 1986
Madolyn Smith in
If Tomorrow Comes

March 22 1986
Bill Cosby of
The Cosby Show

March 29 1986
Sexual Harassment in
Hollywood

April 05 1986
Justine Bateman, Tina Yothers, and Michael J. Fox of *Family Ties*

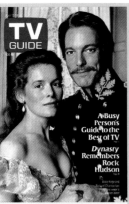

April 12 1986
Alice Krige and Richard Chamberlain in *Dream West*

April 19 1986
Tom Selleck; Pierce Brosnan; Don Johnson – The 10 Most Attractive Men on TV

April 26 1986
Jane Curtin and Susan Saint James of *Kate & Allie*

May 03 1986
James Read and Patrick Swayze in *North and South, Book II*; Mark Harmon in *Deliberate Stranger*

May 10 1986
Cast Members of *Cheers*

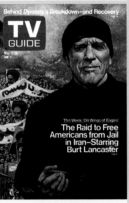

May 17 1986
Burt Lancaster in *On Wings of Eagles*

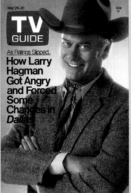

May 24 1986
Larry Hagman of *Dallas*

May 31 1986
Richard Dean Anderson of *MacGyver*

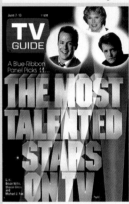

June 07 1986
Bruce Willis; Sharon Gless; Michael J. Fox – The Most Talented Stars on TV

June 14 1986
Emmanuel Lewis of *Webster*

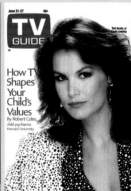

June 21 1986
Teri Austin of *Knots Landing*

June 28 1986
Nancy and Ronald Reagan – What We've Learned About America from Our Years in the White House

July 05 1986
The Goodwill Games

July 12 1986
Joan Collins; *Moonlighting*; Don Johnson – The Best and Worst We Saw

July 19 1986
Robert Urich and Barbara Stock of *Spenser: For Hire*

July 26 1986
Bill Cosby, Richard Chamberlain, Linda Evans, and John Forsythe – TV's Top Moneymakers

August 02 1986
Shelley Long and Ted Danson of *Cheers*; Bruce Willis and Cybill Shepherd of *Moonlighting*

August 09 1986
The Cast of *Growing Pains*

August 16 1986
Suzanne Somers – The Rise and Fall of a TV Sex Symbol

August 23 1986
Valerie Harper of
Valerie

August 30 1986
Victoria Principal
and Patrick Duffy of
Dallas

September 06 1986
Miss America Pageant;
Monday Night Football

September 13 1986
Fall Preview:
Special Issue

September 20 1986
*George Washington:
The Forging of a Nation*

September 27 1986
Bronson Pinchot and
Mark Linn-Baker of
Perfect Strangers

October 04 1986
Lucille Ball and Andy Griffith –
Two Old Favorites Return
to Series TV

October 11 1986
Harry Hamlin, Jill Eikenberry,
and Corbin Bernsen of
L.A. Law

October 18 1986
Michael J. Fox and
Brian Bonsall of
Family Ties

October 25 1986
Kim Novak of
Falcon Crest

November 01 1986
Ken Howard and
Jaclyn Smith in
Rage of Angels II

November 08 1986
Joan Collins and
George Hamilton of
Monte Carlo

November 15 1986
The Cast of
Fresno

November 22 1986
Farrah Fawcett – From Charlie's
Angel to Avenging Angel

November 29 1986
Tom Mason and
Shelley Hack of
Jack and Mike

December 06 1986
Delta Burke of
Designing Women

December 13 1986
James Garner and
James Woods in
Promise

December 20 1986
The Cast of
Our House

December 27 1986
Heather Locklear of
Dynasty

January 03 1987
Angela Lansbury of
Murder, She Wrote

January 10 1987
Ted Koppel of
Nightline

January 17 1987
Clifton Davis and
Sherman Hemsley of
Amen

January 24 1987
Nicollette Sheridan of
Knots Landing

January 31 1987
Estelle Getty, Bea Arthur, Betty
White, and Rue McClanahan of
The Golden Girls

February 07 1987
Ann-Margret in
The Two Mrs. Grenvilles

February 14 1987
Robert Urich and
Kris Kristofferson in
Amerika

February 21 1987
Tom Selleck and
Frank Sinatra of
Magnum, P.I.

February 28 1987
Valerie Bertinelli in
I'll Take Manhattan

March 07 1987
Justine Bateman and
Michael J. Fox of
Family Ties

March 14 1987
Victoria Principal of
Dallas

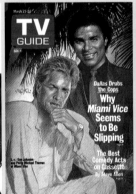

March 21 1987
Don Johnson and
Philip Michael Thomas of
Miami Vice

March 28 1987
Kirk Cameron of
Growing Pains

April 04 1987
Susan Dey and
Harry Hamlin of
L.A. Law

April 11 1987
The Cast of
Newhart

April 18 1987
Tony Danza of
Who's The Boss?

April 25 1987
Fred Dryer and
Stephanie Kramer of
Hunter

May 02 1987
The Cast of
Cheers

May 09 1987
Pam Dawber and
Rebecca Schaeffer of
My Sister Sam

May 16 1987
The Cast of
Head of the Class

May 23 1987
Edward Woodward of
The Equalizer

May 30 1987
Cybill Shepherd of
Moonlighting

June 06 1987
Keshia Knight Pulliam of *The Cosby Show*; Jason Bateman of *Valerie*; Jeremy Miller of *Growing Pains*

June 13 1987
Al Waxman and
Sharon Gless of
Cagney & Lacey

June 20 1987
Markie Post of
Night Court

June 27 1987
L.A. Law; *Amerika*; *ALF*;
I'll Take Manhattan – The Best
and Worst We Saw

July 04 1987
Barbara Walters with Angela
Lansbury, Patrick Duffy,
and Betty White

July 11 1987
Tempestt Bledsoe and
Malcolm Jamal Warner of
The Cosby Show

July 18 1987
Kate Jackson, Victoria Principal,
and Oprah Winfrey – Ambition
in Hollywood

July 25 1987
Blair Brown of
*The Days and Nights of
Molly Dodd*

July 4-10   60¢

TV GUIDE

Interviewees Answer
Does She Push Too Hard?
Their Report Card on Barbara Walters
Page 2

Angela Lansbury: 'I don't think she went for my throat. But once she __had__ it, oh boy!'

Patrick Duffy: The interview 'was the most honest I've ever been treated.'

Betty White: 'You're dealing with somebody who's going to cut right to the heart.'

Barbara Walters is responsible for breaking the gender barrier in network news. She was the first official female co-host of the *Today Show* and, in 1976, became the first woman to hold the position of "anchorman" on evening network news. Currently, she concentrates on her famous interview specials.

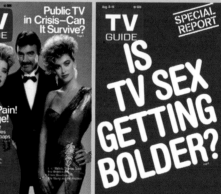

August 01 1987
Melody Thomas Scott, Eric
Braeden, and Eileen Davidson of
The Young and the Restless

August 08 1987
Is TV Sex Getting Bolder?

August 15 1987
ALF

August 22 1987
TV is Opening Up the Soviet
Bloc Nations

August 29 1987
Sherman Hemsley and
Anna Maria Horsford of
Amen

September 05 1987
Terri Garber of
Dynasty

September 12 1987
Fall Preview:
Special Issue

September 19 1987
Brooke Shields – Why Not
Brooke Shields for
Miss America!

September 26 1987
Michael Tucker and
Jill Eikenberry in
Assault and Matrimony

October 03 1987
Victoria Principal in
Mistress

October 10 1987
Cast Members of *Growing Pains*;
Michael J. Fox of *Family Ties*;
Bob Newhart of *Newhart*

October 17 1987
Dolly Parton of
Dolly

October 24 1987
Bruce Willis and
Cybill Shepherd of
Moonlighting

October 31 1987
Courteney Cox and
Michael J. Fox of
Family Ties

November 07 1987
Jacqueline Bisset and Armand
Assante in *Napoleon and
Josephine: A Love Story*

November 14 1987
Ted Danson and
Kirstie Alley of
Cheers

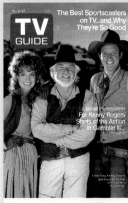

November 21 1987
Linda Gray, Kenny Rogers,
and Bruce Boxleitner in
Gambler III

November 28 1987
David Birney and
Meredith Baxter Birney in
The Long Journey Home

December 05 1987
Connie Sellecca in
Downpayment on Murder

December 12 1987
John Ritter of
Hooperman

December 19 1987
Keshia Knight Pulliam in
The Little Match Girl

December 26 1987
Amanda Peterson, Trey Ames,
and Richard Kiley of
A Year in the Life

1988

January 02 1988
The Women of
Falcon Crest

January 09 1988
Emma Samms of
Dynasty

January 16 1988
Sharon Gless and
Tyne Daly of
Cagney and Lacey

131

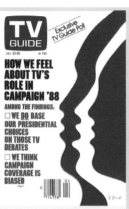

January 23 1988
Campaign '88

January 30 1988
Priscilla Beaulieu Presley –
My Life With Elvis

February 06 1988
Jaclyn Smith and
Robert Wagner in
Windmills of the Gods

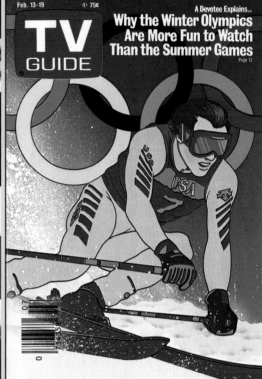

February 13 1988
The Wnter Olympic Games

February 20 1988
Pierce Brosnan and
Deborah Raffin in
Noble House

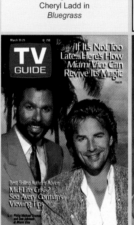

February 27 1988
Cheryl Ladd in
Bluegrass

Although what are known as the first official Olympic games were held in Athens in 1896, their roots go back to a footrace that took place in Olympia in honor of Zeus in 776 BC. The first event telecast was in 1960. In 1994, the Olympics switched from a four year schedule to two years, mostly for financial reasons.

March 05 1988
Oprah Winfrey of
The Oprah WInfrey Show

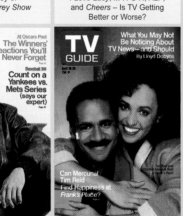

March 12 1988
I Love Lucy, *M*A*S*H*, *ALF*,
and *Cheers* – Is TV Getting
Better or Worse?

March 19 1988
Philip Michael Thomas
and Don Johnson of
Miami Vice

March 26 1988
Sheree J. Wilson of
Dallas

April 02 1988
Kirk Cameron and
Tracey Gold of
Growing Pains

April 09 1988
Harry Hamlin of
L.A. Law

April 16 1988
Tim Reid and
Daphne Maxwell Reid of
Frank's Place

April 23 1988
Jason Bateman of
Valerie's Family

April 30 1988
Dr. Ruth Westheimer and
The Golden Girls

May 07 1988
Richard Chamberlain
and Jaclyn Smith in
The Bourne Identity

May 14 1988
Lesley Stahl; Sam Donaldson; Chris Wallace – Beat The Press

May 21 1988
Princess Diana and Prince Charles – Why We're So Taken with British Royalty

May 28 1988
Brian Bonsall and Michael J. Fox of *Family Ties*

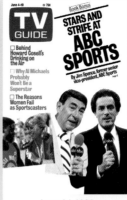

June 04 1988
Carl Lewis and Donna de Varona; Howard Cosell; Al Michaels – Stars and Strife at ABC Sports

June 11 1988
Mel Harris, Brittany Craven, and Ken Olin of *thirtysomething*

June 18 1988
The 1988 Network News All-Star Team

June 25 1988
Olympics; Tom Selleck; Oliver North; *Cheers* – The Best and Worst We Saw

July 02 1988
Delta Burke, Annie Potts, Dixie Carter, and Jean Smart of *Designing Women*

July 09 1988
The Cast of *Head of the Class*

July 16 1988
Kim Alexis and Nicollette Sheridan – The Six Most Beautiful Women on TV

July 23 1988
How TV is Shaking Up the American Family

July 30 1988
Leann Hunley – Was She Right To Walk Away from *Dynasty*?

August 06 1988
Susan Lucci; Peter Barton & Lauralee Bell; Drake Hogestyn; Tristan Rogers – Daytime Soaps

August 13 1988
ALF

August 20 1988
Johnny Depp and Holly Robinson of *21 Jump Street*

August 27 1988
Mariel Hemingway in *Steal the Sky*

September 03 1988
Kaye Lani Rafko; Phoebe Mills; *Peanuts*; Charlie Sheen

September 10 1988
Kaye Lani Rafko – Inside the Mind of Miss America

September 17 1988
Olympics '88 Viewers Guide

September 24 1988
Cast Members of *The Cosby Show*

October 01 1988
Fall Preview:
Special Issue

October 08 1988
NBC Entertainment President
Brandon Tartikoff with New
Series Stars

October 15 1988
Kevin Costner and
Susan Sarandon in
Bull Durham

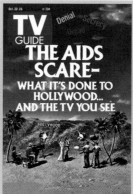

October 22 1988
The AIDS Scare – What It's
Done to Hollywood…And the
TV You See

October 29 1988
Linda Kozlowski and
Harry Hamlin in
Favorite Son

November 05 1988
Election Day: Which Network
You Should Watch

November 12 1988
Cast Members in
War and Remembrance

November 19 1988
John F. Kennedy and Family –
Remembering JFK…Our First
TV President

November 26 1988
Barbara Walters and Stars From
Her Specials

December 03 1988
Our Viewer's Guide to the
Holiday Specials

December 10 1988
Dinah Manoff, Kristy McNichol,
Richard Mulligan and Dreyfuss
of *Empty Nest*

December 17 1988
Stepfanie Kramer,
Shari Belafonte,
and Sheree J. Wilson

December 24 1988
Angela Lansbury of
Murder, She Wrote

December 31 1988
Sandy Duncan and
Jason Bateman of
Hogan Family

1989

January 07 1989
Bryant Gumbel; Jane Fonda;
Geraldo Rivera – Our 8th Annual
J. Fred Muggs Awards

January 14 1989
Cybill Shepherd and
Bruce Willis of
Moonlighting

January 21 1989
Elvis Presley, Bruce Springsteen,
Madonna, and Michael Jackson –
Elvis is Still King!

January 28 1989
John Goodman and
Roseanne Barr in
Roseanne

February 04 1989
Get Ready for a Hot February

February 11 1989
Larry Hagman of
Dallas

February 18 1989
Parents' Guide – The Best
Children's Shows on TV

February 25 1989
Victoria Principal in
Naked Lies

March 04 1989
Vanna White of
The Wheel of Fortune

March 11 1989
One-Upmanship Guide –
thirtysomething; *Murphy Brown*;
L.A. Law

March 18 1989
Oprah Winfrey, Robin Givens,
and Jackee in
The Women of Brewster Place

March 25 1989
Jodie Foster; Melanie Griffith;
Gene Hackman; Dustin Hoffman

April 01 1989
Susan Ruttan, Susan Dey, Michele
Greene, and Jill Eikenberry
of *L.A. Law*

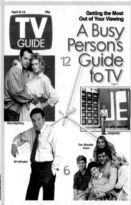

April 08 1989
Moonlighting; *60 Minutes*; *The
Wonder Years*; *Jeopardy* – A Busy
Person's Guide to TV

April 15 1989
John Forsythe and
Joan Collins of
Dynasty

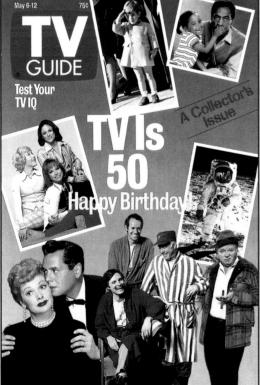

If only **Philo Farnsworth** and **Vladimir Zworykin**
could see what they started! Although the first
play broadcast by television was *The Queen's
Messenger* on September 11, 1928, television sets
were not mass produced and commercially available
until 1939. We've come a long way since then.

April 22 1989
Kirk Cameron of *Growing Pains*
and Jason Bateman of
The Hogan Family

April 29 1989
Guts & Glory; *War and
Remembrance*; *Murder by
Moonlight*; *Roe vs. Wade*

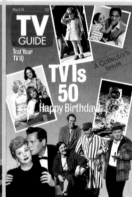

May 06 1989
TV is 50 – Happy Birthday!

May 13 1989
Tracy Scoggins of
Dynasty

May 20 1989
Roseanne Barr of
Roseanne

May 27 1989
Ted Danson and
Kirstie Alley of
Cheers

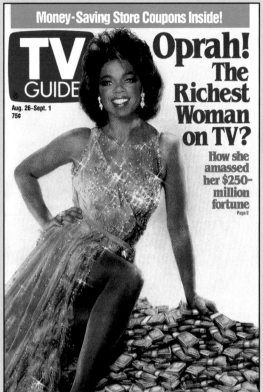

Money-Saving Store Coupons Inside!

Oprah! The Richest Woman on TV?

How she amassed her $250-million fortune
Page 2

TV GUIDE
Aug. 26–Sept. 1
75¢

Oprah Winfrey – actress, talk show host, producer and creator, author, magazine editor, cable network founder, philanthropist, inspirational leader, award winner, and the richest woman on TV.
What else needs to be said?

June 03 1989
Oprah Winfrey of
The Oprah Winfrey Show

June 10 1989
Fred Savage and
Danica McKellar of
The Wonder Years

June 17 1989
Donna Mills of
Knots Landing

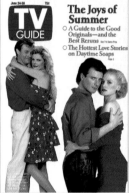

June 24 1989
Tristan Rogers and Edie Lehmann
(*General Hospital*); James DePaiva
and Jessica Tuck (*One Life to Live*)

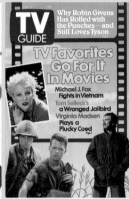

July 01 1989
Virginia Madsen; Michael J. Fox;
Tom Selleck – TV Favorites Go
For It in the Movies

July 08 1989
The Best and Worst We Saw

July 15 1989
Tom Brokaw (NBC); Peter
Jennings (ABC); Lesley Stahl
(CBS); Andrea Mitchell (NBC)

July 22 1989
Roseanne Barr and
Nicollette Sheridan – TV Stars
to Watch and Ignore

July 29 1989
David Faustino, Christina
Applegate, Katey Sagal, and Ed
O'Neill of *Married... With Children*

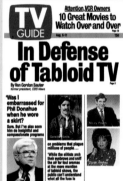

August 05 1989
Phil Donahue; Geraldo Rivera;
Maury Povich; Oprah Winfrey –
In Defense of Tabloid TV

August 12 1989
Mary Alice Williams, Connie Chung,
Maria Shriver, and Diane Sawyer –
TV's New News Queens

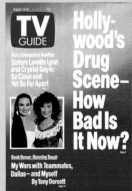

August 19 1989
Sisters Loretta Lynn and
Crystal Gayle: So Close
and Yet So Far Apart

August 26 1989
Oprah Winfrey – Oprah! The
Richest Woman on TV?

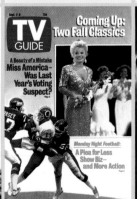

September 02 1989
Two Fall Classics –
Miss America Pageant and
Monday Night Football

September 09 1989
Fall Preview:
Special Issue

September 16 1989
Roseanne Barr of *Roseanne*
and Bill Cosby of
The Cosby Show

September 23 1989
Kimberly Foster (*Dallas*), Khrystyne Haje (*Head of the Class*), and Richard Tyson (*Hardball*)

September 30 1989
Elizabeth Taylor and Mark Harmon in *Sweet Bird of Youth*

October 07 1989
Gerald McRaney & Delta Burke – The Ultimate Prime-Time Love Story

October 14 1989
The World Series, *The Prize Pulitzer* and Faye Dunaway's TV Comeback

October 21 1989
Jamie Lee Curtis of *Anything But Love*

October 28 1989
Lane Smith in *The Final Days* and Richard Grieco of *Booker*

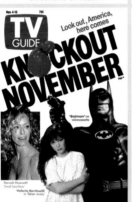

November 04 1989
Farrah Fawcett in *Small Sacrifices*, Valerie Bertinelli in *Taken Away*, and *Batman* on Videocassette

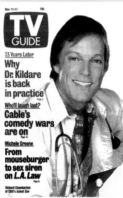

November 11 1989
Richard Chamberlain of *Island Son*

November 18 1989
Courteney Cox and Barry Bostwick in *Till We Meet Again*

November 25 1989
Victoria Principal in *Blind Witness*

December 02 1989
Viewer's Giude to the Holiday Specials

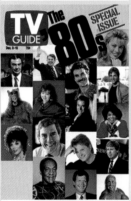

December 09 1989
The '80s: Special Issue

December 16 1989
Neil Patrick Harris of *Doogie Howser, M.D.*; Lucille Ball

December 23 1989
Candice Bergen of *Murphy Brown*; Scott Bakula of *Quantum Leap*

December 30 1989
Julia Duffy of *Newhart* and Jean Smart of *Designing Women*; Susan Lucci of *All My Children*

Memorable TV Show Quotes from the 1980s

"You know, America is a great place, but it doesn't have a place where you can get rid of your kids." Dr. Cliff Huxtable, *The Cosby Show*

"You've got to know the rules before you can break 'em. Otherwise, it's no fun." Sonny Crockett, *Miami Vice*

"Don't do anything I wouldn't do. And if you do, take pictures." Al Calavicci, *Quantum Leap*

"Never take a 'no' from somebody who isn't in a position to give you a 'yes' in the first place." Oprah Winfrey, *The Oprah Winfrey Show*

"Peg, kids, get ready to torture me…I'm home." Al Bundy, *Married...with Children*

"You ate my homework? I didn't know dogs really did that." Bart Simpson, *The Simpsons*

The Nineties

"TVG: Has television lived up to its potential? Gore Vidal: No, of course not. But then, what does?"
November 4, 1995

"Kelsey Grammer sets the tone of kindness, but there are times we all know that the dog is the real star."
Frasier's Peri Gilpin
March 18, 1995

"I would say the biggest change for *Columbo* between now and the '70s is that it's tougher for him to find an ashtray."
Peter Falk
December 1, 1990

"The world is in a shocking state. So a bit of frothy escapism, with women dressed in preposterous clothes and getting into slightly bizarre situations, fits perfectly."
Dynasty's Joan Collins
October 19, 1991

"Every woman on television over the age of 25 has had something done. Plastic surgery is like a tool in a career tool chest."
Joan Rivers
October 26, 1991

1990

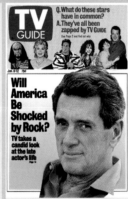

January 06 1990
Rock Hudson; John Tesh, Zsa Zsa Gabor, Andrew Dice Clay, Cher, Roseanne Barr & Tom Arnold

January 13 1990
Roseanne Barr of *Roseanne* and Craig T. Nelson of *Coach*

January 20 1990
Catherine Crier, Arsenio Hall, and Dana Delaney – Dynamite Dozen

January 27 1990
Harrison Ford as Indiana Jones

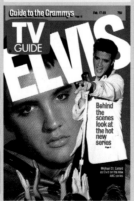

February 03 1990
Lesley Ann Warren; Sammy Davis Jr. and Friends; *Amen*; Jennifer Grey

February 10 1990
Maury Povich & Connie Chung; Michael Tucker & Jill Eikenberry; Patricia Wettig & Ken Olin

February 17 1990
Michael St. Gerard as Elvis on the New ABC Series

February 24 1990
Cast Members in *Challenger*

March 03 1990
Parent's Guide to Children's Television

March 10 1990
The Cast of
L.A. Law

March 17 1990
The Simpsons

March 24 1990
Billy Crystal, Host of This
Year's Academy Awards Show;
Paula Zahn

March 31 1990
Bob Saget of
America's Funniest Home Videos

April 07 1990
Valerie Bertinelli (*Sydney*);
Cast Members of *Capital News*;
Carol Burnett (*Carol & Company*)

April 14 1990
America's Top TV Critics Tell:
What's In, What's Out

April 21 1990
Arnold Schwarzenegger Directs
Tales from the Crypt

April 28 1990
May Sweeps – *The Little Mermaid*;
The Beach Boys; *HBO's Comic
Relief '90*; The Kentucky Derby

May 05 1990
Oprah Winfrey –
Oprah Opens Up

May 12 1990
Barbara Cameron with Kirk
Cameron and Joanna Kerns
of *Growing Pains*

May 19 1990
Carol Burnett of
Carol & Company

May 26 1990
Madonna in *Dick Tracy*;
Women and Men; the
Back to the Future Trilogy

June 02 1990
Steve Bond of *Santa Barbara* and
Barbara Crampton of *The Young
and the Restless*

June 09 1990
Bart Simpson of *The Simpsons*,
Teenage Mutant Ninja Turtles,
and *The Little Mermaid*

June 16 1990
Dana Delaney of
China Beach

June 23 1990
Arsenio Hall – TV Person
of the Year

The first cartoon broadcast was **Disney**'s *Donald's
Cousin Gus* in May 1939, and in December 1955, *The
Mighty Mouse Playhouse* was the first Saturday morning cartoon show. *The Flintstones* was the first prime
time cartoon show in 1960, and *The Simpsons* holds
the record for the longest running evening cartoon.

June 30 1990
Your TV Summer Survival Guide –
61st All-Star Game; *The Last
Elephant*; *Licence to Kill*

July 07 1990
The Best and Worst

July 14 1990
Sinbad, Kadeem Hardison, Jasmine
Guy, and Dawnn Lewis of
A Different World

July 21 1990
Malcolm-Jamal Warner, David
Faustino, Neil Patrick Harris,
and Alyssa Milano

July 28 1990
Guide to Home Video's
High-Flying New Season

August 04 1990
Candice Bergen (*Murphy Brown*),
Nicollette Sheridan (*Knots Landing*),
and Kirstie Alley (*Cheers*)

August 11 1990
Joe Montana, Michael Jordan,
and Bo Jackson – TV, Sports
and Money

August 18 1990
Annie Potts, Delta Burke, Dixie
Carter, and Jean Smart of
Designing Women

August 25 1990
Nicollette Sheridan, Dana Delaney,
and Jaclyn Smith – Results of our
1990 TV Beauty Poll

September 01 1990
Janet Jackson and Paula Abdul;
Madonna – MTV: Why Women
Now Rule Rock

September 08 1990
Sheryl Lee, Lara Flynn Boyle,
and Peggy Lipton of
Twin Peaks

September 15 1990
Fall Preview:
Special Issue

September 22 1990
Bart Simpson and Bill Cosby –
Fall Preview II

September 29 1990
Laila Robins, Lenny Clarke,
and Will Smith –
Fall Preview III

October 06 1990
What's Best... and What's
Waiting in the Wings

October 13 1990
Pretty Woman; World Series;
Corin Nemec; Will Smith;
Charlie Schlatter

October 20 1990
Marge Simpson, Oprah Winfrey,
and Delta Burke – The Best and
Worst Dressed on TV

October 27 1990
Ari Lehman, The Crypt-Keeper,
Ben Cross, and Robert Englund –
Yikes!

November 03 1990
The Cast of
Cheers Celebrates
It's 200th Episode

November 10 1990
Susan Lucci of
All My Children

A NOVEMBER TO REMEMBER

Your guide to the biggest month of the fall season

Nov. 3-9
75¢

The cast of *Cheers* celebrates its 200th episode

Airing from 1982 to 1993, *Cheers*'s entire first season was staged in the bar. In 1990, the place "where everybody knows your name" sparked a chain of bars in airports and hotels. *Cheers* was cancelled in 1993 after **Ted Danson** left the show, and its final episode is one of the highest rated series finales.

November 17 1990
Andy Griffith of *Matlock*;
The Muppets and Jim Henson

November 24 1990
Linda Evans in
She'll Take Romance;
Malcolm-Jamal Warner

December 01 1990
Cast Members of *A Different World*;
Dolly Parton (*Home for Christmas*);
Chevy Chase (*Christmas Vacation*)

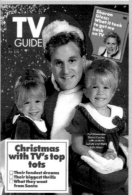

December 08 1990
David Coulier and Ashley and Mary Kate Olsen of
Full House; Sharon Gless

December 15 1990
Dixie Carter of
Designing Women

December 22 1990
Batman, Dick Tracy, and the Flash – How Hollywood Brings Our Comic Book Heroes to Life

December 29 1990
The Cast of
Murphy Brown

1991

January 05 1991
Jane Pauley of *Real Life*;
Beatrice Arthur of *The Golden Girls*

January 12 1991
Farrah Fawcett and
Ryan O'Neal of
Good Sports

January 19 1991
Morley Safer, Harry Reasoner,
Mike Wallace, and Ed Bradley of
60 Minutes

January 26 1991
Cybill Shepherd in
Which Way Home

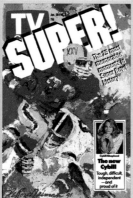

January 26 1991
Super Bowl: 25 Memorable
Moments

February 02 1991
Julia Roberts, M.C. Hammer,
Gary Cole – It's TV's Fab Feb!

February 09 1991
*Lucy and Desi: Before
the Laughter*

February 16 1991
Watching the War

141

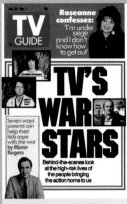

February 23 1991
TV's War Stars

March 02 1991
Jaleel White of
Family Matters

March 09 1991
Dreyfuss of *Empty Nest*;
Fred Dryer of *Hunter*

March 16 1991
Barbara Walters and the
Teenage Mutant Ninja Turtles

March 23 1991
Whoopi Goldberg (*Ghost*), Julia
Roberts (*Pretty Woman*), and Kevin
Costner (*Dances with Wolves*)

March 30 1991
Cheryl Ladd of *Changes*;
Whitney Houston

April 06 1991
Baseball TV Preview

April 13 1991
Delta Burke of
Designing Women

April 20 1991
Burt Reynolds and
Marilu Henner of
Evening Shade

April 27 1991
Dinosaurs; Magic Johnson;
Patrick Bergin in *Robin Hood*

May 04 1991
Larry Hagman of
Dallas

May 11 1991
Old and New Cast Members of
L.A. Law

May 18 1991
Robin Thomas, Candice Bergen,
and Jay Thomas of
Murphy Brown

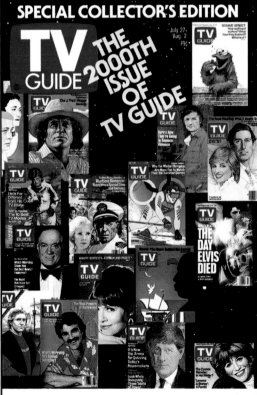

May 25 1991
101 Dalmatians; Julia Roberts;
Arnold Schwarzenegger in
The Terminator

June 01 1991
Jasmine Guy of
A Different World

June 08 1991
Michael Landon – We're With
You, Michael

On July 27, 1991, **TV Guide** published their 2000th
issue, establishing itself as a permanent fixture in the
lives of the American public. The Special Edition,
which includes an article on TV Legends Then & Now,
is a "must have" for all serious collectors.

June 15 1991
The Wizard of Oz; *Mary Poppins*; *Casablanca*; *Tootsie*; *Star Wars*

June 22 1991
Husband and Wife Stars Gerald McRaney and Delta Burke

June 29 1991
Arsenio Hall, Johnny Carson, David Letterman, and Jay Leno – The Battle for Carson's Crown

July 06 1991
The Best and The Worst

July 13 1991
Michael Landon – What Michael Means To Us

July 13 1991
Michael Landon – What Michael Meant To Us

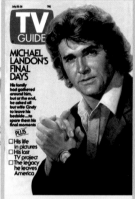

July 20 1991
Michael Landon – Michael Landon's Final Days

July 27 1991
The 2000th Issue of TV Guide

August 03 1991
Madonna – The MTV Revolution

August 10 1991
Jaclyn Smith, Candice Bergen, and Vanna White – TV's Most Beautiful Women

August 17 1991
Kevin Costner in *Dances With Wolves* and Macaulay Culkin in *Home Alone*

August 24 1991
Shannen Doherty of *Beverly Hills, 90210*

August 31 1991
Patrick Stewart and William Shatner – It's Kirk vs. Picard

September 07 1991
Janine Turner of *Northern Exposure*

September 14 1991
Fall Preview: Special Issue

September 21 1991
Jan Hooks and Julia Duffy of *Designing Women*

September 28 1991
Where's Waldo?, *Hammerman*, *Darkwing Duck*, and *Doug*

October 05 1991
Sharon Gless and Arsenio Hall – TV's Fashion Standouts

October 12 1991
Jacqueline Kennedy Onassis, the Subject of This Week's Six-Hour NBC Miniseries

October 19 1991
Linda Evans and Joan Collins in *Dynasty: The Reunion*

October 26 1991
Joan Rivers: Can We Tuck?

November 02 1991
Michael Jackson – The Making of
Michael Jackson's New Video

November 09 1991
Tom Brokaw, Peter Jennings,
and Dan Rather – Is Network
News Crumbling?

November 16 1991
Valerie Bertinelli in
In A Child's Name

November 23 1991
Madonna

November 30 1991
Naomi Judd and
Wyonna Judd –
Breaking Up is Hard to Do

December 07 1991
Christmas

December 14 1991
Luke Perry and
Jason Priestly of
Beverly Hills, 90210

December 21 1991
John Corbett of
Northern Exposure

December 28 1991
John Goodman of
Roseanne

1992

January 04 1992
Roseanne Barr – Is Roseanne
the New Lucy?

January 11 1992
Henry Fonda and Jane Fonda –
Fonda on Fonda

January 18 1992
Dreyfuss of
Empty Nest

January 25 1992
Your Number 1 Guide to
Super Bowl XXVI;
Cybill Shepherd in *Memphis*

February 01 1992
Jessica Lange in
O Pioneers!

February 08 1992
Kristi Yamaguchi;
Grant Shaud of *Murphy Brown*

February 15 1992
Regis Philbin and
Kathie Lee Gifford of
Live with Regis & Kathie Lee

February 22 1992
Garth Brooks; Natalie Cole;
Alison Doody and Benedict
Taylor in *Duel of Hearts*

February 29 1992
Corey Carrier of
Young Indiana Jones

March 07 1992
Macaulay Culkin: What I Watch
When I'm Home Alone

March 14 1992
Jane Pauley of
Dateline NBC

March 21 1992
Magic Johnson – Magic Talks
to Our Kids

May 23 1992
Jerry Seinfeld of *Seinfeld*

Plus: A Guide
to the Summer's
Hot Videos

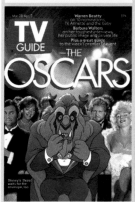

March 28 1992
Disney's *Beauty and the Beast*
at The Oscars

April 04 1992
Ronn Moss and
Katherine Kelly Lang of
The Bold and the Beautiful

April 11 1992
Jay Leno of
The Tonight Show;
S.O.S. – Save Our Shows

Seinfeld debuted in 1990 and the self-proclaimed "show about nothing" became a favorite. In its eight year run, it won a total of more than 50 awards from critics, peers, and the viewers. Remember "The Contest" and George's father's **TV Guide** collection? On Friday mornings, the talk at the water cooler was about Seinfeld.

April 18 1992
Patricia Richardson and
Tim Allen of
Home Improvement

April 25 1992
Burt Reynolds of
Evening Shade

May 02 1992
Woody Harrelson and
Jackie Swanson of
Cheers

May 09 1992
Johnny Carson –
Carson Countdown: Two
Weeks and Ticking…

May 16 1992
Oprah Winfrey debuts
Oprah: Behind the Scenes

May 23 1992
Jerry Seinfeld of
Seinfeld

May 30 1992
Dan Lauria, Alley Mills, Jason
Hervey, and Fred Savage of
The Wonder Years

June 06 1992
Grant Show of *Melrose Place*;
Drew Barrymore of 2000
Malibu Road

June 13 1992
Bob Saget of
Full House

June 20 1992
The Year's Best and Worst

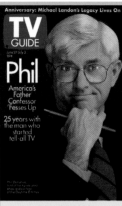

June 27 1992
Phil Donahue – Host of His
Syndicated Show and Co-Host of
the Daytime Emmys

July 04 1992
Delta Burke of
Delta

July 11 1992
Luke Perry and
Shannen Doherty of
Beverly Hills, 90210

July 18 1992
Cindy Crawford of MTV and
Patrick Stewart of
Star Trek: The Next Generation

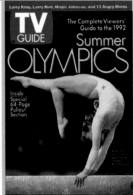

July 25 1992
American Gymnast
Kim Zmeskal

August 01 1992
Dana Carvey and David
Letterman – Why Are These
Guys Smiling?

August 08 1992
Princess Diana and Prince
Charles: Di vs. Chuck
The Soap Opera

August 15 1992
Roseanne Arnold, Whoopi
Goldberg, Homer Simpson, Ted
Koppel, and Michele Pfeiffer

August 22 1992
Is TV Violence Battering
Our Kids?

August 29 1992
Roseanne Barr – An Emmy? Moi?

September 05 1992
Joan Lunden of
Good Morning America

September 12 1992
Fall Preview:
Special Issue

September 19 1992
Candice Bergen of
Murphy Brown

September 26 1992
Billy Ray Cyrus and
Reba McEntire –
Country Music Awards

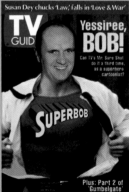

October 03 1992
Bob Newhart of
Bob!

October 10 1992
Helen Hunt and Paul Reiser of
Mad About You; Markie Post
and John Ritter of *Hearts Afire*

October 17 1992
Leeza Gibbons of *Entertainment
Tonight* and Jay Leno of
The Tonight Show

October 24 1992
Goofy and Son Max of
Goof Troop;
Kathie Lee Gifford

October 31 1992
Julia Roberts, Peter Falk, and
Jaclyn Smith – Your Guide To
Fall's Biggest Month

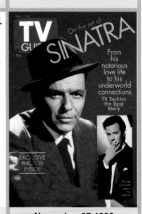

November 07 1992
Frank Sinatra;
Philip Casanoff in *Sinatra*

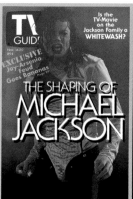

November 14 1992
Michael Jackson – The Shaping of
Michael Jackson

November 21 1992
Diane Sawyer of
Prime Time Live

November 28 1992
Maggie Simpson and Bart Simpson;
John Ritter and Markie Post
of *Hearts Afire*

December 05 1992
John Stamos and Blake
and Dylan Tuomy-Wilhoit of
Full House

December 12 1992
Katey Sagal of
Married...With Children

December 19 1992
Tiny Toon Adventures

December 26 1992
Angela Lansbury of
Murder, She Wrote

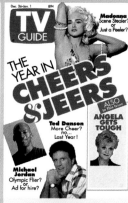

December 26 1992
Madonna; Michael Jordan; Ted
Danson; Angela Lansbury – The
Year in Cheers & Jeers

January 02 1993
Avery Brooks (*Star Trek: Deep
Space Nine*); Patrick Stewart (*Star
Trek: The Next Generation*)

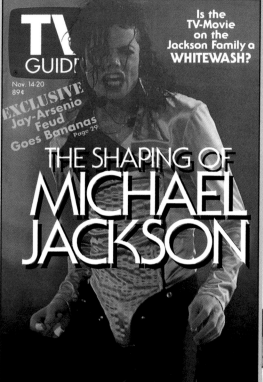

January 09 1993
Hillary and Bill Clinton –
Inaugural Exclusive

January 16 1993
Dana Carvey and
Phil Hartman of
Saturday Night Live

January 23 1993
Will Smith of
The Fresh Prince of Bel Air

The first music videos could be said to actually
be some of the first sound films which featured
musicians performing or had accompanying musical
scores. In the early 1940's, short one-song films
were made. MTV debuted in 1981 and is responsible
for the success of many top performers like
Michael Jackson and **Madonna**.

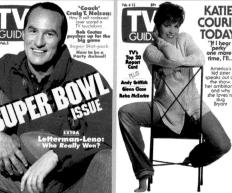

January 30 1993
Craig T. Nelson of
Coach

February 06 1993
Katie Couric of
Today

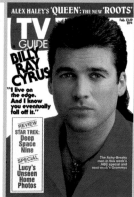

February 13 1993
Billy Ray Cyrus – The Achy-
Breaky Man in This Week's
ABC Special

February 20 1993
Jane Seymour of
Dr. Quinn, Medicine Woman

February 27 1993
Jane Pauley and Barney

March 06 1993
Fitness on TV – Regis Philbin
of *Live with Regis & Kathie Lee*;
Cher

March 13 1993
Mary Tyler Moore –
Mary Opens Up

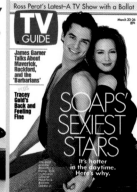

March 20 1993
Antonio Sabato Jr. of *General
Hospital* and Hunter Tylo of *The
Bold and the Beautiful*

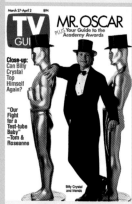

March 27 1993
Billy Crystal and Friends –
Mr. Oscar

April 03 1993
Heather Locklear of
Melrose Place

April 10 1993
When the Cheering Stops –
Ted Danson; Shelley Long

April 17 1993
40th Anniversary Issue

April 24 1993
Patricia Richardson and
Tim Allen of
Home Improvement

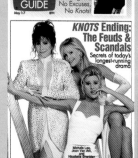

May 01 1993
Donna Mills and Michele Lee,
Joan Van Ark, and Nicollette
Sheridan of *Knots Ending*

May 08 1993
Arsenio Hall of *The Arsenio
Hall Show*; Tori Spelling of
Beverly Hills, 90210

May 15 1993
The Cast of *Cheers*:
Kirstie Alley, Ted Danson,
Woody Harrelson,

Fold Out
Rhea Perlman,
Kelsey Grammer,
John Ratzenberger,

Fold Out
and
George Wendt

May 22 1993
Linda Ellerbee – TV's Joyful
Survivor

May 29 1993
Here Comes Richard Simmons

June 05 1993
Connie Chung of
Eye to Eye with Connie Chung

June 12 1993
Joey Lawrence of
Blossom

June 19 1993
A Martinez of *L.A. Law*
and His Son, Cody;
Little House on the Prairie

June 26 1993
Cindy Crawford, Lauren Hutton, Naomi Campbell, and Beverly Johnson; Marge of *The Simpsons*

July 03 1993
Vanna White of *The Wheel of Fortune*

July 10 1993
Larry Hagman of *Staying Afloat*

July 17 1993
Julia Roberts & Lyle Lovett – Hot-Blooded Hollywood

July 24 1993
Armin Shimerman of *Star Trek: Deep Space Nine*

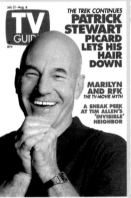

July 31 1993
Patrick Stewart of *Star Trek: The Next Generation*

August 07 1993
Mary-Kate and Ashley Olsen – Tycoon Tots

August 14 1993
The Furor Over R-Rated Network TV

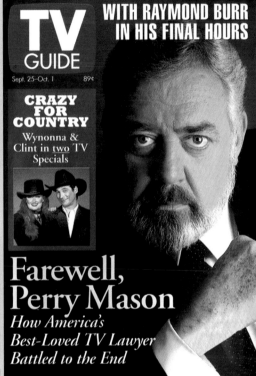

His first film roles were as villains, and **Raymond Burr** was originally asked to audition for the bad guy, D.A. Hamilton Burger, in *Perry Mason*. He won the lead role instead and began his long TV career. He was also the founder, with **Robert Benevides**, of Raymond Burr Vineyards. He died on 9/12/93 from cancer.

August 21 1993
Loni Anderson – Loni's Story

August 28 1993
Late Night Star Wars!
Jay Leno, Chevy Chase, David Letterman,

Fold Out
Ted Koppel, Conan O'Brien, and Arsenio Hall

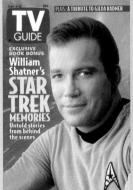

September 04 1993
William Shatner – *Star Trek* Memories

September 11 1993
Kelsey Grammer of *Frasier*

September 18 1993
Fall Preview: Special Issue

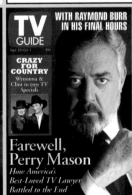

September 25 1993
Raymond Burr – With Raymond Burr in His Final Hours; Wynonna Judd and Clint Black

September 25 1993
Wynonna Judd and Clint Black

October 02 1993
Victoria Principal in
River of Rage

October 09 1993
John Larroquette of *The John
Larroquette Show*; Harry
Anderson of *Dave's World*

October 16 1993
Anthony Geary and
Genie Francis of
General Hospital

October 23 1993
Kelly Rutherford, Paula
Poundstone, Jason Alexander,
and Faye Dunaway

October 30 1993
Ernie and Bert of
Sesame Street

November 06 1993
Mike Wallace of
60 Minutes

November 13 1993
Hillary Rodham Clinton
and Big Bird;
Mariah Carey

November 20 1993
Ralph Waite, Richard Thomas,
and Michael Learned in
A Walton Thanksgiving Reunion

November 27 1993
Dolly Parton – Good Golly,
Miss Dolly!

December 04 1993
The Grinch and Max unwrap *It's
a Wonderful Life*, Will Smith,
and Jennie Garth

December 11 1993
Bette Midler in *Gypsy*;
Daryl Hannah in *Attack of
the 50 Ft. Woman*

December 18 1993
Our 40th Anniversary Show

December 25 1993
Johnny Carson in
The Kennedy Center Honors

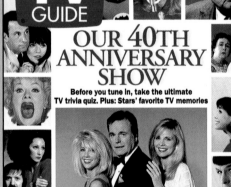

January 01 1994
Tim Allen of
Home Improvement

January 08 1994
David Caruso of
NYPD Blue

To celebrate their 40th anniversary, on December
20, 1993, **TV Guide** ran a special on CBS hosted
by **Heather Locklear**, **Robert Wagner**, and
Lindsay Wagner. The show featured classic
stars such as **Lucille Ball** (in archival footage)
and a variety of current stars.

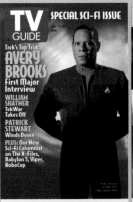

January 15 1994
Avery Brooks of
Star Trek: Deep Space Nine

January 22 1994
Henry Winkler; Dan Cortese;
Ellen DeGeneres; Ed Begley Jr.;
Sister, Sister – Winter Preview

January 29 1994
Valerie Bertinelli – Crazy for
Football

February 05 1994
Courtney Thorne-Smith
and Heather Locklear of
Melrose Place; Fabio

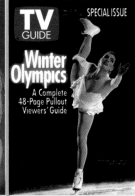

February 12 1994
Nancy Kerrigan, American
Figure Skater

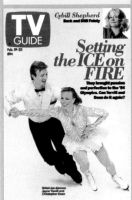

February 19 1994
Jane Torvill and Christopher
Dean, British Ice Dancers;
Cybill Shepherd

February 26 1994
Whitney Houston

March 05 1994
Dennis Franz of
NYPD Blue

March 12 1994
Erin Davis of
The Sinbad Show

March 19 1994
Barbara Walters Hosts Pre-Oscar
Special; Whoopi Goldberg Emcees
the Academy Awards

March 26 1994
Diane Sawyer – Diane's Big Deal

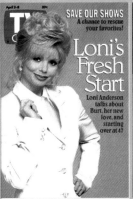

April 02 1994
Loni Anderson – Loni's Fresh Start

April 09 1994
Kirstie Alley in
David's Mother

April 16 1994
Nicollette Sheridan in
A Time To Heal

April 23 1994
Jason Alexander of
Seinfeld

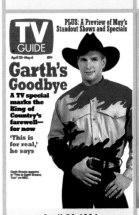

April 30 1994
Garth Brooks in
This is Garth Brooks, Too!

May 07 1994
Rob Lowe and
Laura San Giacomo in
The Stand

May 14 1994
The Cast of
Star Trek: The Next Generation

May 21 1994
Farrah Fawcett in
The Substitute Wife

May 28 1994
Andrew Shue of
Melrose Place

June 04 1994
Elizabeth Taylor – Liz on Liz

June 11 1994
David Caruso; Laura Leighton;
Madonna; Brett Butler – The Best
and Worst Of The Year in TV

June 18 1994
Eddie of *Frasier* and
Murray of *Mad About You*

June 25 1994
Jane Seymour, Tim Allen, and
Jay Leno – Who are Hollywood's
Best-Loved Stars?

July 02 1994
Gillian Anderson and David
Duchovny of *The X-Files*;
Reba McEntire

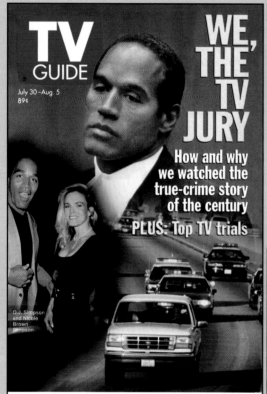

On June 17, 1994 all network stations showed us
his Bronco chase, and **O.J. Simpson**'s trial lasted
4 months, most of it televised. During that time,
the most common question heard was "Do you think
O.J. did it?" "The Juice" was acquitted but not before
giving **Kato Kaelin** his 15 minutes of fame.

July 02 1994
Reba McEntire: Is There Life
Out There?

July 09 1994
Go, Go, Power Rangers!

July 16 1994
Cindy Crawford of
House of Style

July 23 1994
Oprah Winfrey – Oprah's
Stormy Summer

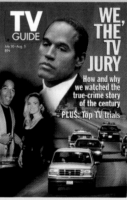

July 30 1994
O.J. Simpson – We, The Jury

August 06 1994
Paul Reiser of
Mad About You

August 13 1994
Alexandra Paul, Pamela Anderson,
David Hasselhoff, and Yasmine
Bleeth of *Baywatch*

August 20 1994
Barbra Streisand – Barbra's
Quest for the Best

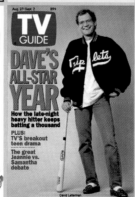

August 27 1994
David Letterman of
Late Show with David Letterman

September 03 1994
John Madden, Coach of
the Raiders

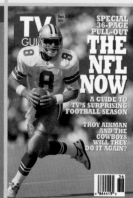

September 03 1994
Troy Aikman of the Cowboys

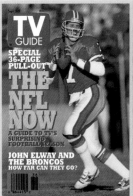

September 03 1994
John Elway of the Broncos

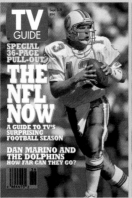

September 03 1994
Dan Marino of the Dolphins

September 03 1994
Joe Montana of the Chiefs

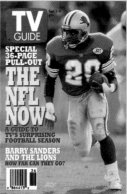

September 03 1994
Barry Sanders of the Lions

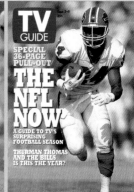

September 03 1994
Thurman Thomas of the Bills

September 10 1994
Tim Allen of *Home Improvement* and David Caruso of *NYPD Blue*

September 17 1994
Fall Preview:
Special Issue

September 24 1994
John Mahoney, David Hyde Pierce, Kelsey Grammer, and Eddie of *Frasier*

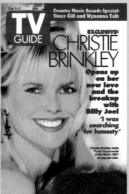

October 01 1994
Christie Brinkley Hosts *Ford's Supermodel of the World 1994*

October 08 1994
Kate Mulgrew of *Star Trek: Voyager*

October 15 1994
Melissa Gilbert of *Sweet Justice*

October 22 1994
Suzanne Somers of *Step by Step*; Jay Leno of *The Tonight Show*

October 29 1994
The Mighty Morphin Power Rangers

November 05 1994
Shannen Doherty in *The Margaret Mitchell Story*

November 12 1994
Joanne Whalley-Kilmer ad Timothy Dalton in *Scarlett*

November 19 1994
Sherry Stringfield, Anthony Edwards, and Noah Wyle of *ER*

November 26 1994
Ellen DeGeneres of *Ellen*; James Garner

December 03 1994
Crystal Bernard of *Wings*

December 10 1994
Jane Pauley of *Dateline NBC*; Matthew Fox and Scott Wolf of *Party of Five*

December 17 1994
Kathie Lee Gifford in *Looking for Christmas*

December 24 1994
Roseanne, Dorothy Letterman, and Burt Reynolds – The Year in Cheers & Jeers

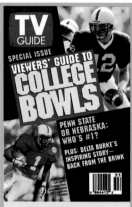

December 31 1994
Penn State QB Kerry Collins; Nebraska RB Lawrence Phillips

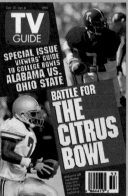

December 31 1994
Alabama QB Jay Barker; Ohio State WR Joey Galloway

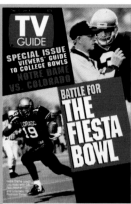

December 31 1994
Notre Dame Coach Lou Holtz with QB Ron Powtus; Colorado RB Rashaan Salaam

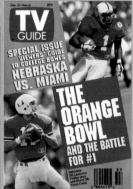

December 31 1994
Nebraska RB Lawrence Phillips; Miami QB Frank Costa

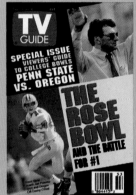

December 31 1994
Penn State Coach Joe Paterno; Oregon QB Danny O'Neil

December 31 1994
Penn State Coach Joe Paterno; QB Kerry Collins

December 31 1994
Florida QB Danny Wuerffel; Florida State QB Danny Kanell

January 07 1995
Oprah Winfrey – "I Feel I'm Finally Growing Up"

January 14 1995
Kate Mulgrew, Tim Russ, and Robert Beltran of *Star Trek: Voyager*

January 21 1995
The Wayans Bros.; Delta Burke; Julia Campbell; John Leguizamo; Richard Grieco – Winter Preview

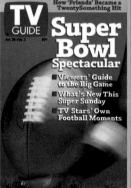

January 28 1995
Super Bowl Spectacular

February 04 1995
Jerry Seinfeld of *Seinfeld*; Roseanne

February 11 1995
Heather Locklear in *Texas Justice*

February 18 1995
Sally Field in *A Woman of Independent Means*

February 25 1995
George Clooney of *ER*

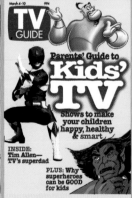

March 04 1995
Parents' Guide to Kids' TV

March 11 1995
Gillian Anderson and David Duchovny of *The X-Files*

March 18 1995
Roseanne; Tim Allen; Oprah; Jerry Seinfeld – TV's 10 Most Powerful Stars

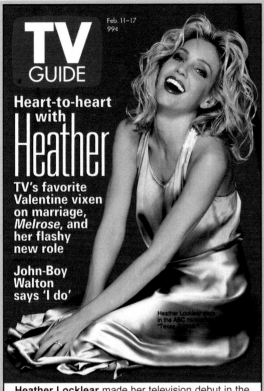

Heart-to-heart with Heather

TV's favorite Valentine vixen on marriage, *Melrose,* and her flashy new role

John-Boy Walton says 'I do'

Feb. 11–17 99¢

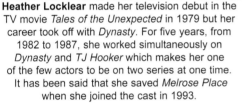

Heather Locklear made her television debut in the TV movie *Tales of the Unexpected* in 1979 but her career took off with *Dynasty*. For five years, from 1982 to 1987, she worked simultaneously on *Dynasty* and *TJ Hooker* which makes her one of the few actors to be on two series at one time. It has been said that she saved *Melrose Place* when she joined the cast in 1993.

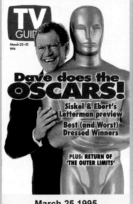

March 25 1995
David Letterman – Dave Does the Oscars

April 01 1995
Jenny Jones, Jerry Springer, Ricki Lake, and Montel Williams – Are Talk Shows Out of Control?

April 08 1995
Jennie Garth of *Beverly Hills, 90210*

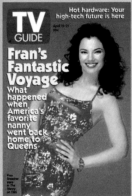

April 15 1995
Fran Drescher of *The Nanny*

April 22 1995
Susan Lucci in *Seduced and Betrayed*

April 29 1995
Kate Mulgrew, Courtney Thorne-Smith, and Roxanne Hart – Boss Ladies

May 06 1995
Jane Seymour and Joe Lando of *Dr. Quinn, Medicine Woman*

May 13 1995
Naomi Judd, Wynonna Judd, and Ashley Judd

May 20 1995
Gail O'Grady and Sharon Lawrence of *NYPD Blue*

May 27 1995
Pamela Anderson of *Baywatch*

June 03 1995
Larry King of *Larry King Live*; Connie Chung

June 10 1995
Summer Preview: Your Guide to the Hot New Shows

June 17 1995
Brett Butler of *Grace Under Fire*; Bryant Gumbel of *Today*

June 24 1995
Jason David Frank of *Mighty Morphin Power Rangers*

July 01 1995
Victoria Principal in *Dancing in the Dark*

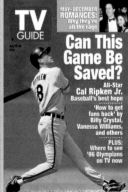

July 08 1995
Cal Ripken Jr. – Baseball's Best Hope; Jerry Seinfeld and Shoshanna Lonstein

July 15 1995

Jennifer Lien and
Ethan Phillips of
Star Trek: Voyager

July 22 1995

Dean Cain of
*Lois and Clark: The New
Adventures of Superman*

July 29 1995

Josie Bissett of
Melrose Place

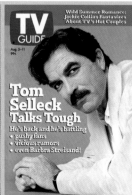

August 05 1995

Tom Selleck Talks Tough

August 12 1995

Cybill Shepherd and Jimmy Smits –
Best Dressed Stars

August 19 1995

Regis Philbin of
Live with Regis & Kathie Lee

August 26 1995

Tiffani-Amber Thiessen and
Brian Austin Green of
Beverly Hills, 90210

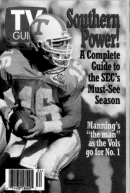

August 26 1995

Tennessee QB Peyton Manning

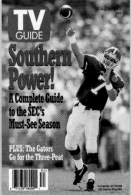

August 26 1995

University of Florida QB
Danny Wuerffel

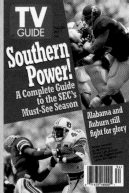

August 26 1995

Alabama tackle Shannon Brown;
Auburn tailback Stephen Davis

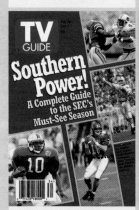

August 26 1995

Stephen Davis; Peyton Manning;
Steve Taneyhill; Moe Williams

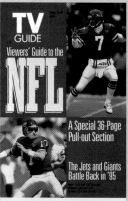

September 02 1995

Boomer Esiason of the Jets; Dave
Brown of the Giants

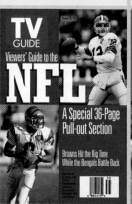

September 02 1995

Vinny Testaverde of the Browns;
Jeff Blake of the Bengals

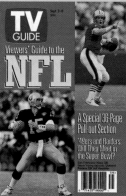

September 02 1995

Steve Young of the 49ers; Jeff
Hostetler of the Raiders

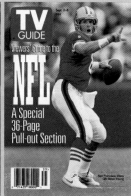

September 02 1995

Steve Young of the 49ers

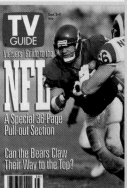

September 02 1995

Chris Zorich of the Bears

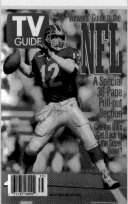

September 02 1995

Jim Kelly of the Bills

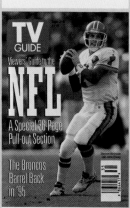

September 02 1995

John Elway of the Broncos

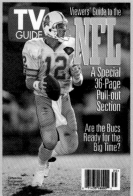

September 02 1995

Trent Dilfer of the Buccaneers

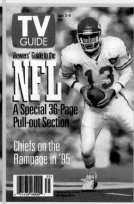

September 02 1995

Steve Bono of the Chiefs

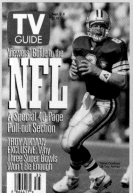

September 02 1995
Troy Aikman of the Cowboys

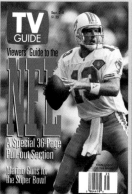

September 02 1995
Dan Marino of the Dolphins

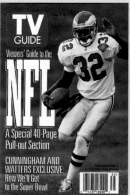

September 02 1995
Ricky Watters of the Eagles

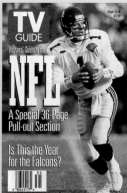

September 02 1995
Jeff George of the Falcons

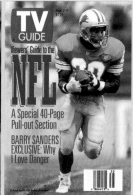

September 02 1995
Barry Sanders of the Lions

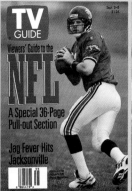

September 02 1995
Steve Beuerlein of the Jaguars

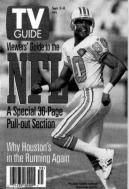

September 02 1995
Haywood Jeffires of the Oilers

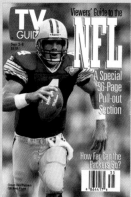

September 02 1995
Brett Favre of the Packers

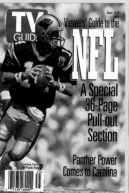

September 02 1995
Frank Reich of the Panthers

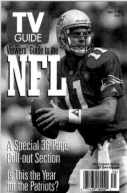

September 02 1995
Drew Bledsoe of the Patriots

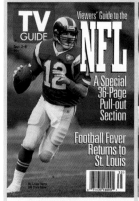

September 02 1995
Chris Miller of the Rams

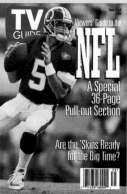

September 02 1995
Heath Shuler of the Redskins

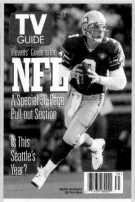

September 02 1995
Rick Mirer of the Seahawks

September 02 1995
Rod Woodson of the Steelers

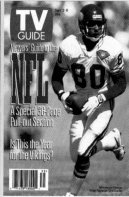

September 02 1995
Cris Carter of the Vikings

September 09 1995
Paul Reiser, Kelsey Grammer, and Garry Shandling; Candice Bergen and John F. Kennedy Jr.

September 16 1995
Fall Preview: Special Issue

September 23 1995
The Cast of *Friends*

September 30 1995
Mary McCormack, Daniel Benzali, and Jason Gedrick of *Murder One*

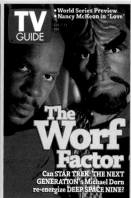

October 07 1995
Avery Brooks and Michael Dorn of *Star Trek: Deep Space Nine*

157

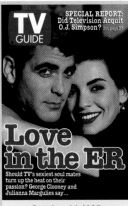

October 14 1995
George Clooney and
Julianna Margulies of
ER

October 21 1995
Andrew Lawrence, Matthew
Lawrence, and Joey Lawrence of
Brotherly Love; Mary Tyler Moore

October 28 1995
Sarah Ferguson, The Duchess
of York

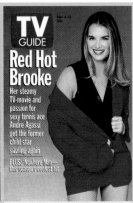

November 04 1995
Brooke Shields in
Nothing Lasts Forever

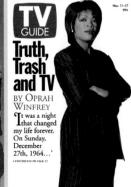

November 11 1995
Oprah Winfrey – Truth, Trash,
and TV

November 11 1995
NCAA Basketball: Mike Krzyzewski,
Duke; Tim Duncan, Wake Forest;
Dante Calabria, North Carolina

November 11 1995
NCAA Basketball: John Wallace,
Syracuse; Kerry Kittles, Villanova;
Ray Allen, Connecticut

November 11 1995
NCAA Basketball: Kentucky's Tony
Delk, Rick Pitino, and Antoine
Walker

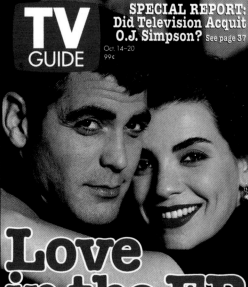

Created by **Michael Crichton**, award winning
author and medical school graduate, *ER* premiered
in September of 1994 and was originally planned
as a film to be directed by **Steven Spielberg**. It was
nominated for an Outstanding Drama Series Emmy
its first season and won it for the second season.

November 11 1995
NCAA Basketball: Chianti Roberts,
Oklahoma State; Ryan Minor,
Oklahoma

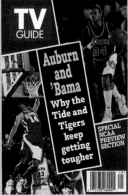

November 11 1995
NCAA Basketball: Moochie Norris,
Auburn; Eric Washington, Alabama

November 11 1995
NCAA Basketball: Maurice Taylor,
Michigan; Quinton Brooks, Michigan
State

November 11 1995
NCAA Basketball: Raef LaFrentz
and Tyrone Davis

November 11 1995
NCAA Basketball: Arizona State's
Ron Riley; Arizona's Joseph Blair

November 18 1995
John Lennon, Paul McCartney,
George Harrison, and Ringo Starr
of The Beatles

November 25 1995
Jane Seymour of
Dr. Quinn, Medicine Woman

December 02 1995
Tea Leoni of
The Naked Truth

December 09 1995
Matthew Fox, Scott Wolf, and
Neve Campbell of *Party of Five*;
Martha Stewart

December 16 1995
Kathie Lee Gifford with Her
Children, Cody and Cassidy;
Howard Stern

December 23 1995
Lisa Kudrow of *Friends*; Jennifer
Aniston; Lorenzo Lamas; Heather
Locklear; Daniel Benzali

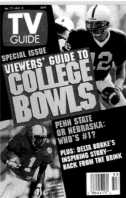

December 30 1995
Penn State's Kerry Collins;
Nebraska's Lawrence Phillips

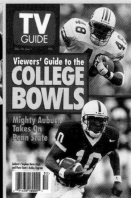

December 30 1995
Auburn's Stephen Davis; Penn
State's Bobby Engram

December 30 1995
Florida's Danny Wuerffel; Florida
State's Danny Kanell

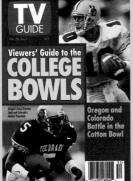

December 30 1995
Oregon's Tony Graziani; Colorado's
Herchel Troutman

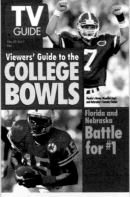

December 30 1995
Florida's Danny Wuerffel;
Nebraska's Tommie Frazier

December 30 1995
Heisman Trophy Winner Eddie
George of Ohio State; Tennessee's
Peyton Manning

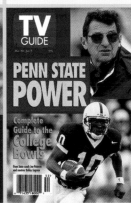

December 30 1995
Penn State coach Joe Paterno;
Receiver Bobby Engram

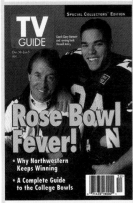

December 30 1995
Northwestern's Coach Gary Barnett
and Darnell Autry

December 30 1995
Texas Quarterback James Brown

January 06 1996
Jerry Seinfeld; Oprah
Winfrey; David Schwimmer;
Cybill Shepherd

January 13 1996
Morgan Fairchild in
The City

January 20 1996
Xena: Warrior Princess; *Hercules –
The Legendary Journeys*; *Space:
Above and Beyond*; William Shatner

January 27 1996
Dallas Cowboys QB Troy Aikman
and Pittsburgh Steelers QB
Neil O'Donnell

February 03 1996
Ted Danson and
Mary Steenburgen in
Gulliver's Travels

February 10 1996
David Schwimmer and
Jennifer Aniston of
Friends

February 17 1996
John de Lancie and Kate
Mulgrew of *Star Trek: Voyager*;
Julia Louis-Dreyfus

159

February 24 1996
Tori Spelling of
Beverly Hills, 90210

March 02 1996
Jimmy Smits and
Dennis Franz of
NYPD Blue

March 09 1996
50 Great Things About
Television Now

March 16 1996
Billy Crystal with Animal,
Kermit, and Gonzo of
Muppets Tonight

March 23 1996
Sharon Stone (*Casino*); Mel
Gibson (*Braveheart*); Babe (*Babe*);
Brad Pitt (*12 Monkeys*)

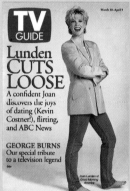

March 30 1996
Joan Lunden of
Good Morning America

April 06 1996
Gillian Anderson and
David Duchovny of
The X-Files

April 13 1996
Anthony Edwards of
ER

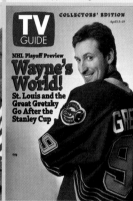

April 13 1996
Wayne Gretzky of the Blues

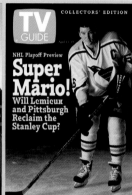

April 13 1996
Mario Lemieux of the Penguins

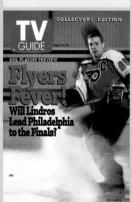

April 13 1996
Eric Lindros of the Flyers

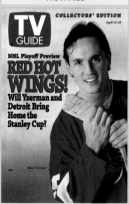

April 13 1996
Steve Yzerman of the Red Wings

April 20 1996
Cybill Shepherd of
Cybill

April 27 1996
The Cast of
60 Minutes

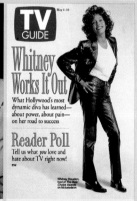

May 04 1996
Whitney Houston Hosts
The Kids' Choice Awards

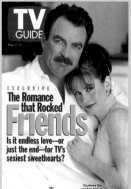

May 11 1996
Courtney Cox and
Tom Selleck of
Friends

May 18 1996
Candice Bergen of
Murphy Brown

May 25 1996
Heather Locklear of
Melrose Place

June 01 1996
Jerry Seinfeld of
Seinfeld

June 08 1996
Jenny McCarthy of
Singled Out

June 15 1996
Teri Hatcher of
*Lois and Clark: The New
Adventures of Superman*

June 22 1996
Conan O'Brien of
Late Night With Conan O'Brien

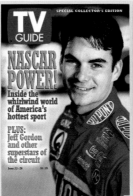

June 22 1996
NASCAR: Jeff Gordon

June 29 1996
100 Most Memorable Moments in
TV History

July 06 1996
Gillian Anderson of
The X-Files

July 13 1996
Jerry Mathers and
Barbara Billingsley of
Leave It to Beaver

July 20 1996
Janet Evans, Four-Time Gold
Medalist

July 27 1996
Lisa Leslie, Rebecca Lobo,
and Dawn Staley – The Other
Dream Team

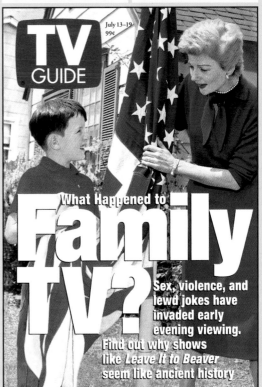

August 03 1996
Dean Cain of *Lois & Clark*
and Jennie Garth of
Beverly Hills, 90210

August 10 1996
Maureen McCormick, Barbara
Feldon, and Chad Everett – Stars
We Still Love

August 17 1996
Matthew Perry of
Friends

The Cleavers of *Leave It to Beaver* are considered
to be the 50's All-American Family. Theodore got
his nickname, Beaver, because Wally, as a child,
couldn't pronounce his proper name. Ward Cleaver
was ranked #28 on **TV Guide**'s list of 50 Greatest
TV Dads of All Time and Eddie Haskell won the
#2 slot on its list of TV's 10 Biggest Brats.

August 24 1996
William Shatner of
Star Trek

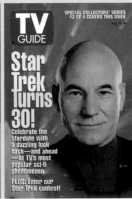

August 24 1996
Patrick Stewart of
Star Trek: The Next Generation

August 24 1996
Kate Mulgrew of
Star Trek: Voyager

August 24 1996
Avery Brooks of
Star Trek: Deep Space Nine

August 31 1996
Drew Carey of
The Drew Carey Show

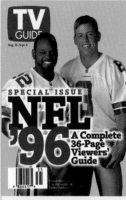

August 31 1996
Emmitt Smith and Troy Aikman
of the Cowboys

August 31 1996
Steve Young of the 49ers and Jeff
Hostetler of the Raiders

August 31 1996
Hugh Douglas of the Jets and Dave
Brown of the Giants

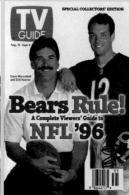

August 31 1996
Dave Wannstedt and Erik Kramer
of the Bears

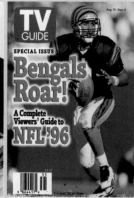

August 31 1996
Jeff Blake of the Bengals

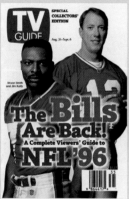

August 31 1996
Bruce Smith and Jim Kelly
of the Bills

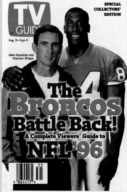

August 31 1996
Mike Shanahan and Shannon
Sharpe of the Broncos

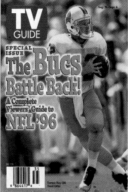

August 31 1996
Trent Dilfer of the Buccaneers

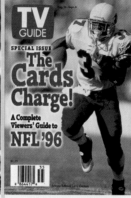

August 31 1996
Larry Centers of the Cardinals

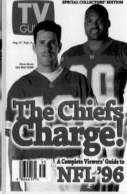

August 31 1996
Steve Bono and Neil Smith
of the Chiefs

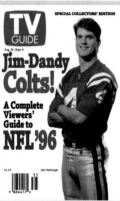

August 31 1996
Jim Harbaugh of the Colts

August 31 1996
Emmitt Smith and Troy Aikman
of the Cowboys

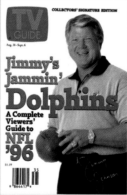

August 31 1996
Coach Jimmy Johnson of the
Dolphins

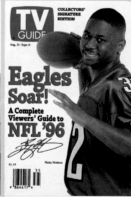

August 31 1996
Ricky Watters of the Eagles

August 31 1996
Eric Metcalf of the Falcons

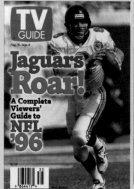

August 31 1996
Mark Brunell of the Jaguars

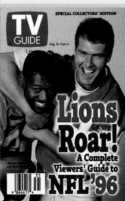

August 31 1996
Herman Moore and Scott Mitchell
of the Lions

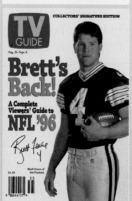

August 31 1996
Brett Favre of the Packers

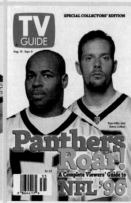

August 31 1996
Sam Mills and Kerry Collins
of the Panthers

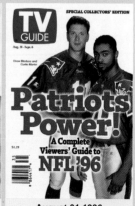

August 31 1996
Drew Bledsoe and Curtis Martin
of the Patriots

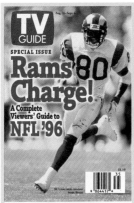

August 31 1996
Isaac Bruce of the Rams

August 31 1996
Vinny Testaverde and Ted
Marchibroda of the Ravens

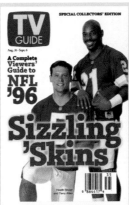

August 31 1996
Heath Shuler and Terry Allen
of the Redskins

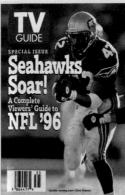

August 31 1996
Chris Warren of the Seahawks

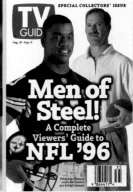

August 31 1996
Kordell Stewart and Coach Bill
Cowher of the Steelers

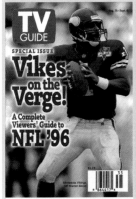

August 31 1996
Warren Moon of the Vikings

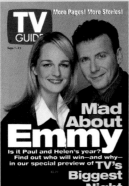

September 07 1996
Helen Hunt and
Paul Reiser of
Mad About You

September 14 1996
Fall Preview:
Special Issue

September 21 1996
Cybill; *Friends*; *Moesha*;
The X-Files; *Lois & Clark*;
Seinfeld – Returning Favorites

September 28 1996
Michael J. Fox of
Spin City

September 28 1996
John Smoltz and Fred McGriff
of the Braves

September 28 1996
Ozzie Smith and Andy Benes
of the Cardinals

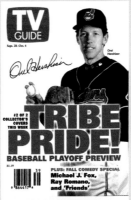

September 28 1996
Orel Hershiser of the Indians

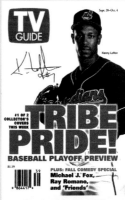

September 28 1996
Kenny Lofton of the Indians

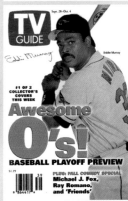

September 28 1996
Eddie Murray of the Orioles

September 28 1996
Cal Ripken Jr. of the Orioles

September 28 1996
Ken Caminiti of the Padres

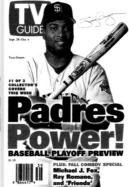

September 28 1996
Tony Gwynn of the Padres

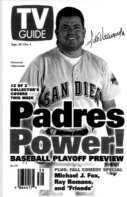

September 28 1996
Fernando Valenzuela of the Padres

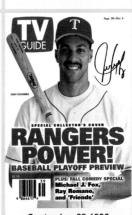

September 28 1996
Juan Gonzalez of the Rangers

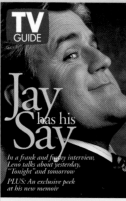

October 05 1996
Jay Leno of
The Tonight Show

October 12 1996
Robyn Lively, Shannon Sturges,
and Jamie Luner of
Savannah

October 19 1996
Brooke Shields of
Suddenly Susan

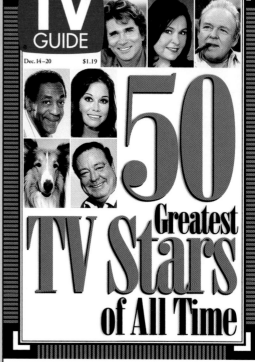

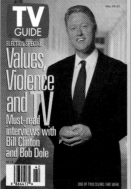

October 19 1996
Bill Clinton – Election Special

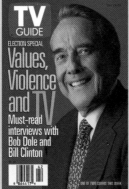

October 19 1996
Bob Dole – Election Special

October 26 1996
Rugrats

TV Guide published its list of the 50 Greatest TV Stars of All Time on December 14, 1996. There are too many great performers on it to list them all here, but we'll tell you that **Lucille Ball** got top honors in the #1 position and **Ed Sullivan** scored the #50 slot.

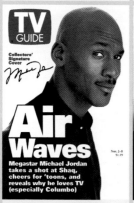

November 02 1996
Michael Jordan – Air Waves

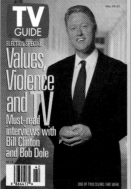

November 09 1996
Robert Urich – His Most
Courageous Battle

November 16 1996
Lance Henriksen of
Millennium

November 23 1996
Carey Lowell of *Law & Order*
and Kyle Chandler of
Early Edition

November 30 1996
Roma Downey of
Touched by an Angel

December 07 1996
Kathy Kinney and
Drew Carey of
The Drew Carey Show

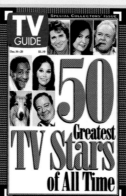

December 07 1996
Selena: Selena's Story

December 14 1996
50 Greatest TV Stars of All Time

December 21 1996
David Duchovny of
The X-Files

December 21 1996
David Duchovny as
Fox Mulder of
The X-Files

December 28 1996
Michelle Forbes, Andre Braugher,
and Kyle Secor of
Homicide: Life on the Street

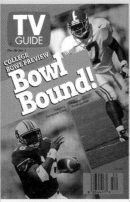

December 28 1996
Auburn's Dameyune Craig;
Alabama's Kevin Jackson

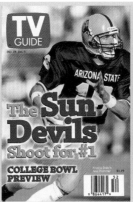

December 28 1996
Arizona State's Jake Plummer

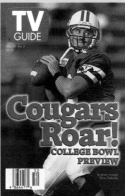

December 28 1996
Brigham Young's Steve Sarkisian

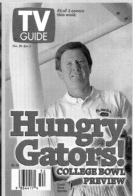

December 28 1996
Florida's Coach Steve Spurrier

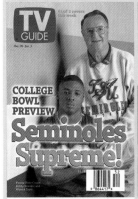

December 28 1996
Florida State Coach Bobby Bowden
and Warrick Dunn

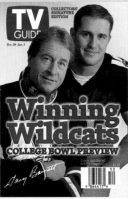

December 28 1996
Northwestern's Coach Gary Barnett
and Pat Fitzgerald

December 28 1996
Ohio State's Pepe Pearson

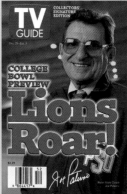

December 28 1996
Penn State Coach Joe Paterno

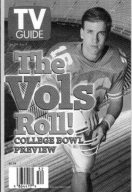

December 28 1996
Tennessee's Peyton Manning

January 04 1997
Oprah Winfrey – Performer
of the Year

January 11 1997
Dilbert

January 18 1997
Winter Preview

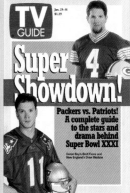

January 25 1997
Brett Favre of the Packers;
Drew Bledsoe of the Patriots

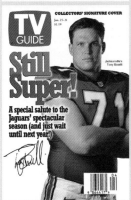

January 25 1997
Tony Boselli of the Jaguars

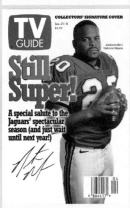

January 25 1997
Natrone Means of the Jaguars

January 25 1997
Reggie White of the Packers

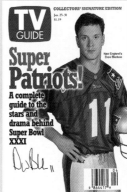

January 25 1997
Drew Bledsoe of the Patriots

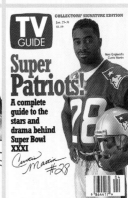

January 25 1997
Curtis Martin of the Patriots

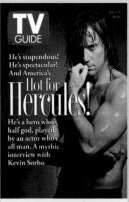

February 01 1997
Kevin Sorbo of
Hercules: The Legendary Journeys

February 08 1997
Neve Campbell of
Party of Five

February 15 1997
David Letterman of
*The Late Show with
David Letterman*

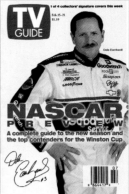

February 15 1997
Dale Earnhardt

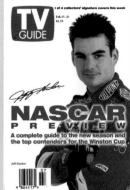

February 15 1997
Jeff Gordon

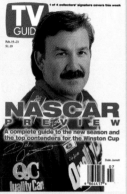

February 15 1997
Dale Jarrett

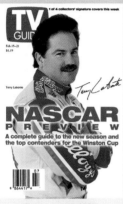

February 15 1997
Terry Labonte

February 22 1997
Chuck Norris of
Walker, Texas Ranger

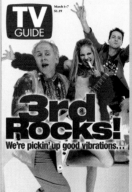

March 01 1997
The Cast of
3rd Rock From the Sun:
John Lithgow, Kristen Johnston,

Fold Out
French Stewart,
Jane Curtin, and
Joseph Gordon-Levitt

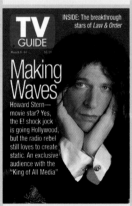

March 08 1997
Howard Stern – Making Waves

March 08 1997
Ekaterina Gordeeva: Victory on Ice

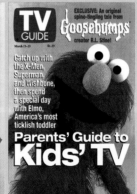

March 15 1997
Elmo of
Sesame Street

Nicolas Cugnot built the first self-propelled road
vehicle in 1769 in France, and when he drove
one of his inventions into a stone wall, he was
probably trying to make it go faster. NASCAR was
formed in 1948 and has since grown into a
billion dollar enterprise. Television viewership for
sports prgramming is second only to the NFL.

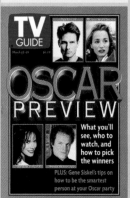

March 22 1997
Tom Cruise; Kristin Scott
Thomas; Barbara Hershey; Woody
Harrelson – Oscar Preview

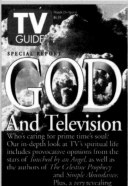

March 29 1997
God and Television

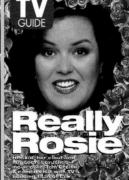

April 05 1997
Rosie O'Donnell of
The Rosie O'Donnell Show

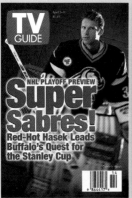

April 05 1997

Dominik Hasek of the Sabres

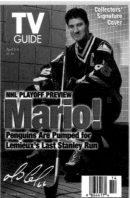

April 05 1997

Mario Lemieux of the Penguins

April 05 1997

Eric Lindros of the Flyers

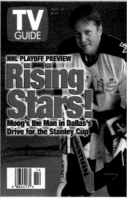

April 05 1997

Andy Moog of the Stars

April 05 1997

Patrick Roy of the Avalanche

April 05 1997

Brendan Shanahan of the
Red Wings

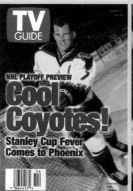

April 05 1997

Keith Tkachuk of the Coyotes

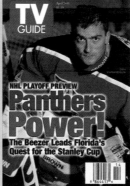

April 05 1997

John Vanbiesbrouck of the Panthers

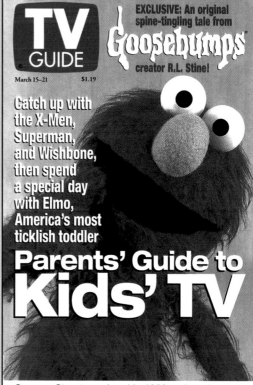

Sesame Street premiered in 1969 and continues to air daily, teaching children the fundamentals of reading, arithmetic, and basic life skills. The show introduced us to **Jim Henson**'s Muppets and has won over 100 Emmy awards. It often parodies other television programs and sometimes uses sly humor, making it interesting for adults to watch with their children.

April 12 1997

Michael Jordan, Hakeem
Olajuwon, Grant Hill, Kevin
Garnett, John Stockton,

Fold Out

Patrick Ewing, Eddie Jones,
Tim Hardaway, Gary Payton,
and Dikembe Mutombo

April 19 1997

Jenny McCarthy of MTV

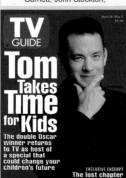

April 26 1997

Tom Hanks – Tom Takes Time
for Kids

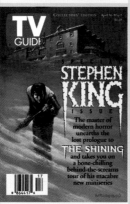

April 26 1997

The Shining

May 03 1997

Lucy Lawless of
Xena: Warrior Princess

May 03 1997

Kentucky Derby: Pulpit and Jockey
Shane Sellers

May 03 1997

Triple Crown: Pulpit and Jockey
Shane Sellers

167

May 10 1997
Kate Mulgrew of
Star Trek: Voyager

May 10 1997
Adam Arkin, Christine Lahtia,
and Mark Harmon of
Chicago Hope

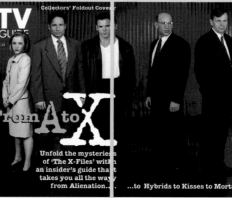

May 17 1997
The Cast of *The X-Files*:
Gillian Anderson, David
Duchovny, Nicholas Lea,

Fold Out
Mitch Pileggi,
William B. Davis,

Fold Out
Dean Haglund, Bruce
Harwood, Chris Carter,
and Tom Braidwood

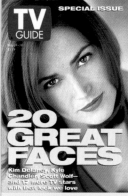

May 24 1997
Kim Delaney of
NYPD Blue

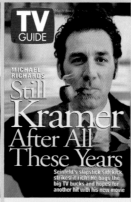

May 31 1997
Michael Richards of
Seinfeld

June 07 1997
Farrah Fawcett – Farrah at 50

June 07 1997
LeAnn Rimes – Country Sensation

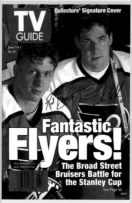

June 07 1997
Rod Brind Amour and John LeClair
of the Flyers

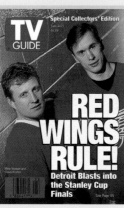

June 07 1997
Mike Vernon and Slava Kozlov of
the Red Wings

June 14 1997
Lea Thompson of
Caroline in the City

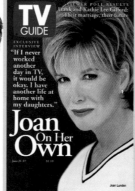

June 21 1997
Joan Lunden – Joan On
Her Own

June 28 1997
100 Greatest Episodes
of All Time

July 05 1997
Claudia Christian, Bruce
Boxleitner, and Jerry Doyle of
Babylon 5

July 12 1997
Hank Hill of *King of the Hill*;
Daria; *Dr. Katz, Professional
Therapist*

July 19 1997
Kathie Lee Gifford of
Live with Regis & Kathie Lee

July 26 1997
Jennifer Aniston of
Friends

August 02 1997
Sarah Michelle Gellar of
Buffy the Vampire Slayer

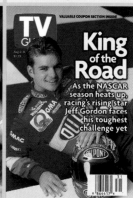

August 02 1997
Jeff Gordon – King of the Road

August 09 1997
Jennifer Love Hewitt of *Party of Five* and French Stewart of *3rd Rock From the Sun*

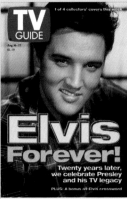

August 16 1997
Elvis Presley – Elvis Forever!

August 16 1997
Elvis Presley – Elvis Forever!

August 16 1997
Elvis Presley – Elvis Forever!

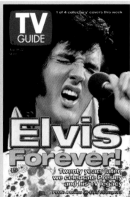

August 16 1997
Elvis Presley – Elvis Forever!

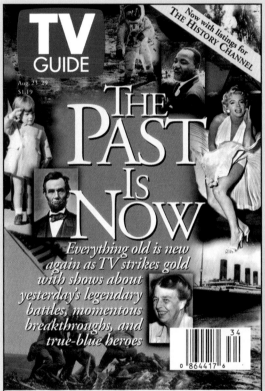

August 23 1997
Madison Michele as Miss Congeniality

August 23 1997
The Past Is Now

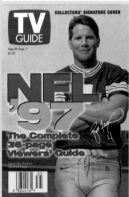

August 30 1997
Brett Favre of the Packers

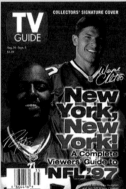

August 30 1997
Rodney Hampton of the Giants and Wayne Chrebet of the Jets

August 30 1997
Steve Young of the 49ers and Jeff George of the Panthers

August 30 1997
Steve Young and Coach Steve Marlucci of the 49ers

To announce adding The History Channel to its listings, **TV Guide** produced a terrific cover. With the popularity of Cable TV, the number of television stations has rapidly increased. Stations like The History Channel and Discovery Channel air reality programs which can teach you about things that you previously would have used books to learn.

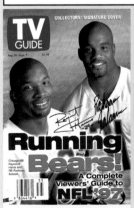

August 30 1997
Raymont Harris and Rashaan Salaam of the Bears

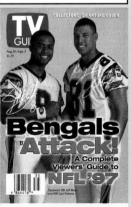

August 30 1997
Jeff Blake and Carl Pickens of the Bengals

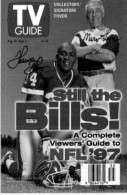

August 30 1997
Thurman Thomas and Coach Marv Levy of the Bills

August 30 1997
Neil Smith and Terrell Davis of the Broncos

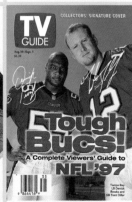

August 30 1997
Derrick Brooks and Trent Dilfer of the Buccaneers

August 30 1997

Simeon Rice and Kent Graham of the Cardinals

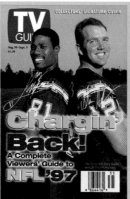

August 30 1997

Tony Martin and Stan Humphries of the Chargers

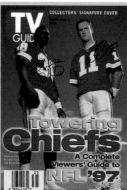

August 30 1997

Kimble Anders and Elvis Grabac of the Chiefs

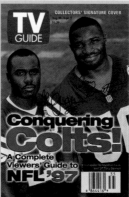

August 30 1997

Marshall Frank and Tony Bennett of the Colts

August 30 1997

Daryl Johnston and S. Darren Woodson of the Cowboys

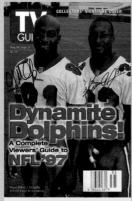

August 30 1997

O.J. McDuffie and Karim Abdul-Jabbar of the Dolphins

August 30 1997

Irving Fryar and Ty Detmer of the Eagles

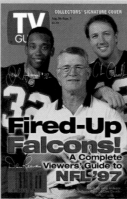

August 30 1997

Jamal Anderson, Coach Dan Reeves, and Chris Chandler of the Falcons

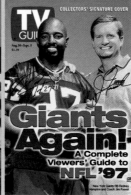

August 30 1997

Rodney Hampton and Coach Jim Fassel of the Giants

August 30 1997

Keenan McCardell and Jimmy Smith of the Jaguars

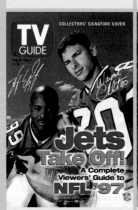

August 30 1997

Hugh Douglas and Wayne Chrebet of the Jets

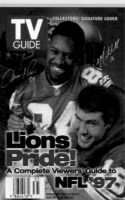

August 30 1997

Herman Moore and Scott Mitchell of the Lions

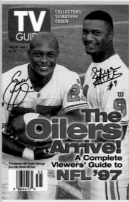

August 30 1997

Eddie George and Steve McNair of the Oilers

August 30 1997

Brett Favre and Coach Mike Holmgren of the Packers

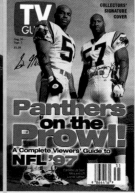

August 30 1997

Sam Mills and Lamar Lathon of the Panthers

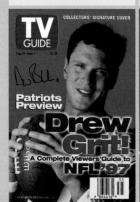

August 30 1997

Drew Bledsoe of the Patriots

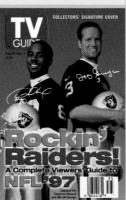

August 30 1997

Desmond Howard and Jeff George of the Raiders

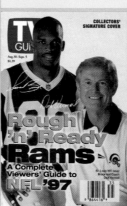

August 30 1997

Isaac Bruce and Coach Dick Vermeil of the Rams

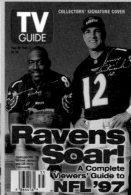

August 30 1997

Michael Jackson and Vinny Testaverde of the Ravens

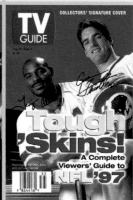

August 30 1997

Terry Allen and Gus Frerotte of the Redskins

August 30 1997
Heath Shuler and Coach Mike Ditka
of the Saints

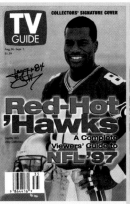

August 30 1997
Joey Galloway of the Seahawks

August 30 1997
Jerome Bettis and Kordell Stewart
of the Steelers

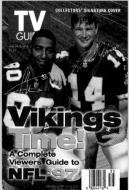

August 30 1997
Cris Carter and Brad Johnson of
the Vikings

September 06 1997
The X-Files; Murphy Brown;
ER; Seinfeld; Spin City –
Returning Favorites

September 13 1997
Fall Preview:
Special Issue

September 20 1997
Princess Diana

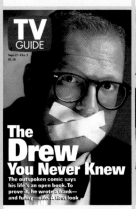

September 27 1997
Drew Carey of
The Drew Carey Show

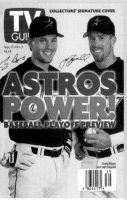

September 27 1997
Craig Biggio and Jeff Bagwell
of the Astros

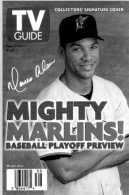

September 27 1997
Moises Alou of the Marlins

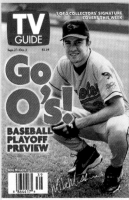

September 27 1997
Mike Mussina of the Orioles

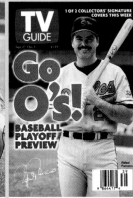

September 27 1997
Rafael Palmeiro of the Orioles

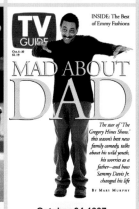

October 04 1997
Gregory Hines of
The Gregory Hines Show

October 11 1997
Ellen DeGeneres of
Ellen

October 18 1997
Melissa Joan Hart of
Sabrina, the Teenage Witch

October 25 1997
Larisa Oleynik of *The Secret World*
of Alex Mack and Irene Ng of *The*
Mystery Files of Shelby Woo

October 25 1997
Sandy Alomar Jr. of the Indians

October 25 1997
Jim Thorne of the Indians

October 25 1997
Omar Vizquel of the Indians

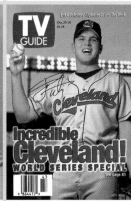

October 25 1997
Jaret Wright of the Indians

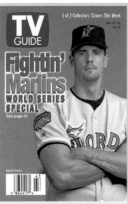

October 25 1997
Kevin Brown of the Marlins

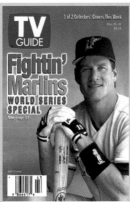

October 25 1997
Jeff Conine of the Marlins

November 01 1997
Larry Bird – Bird's Back!

November 01 1997
Brandy Norwood and Whitney
Houston in *Cinderella*; Calista
Flockhart of *Ally McBeal*

November 08 1997
Jeri Ryan of
Star Trek: Voyager

November 08 1997
Terry Farrell of
Star Trek: Deep Space Nine

November 15 1997
Gillian Anderson, Creator Chris
Carter, and David Duchovny of
The X-Files

November 22 1997
Jenna Elfman of
Dharma & Greg

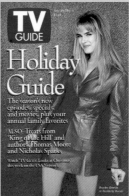

November 29 1997
Brooke Shields of
Suddenly Susan

December 06 1997
Roma Downey of
Touched by an Angel

December 13 1997
Peri Gilpin of *Frasier*;
Mike Tyson; Lucy Lawless;
Marv Albert

December 20 1997
Katie Couric and
Matt Lauer of
Today

December 27 1997
Michigan's Brian Griese;
Nebraska's Scott Frost

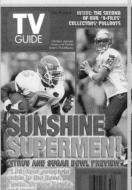

December 27 1997
Florida's Jacquez Green;
Florida State's Thad Busby

December 27 1997
Florida's Jacquez Green;
Florida State's Thad Busby;
Ann Bishop

December 27 1997
Michigan's Brian Griese

The X-Files debuted on September 10, 1993 and
in 1998 was adapted for a feature film. "The Truth
Is Out There" became a favorite T-shirt slogan,
and three years after its demise, over five million
websites devoted to *The X-Files* still exist. The
series sparked several TV specials, such as
Secrets of the X-Files in 1995.

December 27 1997
Michigan's Charles Woodson

December 27 1997
Michigan's Brian Griese and
Charles Woodson

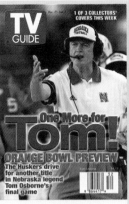

December 27 1997
Nebraska's Coach Tom Osborne

December 27 1997
Nebraska's Scott Frost

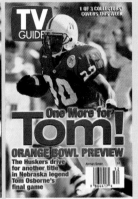

December 27 1997
Nebraska's Ahman Green

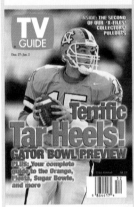

December 27 1997
North Carolina's Chris Keldorf

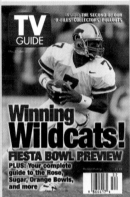

December 27 1997
Northwestern's Michael Bishop

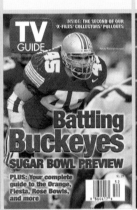

December 27 1997
Ohio's Andy Katzenmoyer

December 27 1997
Tennessee's Peyton Manning and
Coach Phillip Fulmer

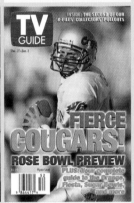

December 27 1997
Washington's Ryan Leaf

January 03 1998
Bart and
Santa's Little Helper of
The Simpsons

January 03 1998
Grampa, Homer, and Selma of
The Simpsons

January 03 1998
Patty and Lisa of
The Simpsons

January 03 1998
Marge and Maggie of
The Simpsons

January 10 1998
Tom Selleck; Vivica A. Fox;
*La Femme Nikita; Dawson's
Creek* – Winter Preview

January 17 1998
Steve Harris, Dylan McDermott,
and Lara Flynn Boyle of
The Practice

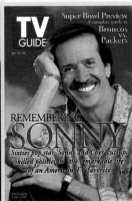

January 24 1998
Sonny Bono – Remembering
Sonny

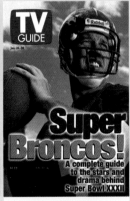

January 24 1998
John Elway of the Broncos

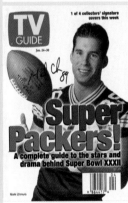

January 24 1998
Mark Chmura of the Packers

173

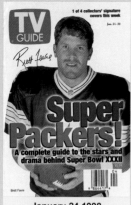

January 24 1998
Brett Favre of the Packers

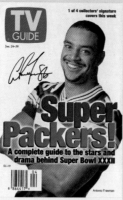

January 24 1998
Antonio Freeman of the Packers

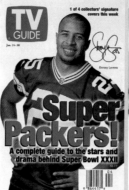

January 24 1998
Dorsey Levens of the Packers

January 31 1998
Yasmine Bleeth in
The Lake

February 07 1998
Olympics-Bound Philadelphia Flyers
Joel Otto and John LeClair

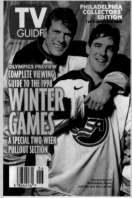

February 07 1998
Olympics-Bound Philadephia Flyers
Joel Otto and John LeClair
(Philadelphia Collectors Edition)

February 07 1998
Figure Skater Michelle Kwan

February 07 1998
Figure Skater Tara Lipinski

February 07 1998
Gold-Medal Skier Tommy Moe

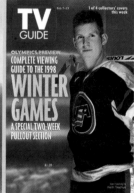

February 07 1998
Ice Hockey's Keith Tkachuk

February 14 1998
Jenna Elfman and
Thomas Gibson of
Dharma & Greg

February 14 1998
Mark Martin and Bobby Allison

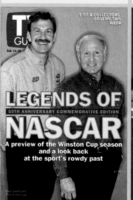

February 14 1998
Dale Jarrett and Cale Yarborough

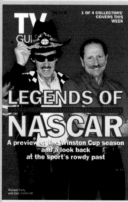

February 14 1998
Richard Petty and Dale Earnhardt

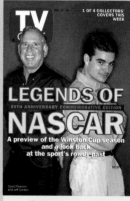

February 14 1998
David Pearson and Jeff Gordon

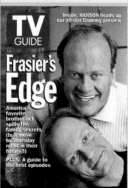

February 21 1998
Kelsey Grammer and
David Hyde Pierce of
Frasier

February 28 1998
Calista Flockhart, Gil Bellows,
and Courtney Thorne-Smith of
Ally McBeal

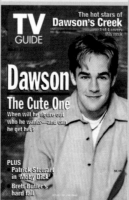

March 07 1998
James Van Der Beek of
Dawson's Creek

March 07 1998
Katie Holmes of
Dawson's Creek

March 07 1998
Michelle Williams of
Dawson's Creek

March 07 1998
Joshua Jackson of
Dawson's Creek

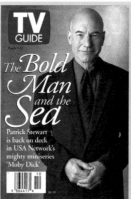

March 07 1998
Patrick Stewart in
Moby Dick

March 07 1998
A Tribute to Harry Caray

March 14 1998
D.W. and Arthur of
Arthur

March 21 1998
Helen Hunt; Leonardo DiCaprio
and Kate Winslet; Matt Damon;
Burt Reynolds – Oscar Preview

March 28 1998
Cartman, Stan, Kyle,
and Kenny of
South Park

March 28 1998
Cast Members of
Law & Order

April 04 1998
45th Anniversary Celebration

April 11 1998
Madonna – Confidential

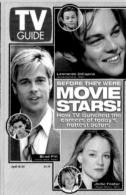

April 18 1998
Leonardo DiCaprio; Brad Pitt;
Jodie Foster – Before They
Were Movie Stars

April 25 1998
Peta Wilson of
La Femme Nikita

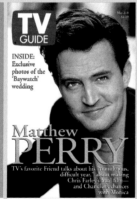

May 02 1998
Matthew Perry of
Friends

May 09 1998
Jerry Seinfeld of
Seinfeld

May 09 1998
Jason Alexander of
Seinfeld

May 09 1998
Julia Louis-Dreyfus of
Seinfeld

May 09 1998
Michael Richards of
Seinfeld

May 16 1998
Julia Roberts

May 23 1998
Tom Hanks; Jim Carrey;
Drew Barrymore – Summer
Movie Preview!

May 30 1998
Frank Sinatra

June 06 1998
Magic Johnson of
The Magic Hour

June 13 1998
Jensen Ackles, Laura Wright,
and Ingo Rademacher – Summer
Soaps Preview

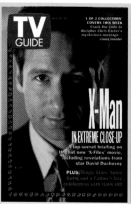

June 20 1998
David Duchovny of
The X-Files

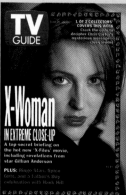

June 20 1998
Gillian Anderson of
The X-Files

June 27 1998
Taylor Hanson, Zac Hanson,
and Isaac Hanson
(42 Different Variations)

July 04 1998
Matt Lauer of
Today
(Multiple Variations)

July 11 1998
TV's 50 Greatest Sports Moments

July 18 1998
Brandy Norwood of *Moesha*;
Phil Hartman of *NewsRadio*

July 25 1998
Jerry Mathers; Johnny Carson;
Ted Nugent; Mary Hart; Soupy
Sales – TV Confidential!

August 01 1998
Drew Carey of
Whose Line Is It Anyway?

August 08 1998
The 50 Greatest Movies on
TV and Video

August 15 1998
Princess Diana

August 22 1998
Joe Mantegna, Ray Liotta, Angus
Macfadyen, Bobby Slayton, and
Don Cheadle in *The Rat Pack*

August 22 1998
Vivica A. Fox of *Getting Personal*
and Thomas Gibson of
Dharma & Greg

August 29 1998
Steve Young of the 49ers; Jeff
George of the Raiders

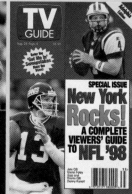

August 29 1998
Glenn Foley of the Jets; Danny
Kanell of the Giants

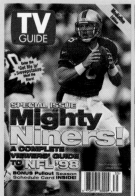

August 29 1998
Steve Young of the 49ers

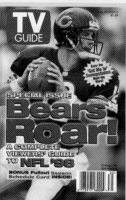

August 29 1998
Erik Kramer of the Bears

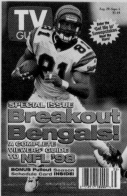

August 29 1998
Carl Pickens of the Bengals

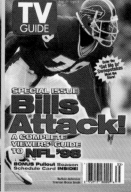

August 29 1998
Bruce Smith of the Bills

August 29 1998
John Elway of the Broncos

August 29 1998

Trent Dilfer of the Buccaneers

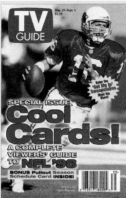

August 29 1998

Jake Plummer of the Cardinals

August 29 1998

Ryan Leaf of the Chargers

August 29 1998

Kimble Anders of the Chiefs

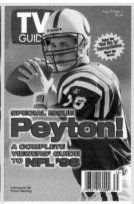

August 29 1998

Peyton Manning of the Colts

August 29 1998

Troy Aikman of the Cowboys

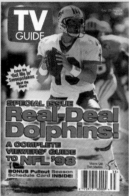

August 29 1998

Dan Marino of the Dolphins

August 29 1998

Bobby Hoying of the Eagles

August 29 1998

Jamal Anderson of the Falcons

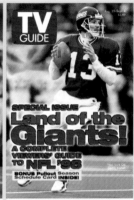

August 29 1998

Danny Kanell of the Giants

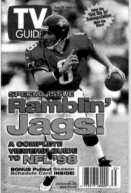

August 29 1998

Mark Brunell of the Jaguars

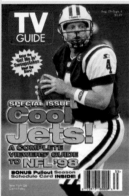

August 29 1998

Glenn Foley of the Jets

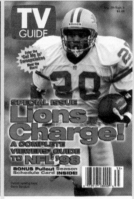

August 29 1998

Barry Sanders of the Lions

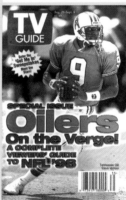

August 29 1998

Steve McNair of the Oilers

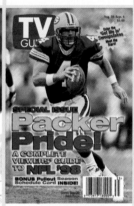

August 29 1998

Brett Favre of the Packers

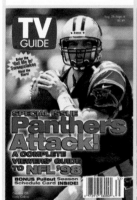

August 29 1998

Kenny Collins of the Panthers

August 29 1998

Drew Bledsoe of the Patriots

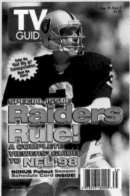

August 29 1998

Jeff George of the Raiders

August 29 1998

Isaac Bruce of the Rams

August 29 1998

Michael Jackson of the Ravens

August 29 1998

Gus Frerotte of the Redskins

August 29 1998

Billy Joe Hobert of the Saints

August 29 1998

Joey Galloway of the Seahawks

August 29 1998

Jerome Betts of the Steelers

August 29 1998

Brad Johnson of the Vikings

September 05 1998

Ally McBeal; Frasier; Cosby; The Practice; ER; Buffy the Vampire Slayer – Returning Favorites

September 12 1998

Fall Preview: Special Issue

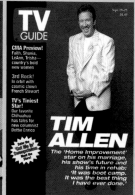

September 19 1998

Tim Allen of *Home Improvement*

September 19 1998

Faith Hill – Bold New Women of Country Music

September 19 1998

LeAnn Rimes – Bold New Women of Country Music

September 19 1998

Shania Twain – Bold New Women of Country Music

September 19 1998

Trisha Yearwood – Bold New Women of Country Music

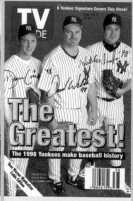

September 19 1998

David Cone, David Wells, and Hideki Irabu of the Yankees

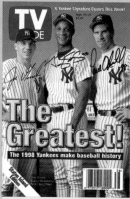

September 19 1998

Joe Girardi, Darryl Strawberry, and Paul O'Neill of the Yankees

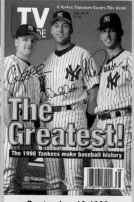

September 19 1998

Chuck Knoblauch, Derek Jeter, and Jorge Posada of the Yankees

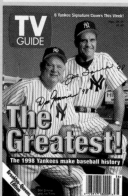

September 19 1998

Don Zimmer and Joe Torre of the Yankees

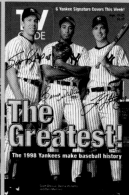

September 19 1998

Scott Brosius, Bernie Williams, and Tino Martinez of the Yankees

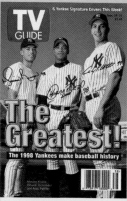

September 19 1998

Mariano Rivera, Orlando Hernandez, and Andy Pettitte of the Yankees

September 26 1998

Lisa Nicole Carson, Calista Flockhart, and Jane Krakowski of *Ally McBeal*

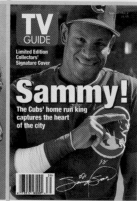

September 26 1998

Sammy Sosa of the Cubs

September 26 1998
Mark McGwire vs. the Los Angeles
Dodgers – 5/31/1998

September 26 1998
Mark McGwire vs. the New York
Mets – 8/20/1998

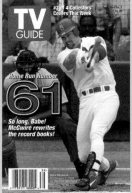

September 26 1998
Mark McGwire vs. the Chicago
Cubs – 9/7/1998

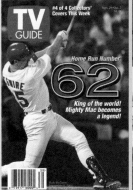

September 26 1998
Mark McGwire vs. the Chicago
Cubs – 9/8/1998

October 03 1998
The Cast of
Frasier

October 03 1998
Linus Roache and
Vincent Perez in
Shot Through the Heart

The longest running prime time cartoon series, *The Simpsons*, debuted in 1989 and has been nominated for Emmy awards every year since 1990. We first met *The Simpsons* in short segments that separated the comedy skits on *The Tracey Ullman Show*. **TV Guide** ranked Bart's "Eat my shorts!" as #3 on its August 2005 list of TV's Top 20 Catchphrases.

October 10 1998
Oprah Winfrey

October 17 1998
The Simpsons

October 24 1998
Walter Cronkite and John Glenn – A
Time For Heroes

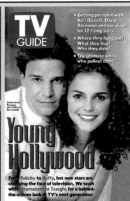

October 31 1998
Steve Burns and Blue of
Blue's Clues

November 07 1998
David Boreanaz of *Buffy the
Vampire Slayer* and
Keri Russell of *Felicity*

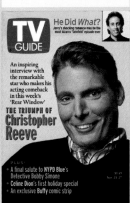

November 14 1998
Robin Williams – Holiday
Movie Preview

November 21 1998
Christopher Reeve in
Rear Window;
Jerry Seinfeld

November 28 1998
Kristen Johnston of
3rd Rock From the Sun

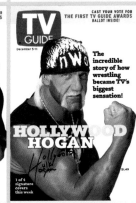

December 05 1998
Wrestler Goldberg

December 05 1998
Wrestler Hollywood Hogan

179

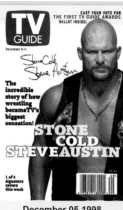

December 05 1998
Wrestler Stone Cold Steve Austin

December 05 1998
Wrestler The Undertaker

December 12 1998
Holly Marie Combs, Shannen
Doherty, and Alyssa Milano of
Charmed

December 19 1998
Darrell Hammond and
Molly Shannon of
Saturday Night Live

December 26 1998
1998 Year-End Tribute

1999

January 02 1999
Diane Sawyer and
Barbara Walters of
20/20

January 02 1999
Florida State's Lamont Green

Everybody Loves Raymond, although his brother,
Robert, resents him sometimes. **Ray Romano**'s
character, Ray Barone, was #10 on **TV Guide**'s list of
the 50 Greatest TV Dads of All Time. The series was
nominated for thirteen Emmys in 2005 and won three,
including Outstanding Comedy Series. We said
goodbye to the Barones in May of 2005.

January 02 1999
Florida State's Corey Simon

January 02 1999
Florida State's Peter Warrick

January 02 1999
Florida State's Jason Whitaker

January 02 1999
Tennessee's Tee Martin

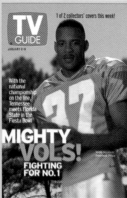

January 02 1999
Tennessee's Peerless Price

January 09 1999
Dilbert; John Larroquette;
Eddie Murphy; Jennifer Grey –
Winter Preview

January 16 1999
Rick Schroder of *NYPD Blue*;
Katie Holmes of *Dawson's Creek*

January 16 1999
Mike Tyson – Tyson's Back

January 23 1999
Jerry Seinfeld; Carol Burnett; Lucille
Ball – The 50 Funniest TV Moments
of All Time

January 30 1999
The TV Guide Awards: You Voted...
Who Won?

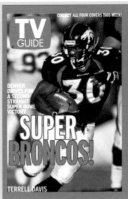

January 30 1999
Terrell Davis of the Broncos

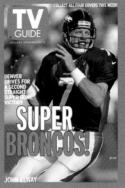

January 30 1999
John Elway of the Broncos

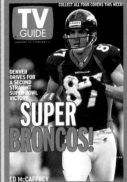

January 30 1999
Ed McCaffrey of the Broncos

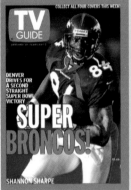

January 30 1999
Shannon Sharpe of the Broncos

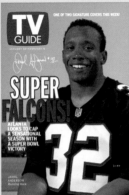

January 30 1999
Jamal Anderson of the Falcons

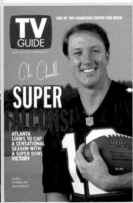

January 30 1999
Chris Chandler of the Falcons

February 06 1999
George Clooney of
ER

February 13 1999
Colm Feore in
Storm of the Century

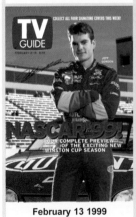

February 13 1999
Jeff Gordon

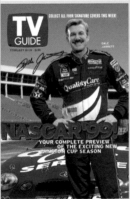

February 13 1999
Dale Jarrett

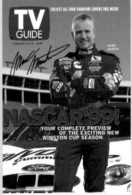

February 13 1999
Mark Martin

February 13 1999
Rusty Wallace

February 20 1999
Patricia Heaton, Ray Romano,
and Brad Garrett of
Everybody Loves Raymond

February 27 1999
Tina Majorino and
Martin Short in
Alice In Wonderland

March 06 1999
The Cast of
7th Heaven

March 13 1999
Jenna Elfman and
Matthew McConaughey in
EDtv

March 13 1999
NCAA's Chamique Holdsclaw,
Tennessee Forward

March 20 1999
Gwyneth Paltrow; Tom Hanks;
Nick Nolte; Meryl Streep –
Oscar Preview

March 27 1999
Peter Krause, Robert Guillaume,
Felicity Huffman, and Josh Charles
of *Sports Night*

March 27 1999
Mankind of
Wrestlemania

March 27 1999
The Rock of
Wrestlemania

March 27 1999
Sable of
Wrestlemania

March 27 1999
Stone Cold Steve Austin of
Wrestlemania

April 03 1999
Bender of
Futurama

April 10 1999
Lucy Lawless of *Xena: Warrior
Princess* and Jeri Ryan of
Star Trek: Voyager

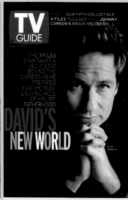

April 17 1999
David Duchovny of
The X-Files

April 24 1999
Heather Locklear; Brandy
Norwood and Diana Ross in
Double Platinum; Garth Brooks

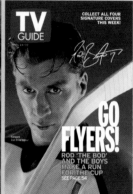

April 24 1999
Rod Brind'Amour of the Flyers

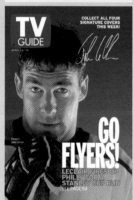

April 24 1999
John LeClair of the Flyers

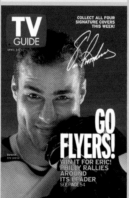

April 24 1999
Eric Lindros of the Flyers

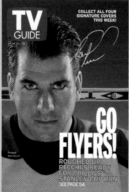

April 24 1999
Mark Recchi of the Flyers

May 01 1999
Calista Flockhart of
Ally McBeal

May 01 1999
Kentucky Derby – General
Challenge and Jockey Gary
Stevens

May 08 1999
Camryn Manheim of
The Practice

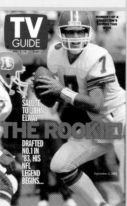

May 08 1999
John Elway – The Rookie!

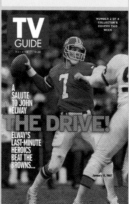

May 08 1999
John Elway – The Drive!

May 08 1999
John Elway – Super '98!

May 08 1999
John Elway – Super Repeat!

May 15 1999
Jake Lloyd in
Star Wars: The Phantom Menace

May 15 1999
Liam Neeson in
Star Wars: The Phantom Menace

May 15 1999
Ewan McGregor in
Star Wars: The Phantom Menace

May 15 1999
Natalie Portman in
Star Wars: The Phantom Menace

May 22 1999
Patricia Richardson and
Tim Allen in
Home Improvement

May 29 1999
The Cast of
Just Shoot Me

May 29 1999
Alexander Siddig, Colm Meaney,
and Cirroc Lofton of
Star Trek: Deep Space Nine

May 29 1999
Nicole deBoer, Michael Dorn, and
Armin Shimerman of
Star Trek: Deep Space Nine

May 29 1999
Avery Brooks of
Star Trek: Deep Space Nine

May 29 1999
Nana Visitor and
Rene Auberjonois of
Star Trek: Deep Space Nine

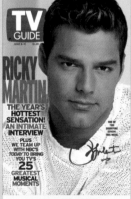

June 05 1999
Ricky Martin – The Year's
Hottest Sensation!

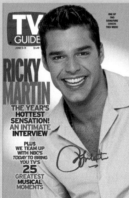

June 05 1999
Ricky Martin – The Year's
Hottest Sensation!

June 05 1999
Theoren Fleury of the Avalanche

June 05 1999
Peter Forsberg of the Avalanche

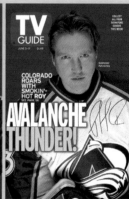

June 05 1999
Patrick Roy of the Avalanche

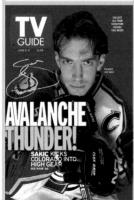

June 05 1999
Joe Sakic of the Avalanche

June 05 1999
Dominik Hasek of the Sabres

June 05 1999
Michael Peca of the Sabres

June 05 1999
Dixon Ward of the Sabres

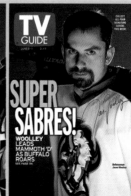

June 05 1999
Jason Woolley of the Sabres

June 12 1999
Jar Jar Binks in
Star Wars: The Phantom Menace

June 12 1999
Jabba the Hutt in
Star Wars: The Phantom Menace

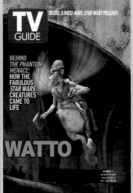

June 12 1999
Watto in
Star Wars: The Phantom Menace

June 12 1999
Boss Nass in
Star Wars: The Phantom Menace

June 19 1999
Laura Prepon, Topher Grace, and
Danny Masterson of
That 70s Show

June 19 1999
Wrestler Sable

June 26 1999
Pamela Anderson Lee of
V.I.P.

July 03 1999
John Gilchrist as Mikey; Taco
Bell's Gidget; Michael Jordan;
the Energizer Bunny

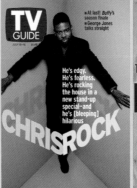

July 10 1999
Chris Rock

July 17 1999
Dennis Franz of
NYPD Blue

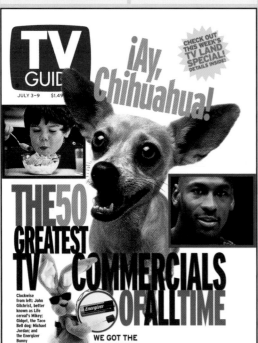

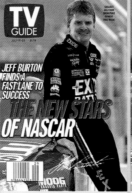

July 17 1999
Jeff Burton Finds a Fast Lane
To Success

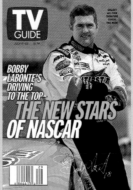

July 17 1999
Bobby Labonte's Driving to the Top

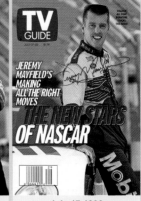

July 17 1999
Jeremy Mayfield's Making All the
Right Moves

With the increased use of remote controls and
VCR's, advertisers were forced to become more
creative. Starring well-known personalities, featuring
catchy jingles and phrases, and with premieres
during the Super Bowl, some commercials have
become almost as good as the TV shows.

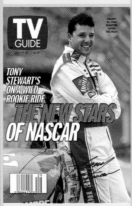

July 17 1999
Tony Stewart's on a Wild Ride

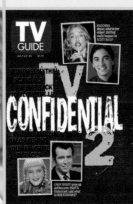

July 24 1999
Madonna; Scott Baio;
Susan Olsen; Bob Eubanks –
TV Confidential 2

July 31 1999
Sarah Michelle Gellar and
David Boreanaz of
Buffy the Vampire Slayer

July 31 1999
Remembering John F. Kennedy Jr.

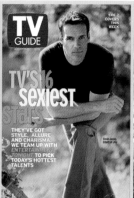

August 07 1999
David James Elliott of
JAG

August 07 1999
Alyssa Milano of
Charmed

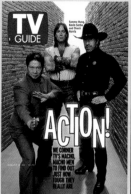

August 14 1999
Sammo Hung, Kevin Sorbo, and
Chuck Norris – Action!

August 14 1999
Intro Girl Kimberly Page

August 14 1999
Wrestler Kevin Nash

August 14 1999
Wrestler Randy Savage

August 14 1999
Wrestler Sting

August 21 1999
Cher

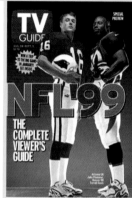

August 28 1999
Jake Plummer of the Cardinals and
Terrell Davis of the Broncos

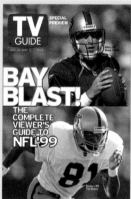

August 28 1999
Steve Young of the 49ers; Tim
Brown of the Raiders

August 28 1999
Amani Toomer of the Giants; Vinny
Testaverde of the Jets

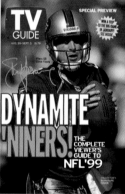

August 28 1999
Steve Young of the 49ers

August 28 1999
Curtis Enis of the Bears

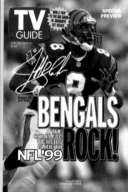

August 28 1999
Jeff Blake of the Bengals

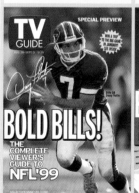

August 28 1999
Doug Flutie of the Bills

August 28 1999
Terrell Davis of the Broncos

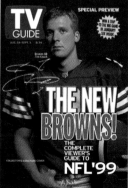

August 28 1999
Tim Couch of the Browns

August 28 1999
Mike Alstott of the Buccaneers

August 28 1999
Jake Plummer of the Cardinals

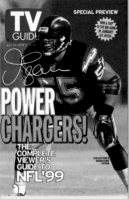

August 28 1999

Junior Seau of the Chargers

August 28 1999

Derrick Thomas of the Chiefs

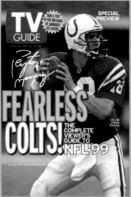

August 28 1999

Peyton Manning of the Colts

August 28 1999

Emmitt Smith of the Cowboys

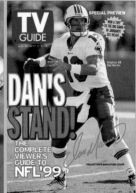

August 28 1999

Dan Marino of the Dolphins

August 28 1999

Duce Staley of the Eagles

August 28 1999

Chris Chandler of the Falcons

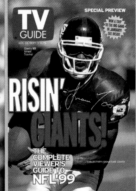

August 28 1999

Amani Toomer of the Giants

August 28 1999

Mark Brunell of the Jaguars

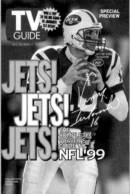

August 28 1999

Vinny Testaverde of the Jets

August 28 1999

Herman Moore of the Lions

August 28 1999

Brett Favre of the Packers

August 28 1999

Muhsin Muhammad of the Panthers

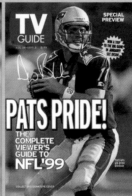

August 28 1999

Drew Bledsoe of the Patriots

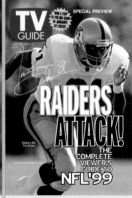

August 28 1999

Tim Brown of the Raiders

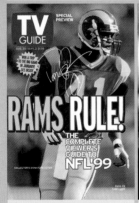

August 28 1999

Todd Lyght of the Rams

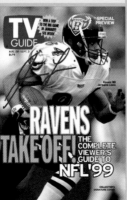

August 28 1999

Jermaine Lewis of the Ravens

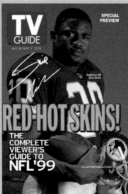

August 28 1999

Skip Hicks of the Redskins

August 28 1999

Ricky Williams of the Saints

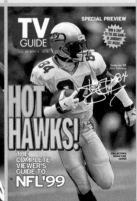

August 28 1999

Joey Galloway of the Seahawks

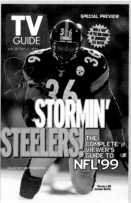

August 28 1999
Jerome Bettis of the Steelers

August 28 1999
Eddie George of the Titans

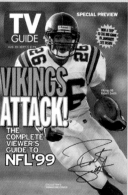

August 28 1999
Robert Smith of the Vikings

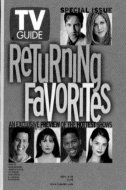

September 04 1999
David Duchovny; Jennifer Aniston;
Ray Romano; Roma Downey;
D.L. Hughley; Katie Holmes

September 11 1999
Fall Preview:
Special Issue

September 18 1999
Faith Hill – Keeping the Faith

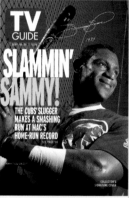

September 18 1999
Sammy Sosa of the Cubs

September 25 1999
Roswell; *Action*; *Freaks and
Geeks*; *Angel*; *Once and Again*;
The West Wing

September 25 1999
Lomas Brown of the Browns

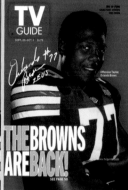

September 25 1999
Orlando Brown of the Browns

September 25 1999
Antonio Langham of the Browns

September 25 1999
Jamir Miller of the Browns

September 25 1999
Edgardo Alfonzo of the Mets

September 25 1999
Al Leiter of the Mets

September 25 1999
Mike Piazza of the Mets

September 25 1999
Robin Ventura of the Mets

October 02 1999
Melissa Joan Hart of
Sabrina, the Teenage Witch

October 02 1999
Roberto Alomar of the Indians

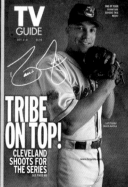

October 02 1999
David Justice of the Indians

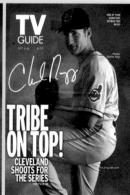

October 02 1999
Charles Nagy of the Indians

October 02 1999
Jim Thome of the Indians

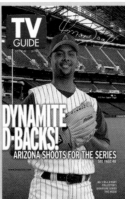

October 02 1999
Omar Daal of the Diamondbacks

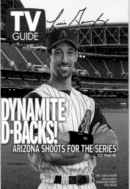

October 02 1999
Luis Gonzalez of the Diamondbacks

October 02 1999
Randy Johnson of the Diamondbacks

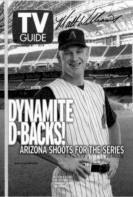

October 02 1999
Matt Williams of the Diamondbacks

October 02 1999
Bernie Williams of the Yankees

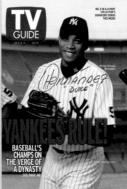

October 02 1999
Orlando Hernandez of the Yankees

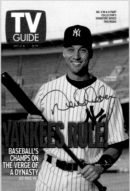

October 02 1999
Derek Jeter of the Yankees

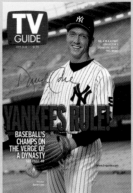

October 02 1999
David Cone of the Yankees

October 02 1999
Nomar Garciaparra of the Red Sox

October 02 1999
Pedro Martinez of the Red Sox

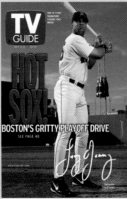

October 02 1999
Troy O'Leary of the Red Sox

October 02 1999
Jason Varitek of the Red Sox

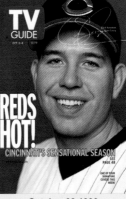

October 02 1999
Sean Casey of the Reds

October 02 1999
Pete Harnisch of the Reds

October 02 1999
Barry Larkin of the Reds

October 02 1999
Eddie Taubensee of the Reds

October 09 1999
Katie Couric of
The Today Show

October 16 1999
Michael Richards (Kramer);
Leonard Nimoy (Mr. Spock); Larry
Hagman (J.R.); Mary Tyler Moore

October 23 1999
Billy Campbell and
Sela Ward of
Once and Again

October 30 1999
Meowth and Togepi of
Pokemon

October 30 1999
Geodude and Payduck of
Pokemon

October 30 1999
Pikachu and Exeggcute of
Pokemon

October 30 1999
Exeggcute, Charmander,
and Voltorb of
Pokemon

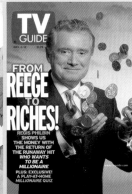

November 06 1999
Regis Philbin of
Who Wants To Be a Millionaire

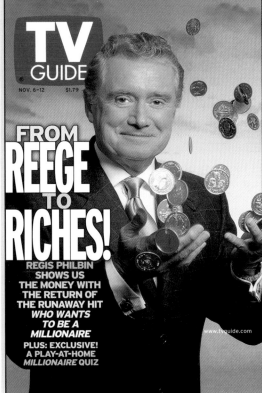

He was named after his father's high school and on August 20, 2004, **Regis Philbin** beat the record for Most Hours on Camera with a total of 15,188. He guest hosted *The Tonight Show* but his first regular gig was on *The Joey Bishop Show* in 1967. He earned a star on the Hollywood Walk of Fame in 2003.

November 06 1999
Tim Duncan of the Spurs

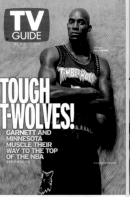

November 06 1999
Kevin Garnett of the Timberwolves

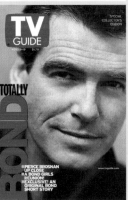

November 13 1999
Pierce Brosnan – Totally Bond

November 20 1999
Celine Dion – Celine Says Goodbye

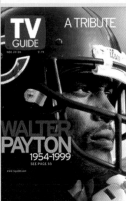

November 20 1999
A Tribute to Walter Payton

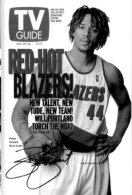

November 20 1999
Brian Grant of the Blazers

November 20 1999
Scottie Pippen of the Blazers

November 20 1999
Steve Smith of the Blazers

November 20 1999
Damon Stoudamire of the Blazers

November 27 1999
Rosie O'Donnell of
The Rosie O'Donnell Show

December 04 1999
Michael Jackson

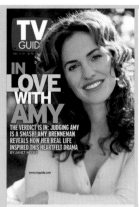

December 11 1999
Amy Brenneman of
Judging Amy

December 18 1999
The Cast of *Ally McBeal*: Lucy Liu,
Peter MacNicol, Greg Germann,
Calista Flockhart, Vonda Shepard,

Fold Out
Jane Krakowski, Courtney Thorne-
Smith, Gil Bellows, Lisa Nicole
Carson, and Portia de Rossi

December 25 1999
Dennis Haysbert, Eric Close,
and Margaret Colin of
Now and Again

Rupert Giles: "The world is going to end." Buffy Summers, Willow Rosenberg, Xander Harris: "Again?" *Buffy the Vampire Slayer*

Memorable TV Show Quotes from the 1990s

"Even if I did get past all my problems, I'm just gonna get out and get new ones."
Ally McBeal, *Ally McBeal*

"Love – a dangerous disease instantly cured by marriage." Lennie Briscoe, *Law & Order*

Angel: "The Gateway for Lost Souls...is under the post office?"
Allen Francis Doyle: "It makes sense, if you think about it."
Angel

"It took us fifteen years and three supercomputers to MacGyver a way to power the gate."
Samantha Carter, *Stargate SG-1*

"What's the point of having a democracy if everybody's going to vote wrong?"
Dick Solomon, *3rd Rock From the Sun*

Jerry: "This isn't a good time."
Telemarketer: "When would be a good time to call back, sir?"
Jerry: "I have an idea, why don't you give me your home number and I'll call you back later?"
Telemarketer: "Umm, we're not allowed to do that."
Jerry: "Oh, I guess because you don't want strangers calling you at home."
Seinfeld

"You want to know the future, Miss Lane? No one works, no one argues, there are 9,000 channels and nothing on!" Tempus, *Lois & Clark: The New Adventures of Superman*

"In the end there can be only one." *Highlander*

"We were on a break!" Ross Geller, *Friends*

"In the old days, I used to come down here all the time. But issues would always come up, I'd end up smiting people..." God, *God, the Devil and Bob*

Ares: "I can't believe you have these mortals convinced that you're this 'Kevin Sorbo' character."
Hercules: "Some people just aren't ready for the truth."
Hercules, the Legendary Journeys

"Homey don't play that." Homey the Clown, *In Living Color*

"Look, it's only a birthday present. It just means I'm glad you didn't die partway through the year." Dave Nelson, *NewsRadio*

"You got a lot of morons in your family? 'Cause that could be genetic."
Andy Sipowicz, *NYPD Blue*

"Good Lord. I can't believe I'm at a public pool. Why doesn't somebody just pee directly on me?" Karen Walker, *Will & Grace*

"It does redefine job insecurity."
Steven Van Zandt, on being a
cast member of *The Sopranos*
March 11, 2001

"World peace?"
Lynda Carter, on what
it would take to get
her into a Wonder
Woman costume
June 27, 2004

"It is safe to say that the
age of innocence is officially over."
MSNBC reporter Ashleigh Banfield,
on covering 9/11
October 13, 2001

"I haven't changed. I still have my assistant put my pants on one leg at a time like
everybody else."
The King of Queens' Kevin James
December 20, 2003

"The nearest my
family came to color
TV in the '60s was
that my grand-
mother lived next to
people who had one.
We'd look through
the window to see it."
Dan Aykroyd
April 6, 2002

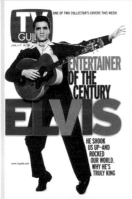

January 01 2000
Elvis Presley: Entertainer
of the Century

January 01 2000
Elvis Presley: Entertainer
of the Century

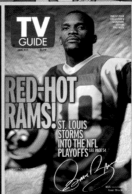

January 01 2000
Isaac Bruce of the Rams

January 01 2000
Marshall Faulk of the Rams

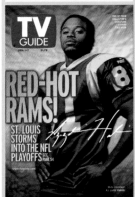

January 01 2000
Az-zahir Hakim of the Rams

January 01 2000
Kurt Warner of the Rams

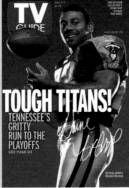

January 01 2000
Blaine Bishop of the Titans

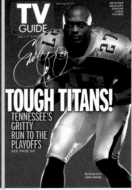

January 01 2000
Eddie George of the Titans

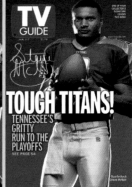

January 01 2000
Steve McNair of the Titans

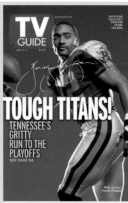

January 01 2000
Yancey Thigpen of the Titans

January 08 2000
The Cast of *The Sopranos*:
D. Chianese, J. Gandolfini, J. L.
Sigler, E. Falco, R. Iler.

Fold Out
M. Imperioli, A. Turturro, D. de
Matteo, D. Proval, S. Van Zandt,
and T. Sirico

January 15 2000
Regis Philbin with Winners of
Who Wants to be a Millionaire

January 22 2000
Barbra Streisand

January 29 2000
Wrestler Chyna

January 29 2000
Wrestler Mankind

January 29 2000
Wrestler The Rock

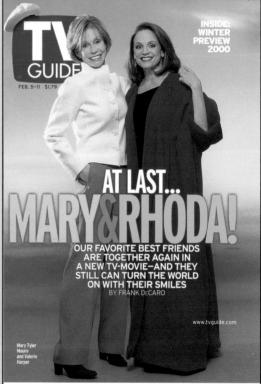

January 29 2000
Wrestler Triple H

February 05 2000
Mary Tyler Moore and
Valerie Harper in
Mary and Rhoda

February 12 2000
Debra Messing, Eric McCormack,
Megan Mullally, and Sean Hayes
of *Will & Grace*

We were introduced to Mary Richards and Rhoda
Morgenstern in 1970 on *The Mary Tyler Moore Show*.
In 1974, *Rhoda* got her own show and eventually got
married. In 2000, **Mary Tyler Moore** and **Valerie
Harper** reunited in *Mary & Rhoda* to let us know what
the two of them had been doing for the last 25 years.

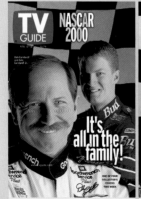

February 12 2000
Dale Earnhardt and
Dale Earnhardt Jr.

February 12 2000
Dale Jarrett, Jason Jarrett,
and Ned Jarrett

February 12 2000
Justin Labonte and
Terry Labonte

February 12 2000
Kyle Petty, Adam Petty,
and Richard Petty

February 19 2000
Sarah Michelle Gellar of
Buffy the Vampire Slayer

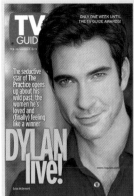

February 26 2000

Dylan McDermott of
The Practice

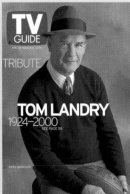

February 26 2000

Tribute to Tom Landry

March 04 2000

The TV Guide Awards – You
Voted…Who Won?

March 11 2000

Josh Charles, Felicity Huffman,
and Peter Krause of
Sports Night

March 18 2000

Frankie Muniz, Jane Kaczmarek,
and Bryan Cranston of
Malcolm in the Middle

March 25 2000

Cybill Shepherd – Cybill Tells All

April 01 2000

Lance Bass of 'N Sync

April 01 2000

JC Chasez of 'N Sync

April 01 2000

Joey Fatone of 'N Sync

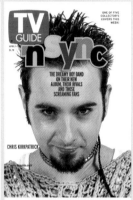

April 01 2000

Chris Kirkpatrick of 'N Sync

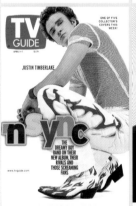

April 01 2000

Justin Timberlake of 'N Sync

April 08 2000

George Clooney in
Fail-Safe

April 15 2000

Larry Fine of
The Three Stooges

April 15 2000

Curly Howard of
The Three Stooges

April 15 2000

Moe Howard of
The Three Stooges

April 15 2000

Evan Handler, John Kassir, Paul
Ben-Victor, and Michael Chiklis in
The Three Stooges

April 22 2000

Emily Robison, Natalie Maines,
and Martie Seidel of
the Dixie Chicks

April 29 2000

Bryant Gumbel of
The Early Show

April 29 2000

Cal Ripken Jr. of the Orioles

May 06 2000

Jeremy Sisto in
Jesus

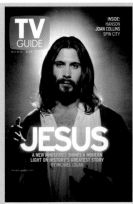

May 06 2000
Jeremy Sisto in
Jesus

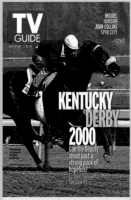

May 06 2000
Kentucky Derby 2000 – The
Deputy in Training

May 13 2000
Michael J. Fox of
Spin City

May 20 2000
Donny Osmond and
Marie Osmond of
Donny & Marie

May 27 2000
Who's Gonna be the
Survivor?

May 27 2000
Tribute to Adam Petty

May 27 2000
Kenny Brack – Indy 1999
Champion

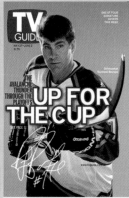

May 27 2000
Raymond Bourque of the Avalanche

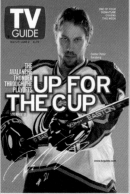

May 27 2000
Peter Forsberg of the Avalanche

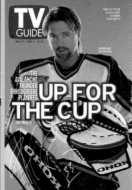

May 27 2000
Patrick Roy of the Avalanche

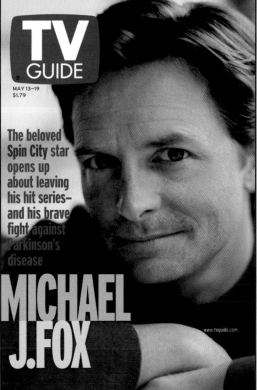

Michael J. Fox earned fame as Alex Keaton on
Family Ties in 1982. He had to leave his successful
series, *Spin City*, in 2000 because of Parkinson's
disease. He continues to make some appearances
and has also been doing voice work. He provided
Stuart Little's voice in all three movies.

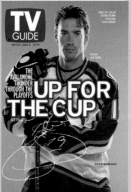

May 27 2000
Joe Sakic of the Avalanche

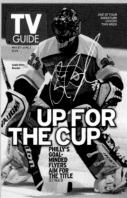

May 27 2000
Brian Boucher of the Flyers

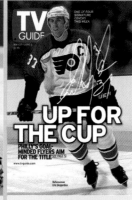

May 27 2000
Eric Desjardins of the Flyers

May 27 2000
John LeClair of the Flyers

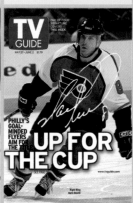

May 27 2000
Mark Recchi of the Flyers

June 03 2000
Britney Spears

June 03 2000
Britney Spears

June 10 2000
Mr. T; Butch Patrick;
Lisa Whelchel; Larry Storch –
Where Are They Now?

June 17 2000
Kim Cattrall of
Sex and the City

Survivor contestants marooned on Pulau Tiga

WHO'S GONNA BE THE SURVIVOR?

GILLIGAN WAS NEVER LIKE THIS!
CASTAWAYS BATTLE EACH OTHER
FOR BIG BUCKS—AND YOU WON'T
BELIEVE THE DESERT ISLAND DRAMA
BY MARK SCHWED

In 1948, *Candid Camera* (under its radio name, *Candid Microphone*) was the first reality show, but in 2000, *Survivor* started the reality game craze. Each year brings new survivors, a new island, and new twists. *Survivor* paved the way for other real-life game shows like *The Amazing Race* and *Fear Factor*.

June 17 2000
Kristin Davis of
Sex and the City

June 17 2000
Cynthia Nixon of
Sex and the City

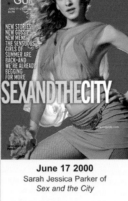

June 17 2000
Sarah Jessica Parker of
Sex and the City

June 24 2000
*The Real World –
Brave New World*

June 24 2000
Kobe Bryant of the Lakers

June 24 2000
Rick Fox of the Lakers

June 24 2000
Shaquille O'Neal of the Lakers

June 24 2000
Glen Rice of the Lakers

July 01 2000
Judy Garland in
The Wizard of Oz

July 01 2000
Ray Bolger in
The Wizard of Oz

July 01 2000
Jack Haley in
The Wizard of Oz

July 01 2000
Bert Lahr in
The Wizard of Oz

July 08 2000
Jenna Lewis, Rudy Boesch,
Kelly Wigglesworth, and
Susan Hawk of *Survivor*

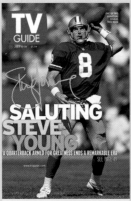

July 08 2000
Steve Young of the 49ers

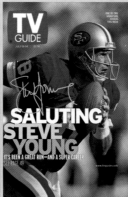

July 08 2000
Steve Young of the 49ers

July 08 2000
Andres Galarraga of the Braves

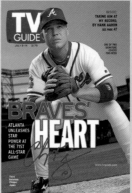

July 08 2000
Chipper Jones of the Braves

July 08 2000
Mark McGwire of the Cardinals

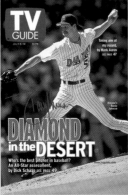

July 08 2000
Randy Johnson of the
Diamondbacks

July 08 2000
Pedro Martinez of the Red Sox

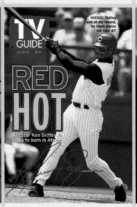

July 08 2000
Ken Griffey Jr. of the Reds

July 15 2000
Halle Berry as
Storm in
X-Men

July 15 2000
Hugh Jackman as
Wolverine in
X-Men

July 15 2000
Famke Janssen as
Jean Grey in
X-Men

July 15 2000
James Marsden as
Cyclops in
X-Men

July 15 2000
Anna Paquin as
Rogue in
X-Men

July 15 2000
Patrick Stewart as Professor
Charles Francis Xavier in
X-Men

July 22 2000
Martin Sheen in
The West Wing

July 29 2000
Claudia Black of
Farscape

July 29 2000
Roxann Dawson of
Star Trek: Voyager

July 29 2000
Gigi Edgley of
Farscape

July 29 2000
Katherine Heigl of
Roswell

July 29 2000
Virginia Hey of
Farscape

July 29 2000
Renee O'Connor of
Xena: Warrior Princess

July 29 2000
Jeri Ryan of
Star Trek: Voyager

July 29 2000
Xenia Seeberg of
Lexx

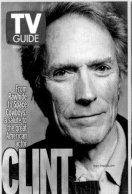

August 05 2000
Clint Eastwood – From
Rawhide to *Space Cowboys*

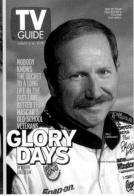

August 12 2000
Dale Earnhardt

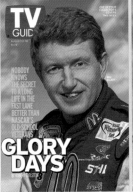

August 12 2000
Bill Elliott

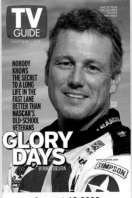

August 12 2000
Ricky Rudd

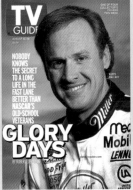

August 12 2000
Rusty Wallace

August 19 2000
The Kat of the WWF

August 19 2000
Chris Jericho of the WWF

August 19 2000
Kurt Angle of the WWF

August 19 2000
Rikishi of the WWF

August 26 2000
Christina Aguilera

August 26 2000
Metallica

August 26 2000
'N Sync

August 26 2000
Sisqo

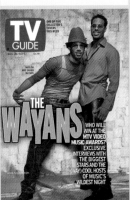

August 26 2000
The Wayans

September 02 2000
Dennis Miller of
Monday Night Football

September 02 2000
Jerry Rice of the 49ers

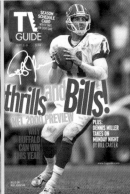

September 02 2000
Rob Johnson of the Bills

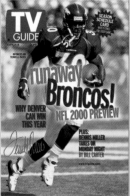

September 02 2000
Terrell Davis of the Broncos

September 02 2000
Tim Couch of the Browns

September 02 2000
Troy Aikman of the Cowboys

September 02 2000
Donovan McNabb of the Eagles

September 02 2000
Charlie Batch of the Lions

September 02 2000
Brett Favre of the Packers

September 02 2000
Steve Beuerlein of the Panthers

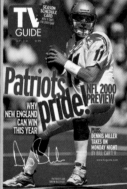

September 02 2000
Drew Bledsoe of the Patriots

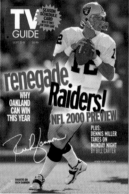

September 02 2000
Rich Gannon of the Raiders

September 02 2000
Kurt Warner of the Rams

September 02 2000
Darrell Green of the Redskins

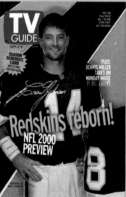

September 02 2000
Brad Johnson of the Redskins

September 02 2000
Deion Sanders of the Redskins

September 02 2000
Bruce Smith of the Redskins

September 02 2000
Levon Kirkland of the Steelers

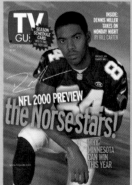

September 02 2000
Randy Moss of the Vikings

September 09 2000
*Malcolm in the Middle; Will &
Grace; The Parkers; Popular;
The Drew Carey Show*

September 16 2000
Soccer Star Julie Foudy

September 16 2000
Track Star Maurice Greene

September 16 2000
Hoops Star Chamique Holdsclaw

NOW! MORE CHEERS AND JEERS!

PLUS! 98° THE FUGITIVE

MORE TODAY THAN YESTERDAY

Katie and Matt dance toward a new day as their show takes a bold step–and their personal lives take inspiring turns By Mary Murphy

OCT. 7–13 $1.99

www.tvguide.com

Katie Couric and Matt Lauer

When the news show, *Today*, premiered back in 1952, the program, which broadcasts live for 3 hours from New York, was seen only for two hours each in the Eastern and Central time zones. **Dave Garroway** was the first host until 1961, and chimpanzee **J. Fred Muggs** was brought on as co-host from 1953 to 1957.

September 16 2000
Track Star Marion Jones

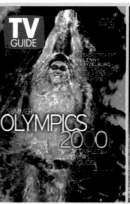

September 16 2000
Backstroker Lenny Krayzelburg

September 16 2000
Swim Star Jenny Thompson

September 23 2000
Tim McGraw;
Richard Hatch and Kelly
Wigglesworth of *Survivor*

September 30 2000
Geena Davis, Michael Richards,
John Goodman, and Bette Midler –
Fall Preview

October 07 2000
Katie Couric and
Matt Lauer of
Today

October 14 2000
Melina Kanakaredes of
Providence

October 21 2000
Apu Nahasapeemapetilon of
The Simpsons

October 21 2000
Barney Gumble of
The Simpsons

October 21 2000
Bumblebee Man of
The Simpsons

October 21 2000
Comic Book Guy of
The Simpsons

October 21 2000
Dr. Julius Hibbert of
The Simpsons

October 21 2000
Ned Flanders of
The Simpsons

October 21 2000
Grampa Abe Simpson of
The Simpsons

October 21 2000
Itchy and Scratchy of
The Simpsons

October 21 2000
Kang of
The Simpsons

October 21 2000
Mrs. Edna Krabappel of
The Simpsons

October 21 2000
Krusty the Clown of
The Simpsons

October 21 2000
Sea Captain McCallister of
The Simpsons

October 21 2000
Millhouse Van Houten of
The Simpsons

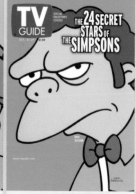

October 21 2000
Moe Szyslak of
The Simpsons

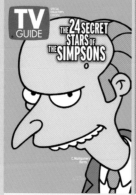

October 21 2000
C. Montgomery Burns of
The Simpsons

October 21 2000
Professor John Frink of
The Simpsons

October 21 2000
Ralph Wiggum of
The Simpsons

October 21 2000
Santa's Little Helper of
The Simpsons

October 21 2000
Selma Bouvier of
The Simpsons

October 21 2000
Sideshow Bob of
The Simpsons

October 21 2000
Principal Seymour Skinner of
The Simpsons

October 21 2000
Waylon Smithers of
The Simpsons

October 21 2000
Chief Clancy Wiggum of
The Simpsons

October 21 2000
Groundskeeper Willie of
The Simpsons

October 28 2000
Lucy Liu, Cameron Diaz, and
Drew Barrymore in
Charlie's Angels

October 28 2000
Cameron Diaz, Drew Barrymore,
and Lucy Liu in
Charlie's Angels

November 04 2000
Gillian Anderson of
The X-Files

November 04 2000
David Duchovny of
The X-Files

November 04 2000
Robert Patrick of
The X-Files

November 11 2000
John Lennon of
The Beatles

November 11 2000
Paul McCartney of
The Beatles

November 11 2000
George Harrison of
The Beatles

November 11 2000
Ringo Starr of
The Beatles

November 11 2000
The Beatles 2000
(Embossed)

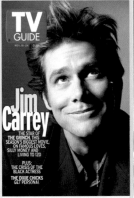

November 18 2000
Jim Carrey

November 25 2000
Jessica Alba of
Dark Angel

December 02 2000
The Cast of
The View

Pokemon originated in Japan as a video game and was first created as a TV show there. It started a national collectors card craze among children and adults alike. The TV show actually holds a Guiness Record for Most Seizures Caused By A TV Program when an episode that aired in Japan caused 700+ fits.

December 09 2000
Firiona Vie from
'Everquest'

December 09 2000
Tony Hawk from
'Tony Hawk's Pro Skater 2'

December 09 2000
Lara Croft from
'Tomb Raider Chronicles'

December 09 2000
The Titan's Eddie George from
'John Madden Football'

December 09 2000
Pikachu from
'Pokemon'

December 09 2000
Ryp and Ling Sha from
'Shenmue'

December 16 2000
Benjamin Bratt

December 23 2000
Vivien Leigh in
Gone With the Wind

December 23 2000
Vivien Leigh in
Gone With the Wind

December 23 2000
Clark Gable in
Gone WIth The Wind

December 23 2000
Clark Gable and
Vivien Leigh in
Gone With The Wind

December 23 2000
Vivien Leigh in
Gone With the Wind

December 30 2000
Mary Hart and
Bob Goen of
Entertainment Tonight

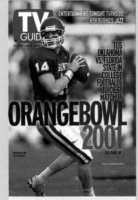

December 30 2000
Oklahoma's QB Josh Heupel

January 06 2001
Darva Conger; Ralph Nader;
Rudy Boesch – The Year in Jeers

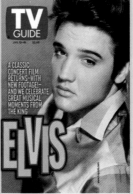

January 13 2001
Elvis Presley
(Hologram)

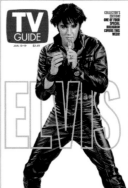

January 13 2001
Elvis Presley
(Hologram)

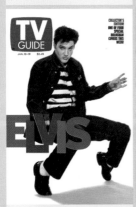

January 13 2001
Elvis Presley
(Hologram)

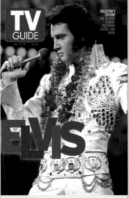

January 13 2001
Elvis Presley
(Hologram)

January 13 2001
Elvis Presley
(Hologram)

January 20 2001
Survivor 2: The Kucha Tribe

January 20 2001
Survivor 2: The Ogakor Tribe

January 27 2001
Alex Trebek of *Jeopardy*
and Regis Philbin of *Who
Wants To be a Millionaire?*

February 03 2001
Anthony Hopkins in
Hannibal

February 10 2001
Jane Kaczmarek (*Malcolm in the
Middle*), Matt LeBlanc (*Friends*),
and Steve Harris (*The Practice*)

February 10 2001
Edie Falco (*The Sopranos*), Conan
O'Brien (*Late Night*), and Carson
Daly (*Total Request Live*)

February 10 2001
Megan Mullally (*Will & Grace*), John
Spencer (*The West Wing*), and Amy
Brenneman (*Judging Amy*)

February 17 2001
Kyle Petty

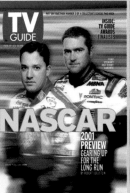

February 17 2001
Tony Stewart and Bobby Labonte

February 17 2001
Matt Kenseth

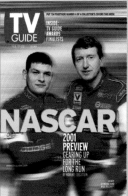

February 17 2001
Casey Atwood and Bill Elliott

February 24 2001
Judy Garland

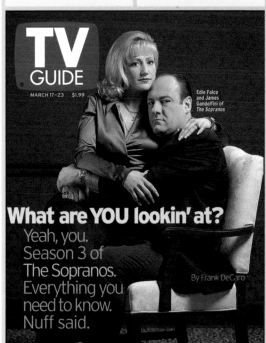

Although the Coalition of Italian-American Associations condemned *The Sopranos* in 2000 for promoting negative stereotypes, the public loves this show about New Jersey mobster Tony Soprano and his family. The program has been nominated for multiple Emmys ever since it premiered in 1999.

February 24 2001
Judy Garland

February 24 2001
Judy Garland

February 24 2001
Judy Garland

February 24 2001
Judy Davis in
Life with Judy Garland: Me and My Shadow

March 03 2001
The TV Guide Awards – You Voted…Who Won?

March 10 2001
Janet Jackson

March 10 2001
Janet Jackson

March 17 2001
Edie Falco and James Gandolfini of
The Sopranos

March 24 2001
The 50 Greatest Movie Moments of All Time

March 31 2001
Rachel Leigh Cook, Tara Reid, and Rosario Dawson in
Josie and the Pussycats

April 07 2001
Ioan Gruffudd in
Horatio Hornblower

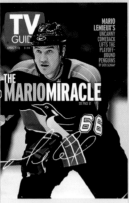

April 07 2001
Mario Lemieux of the Penguins

April 14 2001
David Letterman

April 21 2001
The Cast of
Once and Again

April 28 2001
Lara Flynn Boyle of
The Practice

April 28 2001
Point Given – Kentucky Derby
Contender

May 05 2001
Paul McCartney – Maybe
We're Amazed

May 12 2001
Poppy Montgomery in
Blonde

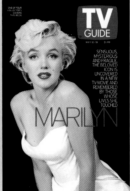

May 12 2001
Marilyn Monroe

May 12 2001
Marilyn Monroe

May 12 2001
Marilyn Monroe

Back Cover
Marilyn Monroe by
Andy Warhol

May 12 2001
Marilyn Monroe by
Andy Warhol

May 19 2001
Jeri Ryan in
Star Trek: Voyager

May 19 2001
Kate Mulgrew in
Star Trek: Voyager

May 19 2001
Jeri Ryan, Alice Krige, and
Kate Mulgrew in
Star Trek: Voyager

Back Cover
Ethan Phillips, Roxann Dawson,
Robert Duncan McNeill,

May 19 2001
Robert Beltran, Kate Mulgrew,
and Tim Russ of
Star Trek: Voyager

May 26 2001
Backstreet Boys

May 26 2001
Nick Carter of
Backstreet Boys

May 26 2001
Howie Dorough of
Backstreet Boys

May 26 2001
Brian Littell of
Backstreet Boys

May 26 2001
A.J. McLean of
Backstreet Boys

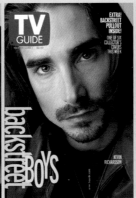

May 26 2001
Kevin Richardson of
Backstreet Boys

The first **Joe Frazier/Muhammad Ali** fight took place on March 8, 1971 and was called the "Fight of the Century." The two sparred again on January 28, 1974. They fought for a third time on October 1, 1975, which was dubbed the "Thrilla in Manilla." On June 8, 2001, their daughters, **Jacqui Frazier-Lyde** and **Laila Ali,** continued the feud.

June 02 2001
Laila Ali and Jacquelyn Frazier-Lyde

June 09 2001
Tiger Woods – His Shot At
Making History

June 09 2001
Tiger Woods – His Shot At
Making History

June 09 2001
Tiger Woods – His Shot At
Making History

June 09 2001
Tiger Woods – His Shot At
Making History

June 16 2001
Bill O'Reilly of
The O'Reilly Factor

June 16 2001
Kobe Bryant of the Lakers

June 16 2001
Rick Fox of the Lakers

June 16 2001
Robert Horry of the Lakers

June 16 2001
Derek Fisher of the Lakers

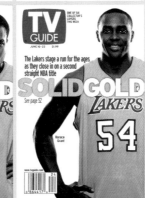

June 16 2001
Horace Grant of the Lakers

June 16 2001
Shaquille O'Neal of the Lakers

June 23 2001
The Women of
ER

June 30 2001
Jerry Seinfeld

July 07 2001
Juliet Mills, McKenzie Westmore,
and Galen Gering of
Passions

July 07 2001
McKenzie Westmore, Galen
Gering, and Juliet Mills of
Passions

July 07 2001
Bozo The Clown Signs Off

July 14 2001
Julianna Margulies in
The Mists of Avalon

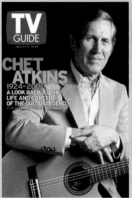

July 21 2001
A Tribute to Chet Atkins

July 21 2001
Angelica of
Rugrats

July 21 2001
Chuckie of
Rugrats

July 21 2001
Lil and Phil of
Rugrats

July 21 2001
Tommy of
Rugrats

Back Cover
Glenn Shadix as Senator Nado
and

July 28 2001
Michael Clarke Duncan
as Attar in
Planet of the Apes

July 28 2001
Tim Roth as
General Thade in
Planet of the Apes

July 28 2001
Mark Wahlberg as
Astronaut Leo Davidson in
Planet of the Apes

July 28 2001
Estella Warren as
Daena in
Planet of the Apes

July 28 2001
Helena Bonham Carter
as Ari in
Planet of the Apes

Guiding Light is the longest running daytime soap
opera. It started as a radio show in 1937 and moved
to a daily TV slot in 1952. In 1974, the Emmy Awards
established a daytime ceremony (the Daytime
Emmys) and *General Hospital* has won the most
frequently for Best Drama Series, with eight awards.

Back Cover
Lisa Marie as Nova
and

July 28 2001
Kris Kristofferson
as Karubi in
Planet of the Apes

August 04 2001
Danny Masterson of
That '70s Show

August 04 2001
Mila Kunis of
That '70s Show

August 04 2001
Ashton Kutcher of
That '70s Show

August 04 2001
Topher Grace of
That '70s Show

August 04 2001
Laura Prepon of
That '70s Show

August 04 2001
Wilmer Valderrama of
That '70s Show

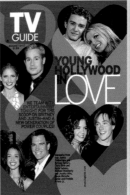

August 11 2001
Justin & Britney; Sarah
Michelle & Freddie; Katie &
Chris; Jessica & Michael

August 18 2001
Kelly Ripa of
Live with Regis & Kelly

Back Cover
Dominic Keating as Lt. Malcolm
Reed, Connor Trinneer as Chief
Engineer Charles "Trip" Tucker III,

August 25 2001
and Linda Park as
Ensign Hoshi
Sato of *Enterprise*

August 25 2001
Scott Bakula as
Captain Jonathan Archer of
Enterprise

August 25 2001
Jolene Blalock as Vulcan
Sub-Commander T'Pol of
Enterprise

August 25 2001
Jolene Blalock and
Scott Bakula of
Enterprise

Back Cover
Anthony Montgomery as
Ensign Travis Mayweather

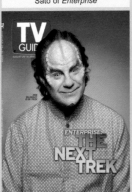

August 25 2001
and John Billingsley
as Dr. Phlox of
Enterprise

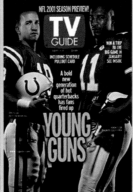

September 01 2001
Peyton Manning of the Colts and
Daunte Culpepper of the Vikings

September 01 2001
Donovan McNabb of the Eagles

September 01 2001
Marshall Faulk of the Rams

207

September 01 2001
Lavar Arrington of the Redskins

September 01 2001
Jerome Bettis of the Steelers

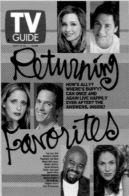

September 08 2001
Ally McBeal; *The West Wing*; *Buffy the Vampire Slayer*; *Once and Again*; *Boston Public*; *Judging Amy*

September 15 2001
Jill Hennessy (*Crossing Jordan*), Kim Delaney (*Philly*), and Jennifer Garner (*Alias*) – Fall Preview

September 22 2001
Tom Hanks and the Cast of *Band of Brothers*; Johnny Carson

September 22 2001
Cal Ripken Jr. –
The Rookie in 1982

September 22 2001
Cal Ripken Jr. –
Baseball's Iron Man in 1995

September 22 2001
Cal Ripken Jr. –
The 2001 Season

September 22 2001
Cal Ripken Jr. with
His Mom, Vi Ripken

September 22 2001
Tony Gwynn –
The Rookie in 1982

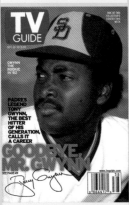

September 22 2001
Tony Gwynn
Calls It a Career

September 29 2001
Terror Hits Home

October 06 2001
Survivor: Africa –
The Boran Tribe

October 06 2001
Ethan Zohn of
Survivor: Africa

October 06 2001
Jessie Camacho of
Survivor: Africa

October 06 2001
Clarence Black of
Survivor: Africa

October 06 2001
Lex van den Berghe of
Survivor: Africa

October 06 2001
Tom Buchanan of
Survivor: Africa

October 06 2001
Kim Johnson of
Survivor: Africa

October 06 2001
Kelly Goldsmith of
Survivor: Africa

October 06 2001
Diane Ogden of
Survivor: Africa

October 06 2001
Survivor: Africa –
The Samburu Tribe

October 06 2001
Brandon Quinton of
Survivor: Africa

October 06 2001
Carl Bilancione of
Survivor: Africa

October 06 2001
Linda Spencer of
Survivor: Africa

October 06 2001
Silas Gaither of
Survivor: Africa

October 06 2001
Kim Powers of
Survivor: Africa

October 06 2001
Lindsey Richter of
Survivor: Africa

October 06 2001
Teresa Cooper of
Survivor: Africa

October 06 2001
Frank Garrison of
Survivor: Africa

October 13 2001
The 50 Funniest Moments of
I Love Lucy –
Lucille Ball

October 13 2001
The 50 Funniest Moments of
I Love Lucy –
Lucille Ball

October 13 2001
The 50 Funniest Moments of
I Love Lucy –
Lucille Ball and Desi Arnaz

October 13 2001
The 50 Funniest Moments of
I Love Lucy –
'Lucy's Italian Movie'

October 13 2001
The 50 Funniest Moments of
I Love Lucy –
'Lucy and Superman'

October 13 2001
The 50 Funniest Moments of
I Love Lucy –
'Lucy Gets in Pictures'

October 13 2001
The 50 Funniest Moments of
I Love Lucy –
'L.A. at Last'

October 13 2001
The 50 Funniest Moments of
I Love Lucy –
'Job Switching'

Back Cover
William Frawley,
Vivian Vance,

October 13 2001
Lucille Ball, and
Desi Arnaz of
I Love Lucy

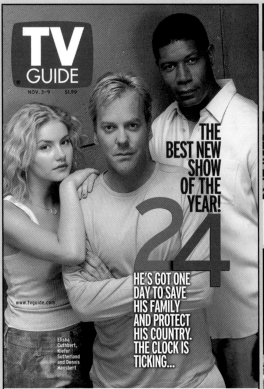

24 is an innovative show in that each episode takes place in real time, and covers one hour of the 24 hours that gave the series its name. Each season covers one day in the life of Jack Bauer, CIA agent. The program first aired on 11/6/2001 and has already been nominated for a total of over 100 awards.

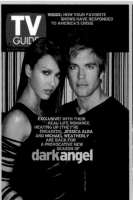

October 20 2001
Jessica Alba and Michael Weatherly of *Dark Angel*

October 27 2001
Daniel Radcliffe in *Harry Potter and the Sorcer's Stone*

October 27 2001
Emma Watson in *Harry Potter and the Sorcer's Stone*

October 27 2001
Rupert Grint in *Harry Potter and the Sorcer's Stone*

October 27 2001
Robbie Coltrane in *Harry Potter and the Sorcer's Stone*

October 27 2001
Barry Bonds – 500th Career Homerun on 4/17/01

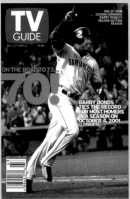

October 27 2001
Barry Bonds – 70th Season Homerun on 10/4/01

October 27 2001
Barry Bonds – 71st Season Homerun on 10/5/01

October 27 2001
Barry Bonds – 73rd Season Homerun on 10/7/01

October 27 2001
Albert Pujols of the Cardinals

November 03 2001
Elisha Cuthbert, Kiefer Sutherland, and Dennis Haysbert of *24*

November 10 2001
Michael Jackson in 1970

November 10 2001
Michael Jackson

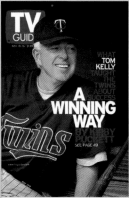

November 10 2001
Tom Kelly of the Twins

November 17 2001
Jennifer Aniston and David Schwimmer of *Friends*

November 24 2001
R2-D2: The Untold Story!

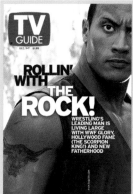

December 01 2001
Rollin' With The Rock!

December 08 2001
Tom Welling
as Clark of
Smallville

December 08 2001
Kristin Kreuk
as Lana of
Smallville

December 08 2001
Michael Rosenbaum
as Lex of
Smallville

December 08 2001
Kal-El as Superman

Born in Europe, **Peter Max** spent the first ten years of his life in Shanghai and travelled the world prior to arriving in America at age sixteen. WIth his bold colors and inspired images, he became "the" artist of the sixties. Following the tragedy of 9/11, **TV Guide** produced five covers reflecting The American Spirit, of which one was created by Peter Max.

Back Cover
Sean Bean
as Boromir
Pleads His Case

December 15 2001
to the Council in
The Lord of the Rings

December 15 2001
Orlando Bloom and
Cate Blanchett in
The Lord of the Rings

December 15 2001
Liv Tyler and
Viggo Mortensen in
The Lord of the Rings

December 15 2001
Ian McKellen in
The Lord of the Rings

December 15 2001
Sean Astin, Elijah Wood, Billy
Boyd, and Dominic Monaghan
in *The Lord of the Rings*

December 22 2001
May It Ever Wave
by Al Hirschfield

December 22 2001
Patriot's Barn
by Jamie Wyeth

December 22 2001
I Love America
by Beata Rubin

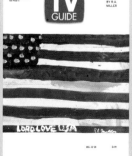

December 22 2001
American Flag
by R.A. Miller

December 22 2001
Flag With Heart
by Peter Max

211

December 29 2001
George Harrison – His Inspired
Musical Legacy and
Spiritual Journey

2002

January 05 2002
Carol Burnett, Tim Conway,
Harvey Korman, and
Vicki Lawrence

January 12 2002
Dave Garroway of
Today

January 12 2002
Hugh Downs and
Barbara Walters of
Today

Carol Burnett's first television appearance was as
a regular on the *Winchell-Mahoney Show* in 1955.
In 1967, she started *The Carol Burnett Show*, and
the much lauded variety show is now considered
a classic. In 2001 the cast members reunited for
a TV special featuring bloopers and famous skits.

January 12 2002
Katie Couric and
Matt Lauer of
Today

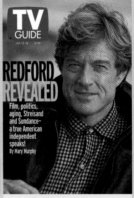

January 12 2002
Robert Redford – Redford
Revealed

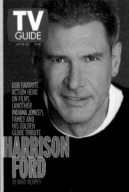

January 19 2002
Harrison Ford

January 26 2002
Rose Red

February 02 2002
Bernie Mac of
The Bernie Mac Show

February 09 2002
Figure Skater Michelle Kwan

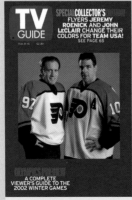

February 09 2002
Jeremy Roenick and
John LeClair of
the Flyers

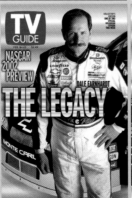

February 16 2002
Dale Earnhardt
(Hologram)

February 16 2002
Dale Earnhardt Jr.
(Hologram)

Back Cover
Dale Earnhardt and
(Hologram)

February 16 2002
Dale Earnhardt Jr.
(Hologram)

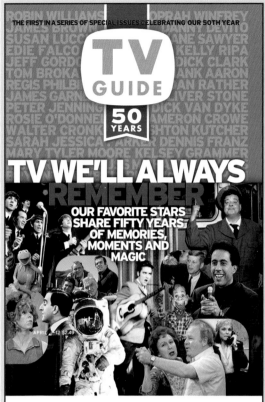

THE FIRST IN A SERIES OF SPECIAL ISSUES CELEBRATING OUR 50TH YEAR

TV WE'LL ALWAYS REMEMBER

OUR FAVORITE STARS SHARE FIFTY YEARS OF MEMORIES, MOMENTS AND MAGIC

APRIL 6-12 $2.49

TV Guide's first issue was only 24 pages and sold for 15¢. As TV grew, so did **TV Guide** and it soon became the ultimate reference for "what's on tonight." In the 2000's, the issues averaged 150+ pages, contained listings for over 80 channels, and circulated over 9 million copies per issue.

February 16 2002
Dale Earnhardt Jr.

February 23 2002
William Petersen and
Marg Helgenberger of
CSI

March 02 2002
Charlie Sheen and
Martin Sheen

March 09 2002
Chi McBride (*Boston Public*), Maura
Tierney (*ER*), and Bryan Cranston
(*Malcolm in the Middle*)

March 09 2002
Tina Fey (*Saturday Night Live*),
Cynthia Nixon (*Sex and the City*),
and Esai Morales (*NYPD Blue*)

March 09 2002
Allison Janney (*The West Wing*),
Peter Krause (*Six Feet Under*),
and Patricia Heaton (*Raymond*)

March 09 2002
Dan Rather (*CBS News*),
Tom Brokaw (*NBC News*),
and Peter Jennings (*ABC News*)

March 16 2002
Frankie Muniz, Christopher
Masterson, Erik Per Sullivan, Justin
Berfield of *Malcolm in the Middle*

March 23 2002
Russell Crowe; Halle Berry;
Marisa Tomei; Ethan Hawke –
Oscar Wild!

March 30 2002
Celine Dion

April 06 2002
TV Guide's 50th Anniversary

April 13 2002
Jay Leno of
The Tonight Show

April 20 2002
James Doohan of
Star Trek

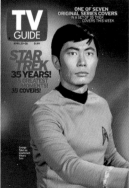

April 20 2002
George Takei of
Star Trek

April 20 2002
Leonard Nimoy of
Star Trek

April 20 2002
William Shatner of
Star Trek

April 20 2002
DeForest Kelley of
Star Trek

April 20 2002
Walter Koenig of
Star Trek

April 20 2002
Nichelle Nichols of
Star Trek

April 20 2002
Marina Sirtis of
Star Trek: The Next Generation

April 20 2002
Brent Spiner of
Star Trek: The Next Generation

April 20 2002
LeVar Burton of
Star Trek: The Next Generation

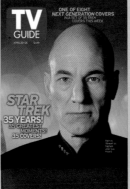

April 20 2002
Patrick Stewart of
Star Trek: The Next Generation

April 20 2002
Jonathan Frakes of
Star Trek: The Next Generation

April 20 2002
Denise Crosby as Sela
and Natasha Yar of
Star Trek: The Next Generation

April 20 2002
Michael Dorn of
Star Trek: The Next Generation

April 20 2002
Wil Wheaton and
Gates McFadden of
Star Trek: The Next Generation

April 20 2002
Nicole deBoer and
Terry Farrell of
Star Trek: Deep Space Nine

April 20 2002
Rene Auberjonois of
Star Trek: Deep Space Nine

April 20 2002
Avery Brooks of
Star Trek: Deep Space Nine

April 20 2002
Nana Visitor and
Alexander Siddig of
Star Trek: Deep Space Nine

April 20 2002
Armin Shimerman of
Star Trek: Deep Space Nine

April 20 2002
Cirroc Lofton and
Colm Meaney of
Star Trek: Deep Space Nine

April 20 2002
Roxann Dawson and
Robert Duncan McNeill of
Star Trek: Voyager

April 20 2002
Jennifer Lien and
Ethan Phillips of
Star Trek: Voyager

April 20 2002
Robert Picardo of
Star Trek: Voyager

April 20 2002
Kate Mulgrew of
Star Trek: Voyager

April 20 2002
Robert Beltran of
Star Trek: Voyager

April 20 2002
Jeri Ryan of
Star Trek: Voyager

April 20 2002
Tim Russ and
Garrett Wang of
Star Trek: Voyager

April 20 2002
John Billingsley and
Linda Park of
Enterprise

April 20 2002
Jolene Blalock and
Connor Trinneer of *Enterprise*

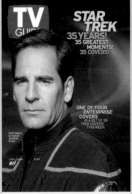

April 20 2002
Scott Bakula of
Enterprise

April 20 2002
Anthony Montgomery and
Dominic Keating of
Enterprise

April 20 2002
Alice Krige of
Star Trek: Voyager

April 20 2002
Ricardo Montalban of
Star Trek

April 20 2002
John de Lancie of
Star Trek: The Next Generation

April 27 2002
Spider-Man by John Romita

April 27 2002
Spider-Man by John Romita Jr.

April 27 2002
Spider-Man by Mark Bagley

April 27 2002
Spider-Man by Alex Ross

April 27 2002
Tobey Maguire in
Spider-Man

May 04 2002
*The Tonight Show; Sopranos; I
Love Lucy; The Dick Van Dyke
Show; Simpsons; Cosby Show*

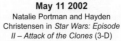

May 11 2002
Hayden Christensen and Ewan
McGregor in *Star Wars: Episode II –
Attack of the Clones* (3-D)

May 11 2002
Natalie Portman and Hayden
Christensen in *Star Wars: Episode
II – Attack of the Clones* (3-D)

May 11 2002
Hayden Christensen in
*Star Wars: Episode II – Attack
of the Clones* (3-D)

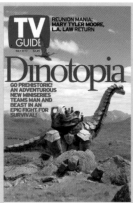

May 11 2002
Dinotopia

May 18 2002
Gillian Anderson and
David Duchovny of
The X-Files

May 18 2002
Robert Patrick and
Annabeth Gish of
The X-Files

May 25 2002
Alex Michel and
Amanda Marsh of
The Bachelor

June 01 2002
Ashley Judd

June 08 2002
Jennifer Aniston of
Friends

June 08 2002
Courtney Cox Arquette of
Friends

June 08 2002
Lisa Kudrow of
Friends

June 08 2002
Matt LeBlanc of
Friends

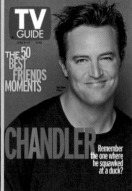

June 08 2002
Matthew Perry of
Friends

June 08 2002
David Schwimmer of
Friends

June 15 2002
50 Greatest TV Guide Covers

June 22 2002
Alexis Bledel and
Lauren Graham of
Gilmore Girls

June 22 2002
Alexis Bledel and
Lauren Graham of
Gilmore Girls

June 29 2002
Sarah Jessica Parker of
Sex and the City

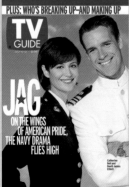

July 06 2002
Catherine Bell and
David James Elliott of
JAG

July 06 2002
P. Diddy & Jennifer Lopez; Gideon
Yago & Kelly Osbourne; Tobey
Maguire & Nicole Kidman

July 13 2002
Contestants Jim Verraros, Tamyra
Gray, and Ryan Starr of
American Idol

July 20 2002
50 Worst Shows of All Time

July 27 2002
Kelly Ripa and
Regis Philbin of
Live with Regis & Kelly

August 03 2002
Charlie Brown of *Peanuts* and Angelica Pickles of *Rugrats*

August 03 2002
Daffy Duck (as Duck Dodgers) and Cadet Porky Pig with the Powerpuff Girls

August 03 2002
Homer Simpson with Rocky and Bullwinkle

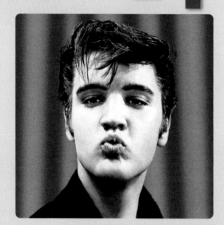

STARS TELL WHY THEY STILL LOVE HIM
WILLIAM F. BUCKLEY JR. ON ELVIS'S LEGACY
THE STORY BEHIND HIS NEW HIT SINGLE

Elvis Presley made his very first recording in 1953. Since then he has sold over 100 million albums and holds the record for the most songs on Billboard's Hot 100. He starred in 31 feature films. Today, his music is still used in films and commercials. Elvis Presley died on August 16, 1977 but he remains "The King."

August 03 2002
Popeye and SpongeBob SquarePants

August 10 2002
Leah Remini, Kevin James, and Jerry Stiller of *The King of Queens*

August 10 2002
Winona Ryder – The Strange Case of Winona Ryder

August 10 2002
Stacey Dales-Schuman, Vicky Bullett, and Chamique Holdsclaw

August 17 2002
Elvis Presley – Elvis Forever!

August 17 2002
Elvis Presley – Elvis Forever!
(3-D)

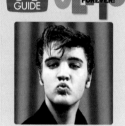

August 17 2002
Elvis Presley – Elvis Forever!
(3-D)

August 17 2002
Elvis Presley – Elvis Forever!
(3-D)

August 24 2002
James Gandolfini of *The Sopranos*

August 24 2002
Edie Falco of *The Sopranos*

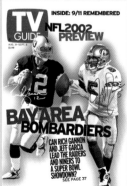

August 31 2002
Donovan McNabb of the Eagles and Tom Brady of the Patriots

August 31 2002
Rich Gannon of the Raiders and Jeff Garcia of the 49ers

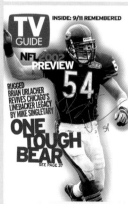

August 31 2002
Brian Urlacher of the Bears

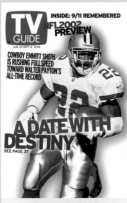

August 31 2002
Emmitt Smith of the Cowboys

August 31 2002
Brett Favre of the Packers

August 31 2002
Kordell Stewart of the Steelers

September 07 2002
Reba McEntire (*Reba*), Christopher Meloni (*Law & Order: SVU*), and Julie Bowen (*ER*)

September 14 2002
Bill Bellamy, Ashley Scott, Kiele Sanchez, David Caruso, and Gail O'Grady – Fall Preview

September 21 2002
Jennifer Garner of *Alias*

September 21 2002
Jennifer Garner of *Alias*

September 21 2002
Jennifer Garner of *Alias*

September 21 2002
Ernie Harwell – Detroit's Sports Legend Signs Off

September 28 2002
Henry Simmmons of *NYPD Blue* and Kim Cattrall of *Sex and the City*

September 28 2002
Henry Simmmons of *NYPD Blue* and Kim Cattrall of *Sex and the City*

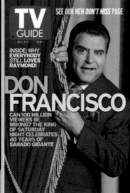

October 05 2002
Don Francisco of *Sabado Gigante*

October 05 2002
The Cast of *Everybody Loves Raymond*

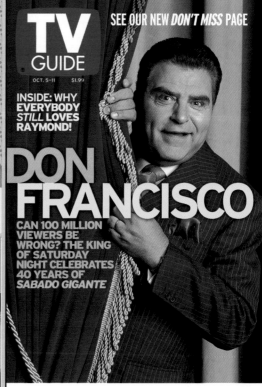

October 05 2002
Unitas Forever – A Tribute by Barry Levinson

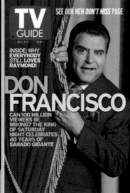

October 12 2002
Maura Tierney, Noah Wyle, Goran Visnjic, and Mehki Phife of *ER*

October 19 2002
Oprah Winfrey, Ozzy Osbourne, Drew Carey, Katie Couric, and David Letterman

The host of *Sabado Gigante*, **Don Francisco (Mario Kreutzberger)**, created the weekly program in 1962 when it aired in Chile. In 1985, he moved it to Florida where it began to air in the United States. At first, two weekly shows were produced, one in the US for the US and UK and one in Chile to air in Chile.

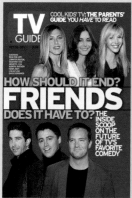

October 26 2002

The Cast of
Friends

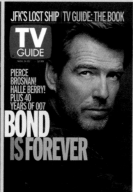

November 09 2002

Pierce Brosnan in
Die Another Day

November 09 2002

Pierce Brosnan in
Die Another Day

November 09 2002

Halle Berry in
Die Another Day

November 09 2002

Pierce Brosnan and
Halle Berry in
Die Another Day

November 02 2002

Shania Twain – Shania's Back!

November 16 2002

Heidi Klum – The Victoria's
Secret Fashion Show

November 16 2002

Tyra Banks – The Victoria's
Secret Fashion Show

November 16 2002

Heidi Klum and Tyra Banks –
The Victoria's Secret
Fashion Show

November 23 2002

Gregory Smith, Brittany Snow,
David Gallagher, and Kathy Cuoco
– Generation Now

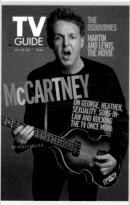

November 23 2002

Paul McCartney

November 30 2002

Austin Powers; *The Lord of
the Rings*; *Shrek*; *The Godfather*;
Sex and the City

November 30 2002

Catherine Dent and
Anton Yelchin in
Taken

December 07 2002

Patrick Stewart and Brent Spiner
of *Star Trek Nemesis*
(3-D)

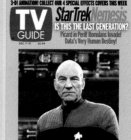

December 07 2002

Patrick Stewart in
Star Trek Nemesis
(3-D)

December 07 2002

The U.S.S. Enterprise of
Star Trek Nemesis
(3-D)

December 07 2002

The U.S.S. Enterprise of
Star Trek Nemesis
(3-D)

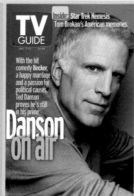

December 07 2002

Ten Danson of
Becker

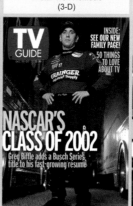

December 14 2002

Greg Biffle

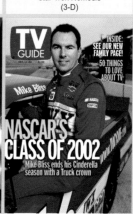

December 14 2002

Mike Bliss

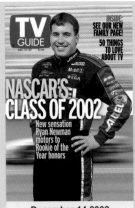

December 14 2002
Ryan Newman

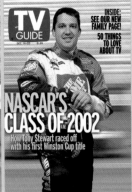

December 14 2002
Tony Stewart

December 14 2002
The Simpsons; Jennifer Garner of *Alias*; Matthew Perry of *Friends*; The Cast of *Seinfeld*

December 21 2002
Shaquille O'Neal of the Lakers

December 28 2002
Holly Marie Combs of *Charmed*

In January of 2003, **TV Guide** joined forces with music station VH-1 to present a special, *100 Greatest Moments That Rocked TV*. It aired for an hour a day over 5 days, counting down from 100. Starting the list at #100 was **Mariah Carey** stripping on *Total Request Live*, and ending the broadcast at #1 was **Bill Clinton** playing sax on *The Arsenio Hall Show* in 1992.

December 28 2002
Rose McGowan of *Charmed*

December 28 2002
Alyssa Milano of *Charmed*

December 28 2002
Rose McGowan, Holly Marie Combs, and Alyssa Milano of *Charmed*

January 04 2003
Kiefer Sutherland of *24*; Michael Chiklis of *The Shield*

January 11 2003
Eminem; Kurt Cobain; Mariah Carey; Ozzy Osbourne; Kelly Clarkson

January 18 2003
Jeff Probst of *Survivor*, Trista Rehn of *The Bachelorette*, and Simon Cowell of *American Idol*

January 25 2003
Jimmy Kimmel of *Jimmy Kimmel Live*; Evan Marriott of *Joe Millionaire*

February 01 2003
Marik of *Yu-Gi-Oh!*
(Foil)

February 01 2003
Seto Kaiba of *Yu-Gi-Oh!*
(Foil)

February 01 2003
Yami Yugi of *Yu-Gi-Oh!*
(Foil)

February 01 2003
Mai of
Yu-Gi-Oh!

February 08 2003
Jennifer Garner and
Ben Affleck in
Daredevil

February 08 2003
Jennifer Garner and
Ben Affleck in
Daredevil

February 15 2003
Homer of
The Simpsons

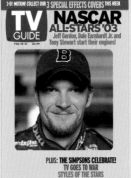

February 15 2003
Dale Earnhardt Jr.
(3-D)

February 15 2003
Jeff Gordon
(3-D)

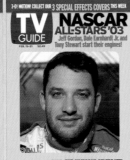

February 15 2003
Tony Stewart
(3-D)

February 22 2003
Nina Vardalos of
My Big Fat Greek Life

March 01 2003
Peter Krause of
Six Feet Under

March 08 2003
David Caruso of
CSI: Miami

March 15 2003
Kelly Clarkson of
American Idol

March 22 2003
Your Oscar Issue

March 29 2003
Debra Messing of
Will & Grace

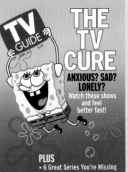

April 05 2003
SpongeBob Squarepants

April 12 2003
Kids & The Television War;
John Walsh

April 19 2003
Paige Davis of
Trading Spaces

The First Annual Academy Awards ceremony took place on May 16, 1929. The first televised ceremony was on March 19, 1953 with **Bob Hope** as MC. Today, the Academy Awards features 25 categories. The annual television specials are extravaganzas that make it one of the most watched award shows.

April 19 2003
Hillary Duff of
Lizzie McGuire

April 26 2003
Your Favorite Shows on DVD

April 26 2003
Jennifer Aniston of
Friends

May 03 2003
Catherine Bell and
David James Elliott of
JAG

May 03 2003
Derby Day 2003 – Front-running
Empire Maker

May 10 2003
Kristin Kreuk and Tom
Welling of *Smallville*;
The Cast of *Enterprise*

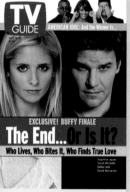

May 17 2003
Sarah Michelle Gellar of *Buffy the
Vampire Slayer* and David
Boreanaz of *Angel*; *American Idol*

May 17 2003
Randy Jackson, Paula Abdul
and Simon Cowell of
American Idol

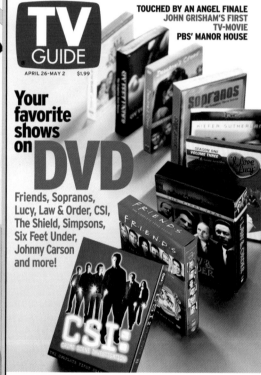

May 24 2003
Willie Nelson; Lisa Kudrow;
Neal McDonough; Patricia
Heaton; Ashton Kutcher

May 31 2003
Arnold Schwarzenegger

June 07 2003
Mariska Hargitay and
Christopher Meloni of
Law & Order: SVU

DVD was first announced in November of 1995.
The first players produced were in Japan a year later,
and they began appearing in the United States in
March, 1997. Today, DVD has become the industry
standard. Now you can see all your favorite shows,
from *I Love Lucy* to *CSI*, whenever you want.

June 14 2003
Kim Cattrall of
Sex and the City

June 14 2003
Kristin Davis of
Sex and the City

June 14 2003
Cynthia Nixon of
Sex and the City

June 14 2003
Sarah Jessica Parker of
Sex and the City

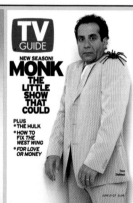

June 21 2003
Tony Shalhoub of
Monk

Motion Effects! Special Edition Collector's Cover!!

THE HULK BREAKS OUT!
Behind the Scenes With the Summer's MONSTER Movie

PLUS
• MONK RETURNS
• HOW TO FIX *THE WEST WING*
• *FOR LOVE OR MONEY*

June 21 2003
The Hulk Breaks Out!
(3-D)

Motion Effects! Special Edition Collector's Cover!!

THE HULK BREAKS OUT!
Behind the Scenes With the Summer's MONSTER Movie

PLUS
• MONK RETURNS
• HOW TO FIX *THE WEST WING*
• *FOR LOVE OR MONEY*

June 21 2003
The Hulk Breaks Out!
(3-D)

3-D! Motion! Collect Our 2 Special Effects Covers This Week

THE HULK BREAKS OUT!
Behind the Scenes With the Summer's MONSTER Movie

PLUS
• MONK RETURNS
• HOW TO FIX *THE WEST WING*
• *FOR LOVE OR MONEY*

June 21 2003
The Hulk Breaks Out!
(3-D)

Motion Effects! Special Edition Collector's Cover!!

THE HULK BREAKS OUT!
Behind the Scenes With the Summer's MONSTER Movie

PLUS
• MONK RETURNS
• HOW TO FIX *THE WEST WING*
• *FOR LOVE OR MONEY*

June 21 2003
The Hulk Breaks Out!
(3-D)

Motion Effects! Special Edition Collector's Cover!!

THE HULK BREAKS OUT!
Behind the Scenes With the Summer's MONSTER Movie

PLUS
• MONK RETURNS
• HOW TO FIX *THE WEST WING*
• *FOR LOVE OR MONEY*

June 21 2003
The Hulk Breaks Out!
(3-D)

CAESAR TV-MOVIE: SEX AND THE CITY'S MR. BIG IN A TOGA?

How Kelly Ripa Keeps Her Marriage Hot
...Even with 3 Kids, 2 TV Series and Husband Mark's Movie Career

June 28 2003
Kelly Ripa and Mark Consuelos

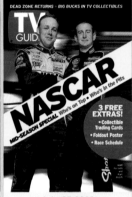

DEAD ZONE RETURNS • BIG BUCKS IN TV COLLECTIBLES

NASCAR
MID-SEASON SPECIAL Who's on Top • Who's in the Pits

3 FREE EXTRAS!
• Collectible Trading Cards
• Foldout Poster
• Race Schedule

July 05 2003
Matt Kenseth and Kurt Busch

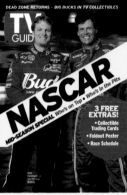

DEAD ZONE RETURNS • BIG BUCKS IN TV COLLECTIBLES

NASCAR
MID-SEASON SPECIAL Who's on Top • Who's in the Pits

3 FREE EXTRAS!
• Collectible Trading Cards
• Foldout Poster
• Race Schedule

July 05 2003
Dale Earnhardt Jr. and
Michael Waltrip

WITHOUT A TRACE
The Real Stories Behind the Show

TV'S NEW TARZAN!
MEET THE HUNK WHO'S SOON TO BE TV'S HOTTEST STAR

July 12 2003
Travis Fimmel of
Tarzan

TV's New TARZAN!
Meet the hunk who's soon to be TV's hottest star

WITHOUT A TRACE
The Real Stories Behind the Shows

July 12 2003
Anthony LaPaglia and
Poppy Montgomery of
Without A Trace

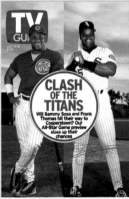

CLASH OF THE TITANS
Will Sammy Sosa and Frank Thomas hit their way to Cooperstown? Our All-Star Game preview sizes up their chances

July 12 2003
Sammy Sosa of the Cubs and
Frank Thomas of the White Sox

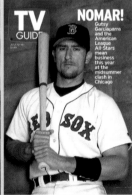

NOMAR!
Gutsy Garciaparra and the American League All-Stars mean business this year at the midsummer clash in Chicago

July 12 2003
Nomar Garciaparra of the
Red Sox

PUJOLS POWER!
Albert Pujols and the National League All-Stars mean business this year at the midsummer clash in Chicago

July 12 2003
Albert Pujols of the Cardinals

LET'S GO, ICHIRO!
Suzuki's sizzling play this season makes him an all-star among All-Stars

July 12 2003
Ichiro Suzuki of the Mariners

ACCORDING TO JIM
Critics Roasted It, You Love It
Belushi wouldn't have it any other way

The Truth About Cedric's Cancellation

Nip/Tuck: The Show That Makes Extreme Makeover Look Tame!

July 19 2003
Courtney Thorne-Smith and
Jim Belushi of
According to Jim

THE RESTAURANT SERVES UP CELEBRITY

IN DEFENSE OF MARTHA

**Forget Trek!
STARGATE SG-1**
is now sci-fi's biggest hit!
(Get ready for an underwater spin-off, too)

July 26 2003
Richard Dean Anderson and
Michael Shanks of
Stargate SG-1

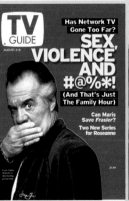

Has Network TV Gone Too Far?

SEX, VIOLENCE, AND #@%*!
(And That's Just The Family Hour)

Can Maris Save *Frasier*?
Two New Series for Roseanne

August 02 2003
Tony Sirico of
The Sopranos

KILLER SHARKS...
HEIDI KLUM IN A BIKINI...
WHAT MORE COULD GUYS WANT? Page 24

HE'S KING OF LATE NIGHT
THEY PAY HIM $17 MILLION

WHY CAN'T JAY LENO JUST RELAX?

August 09 2003
Jay Leno of
The Tonight Show;
Heidi Klum

MORE TRADING SPACES
Spin-offs, Specials, DVDs, Books, Furniture

IS NOAH WYLE LEAVING ER?

JAMIE KENNEDY INTERVIEW

THE BEST OF BOB HOPE'S TV SHOWS

August 16 2003
Paige Davis of
Trading Spaces;
Bob Hope

THE BEST OF BOB HOPE'S TV SHOWS

TRADING SPACES IS BUSTING OUT!
SPIN-OFFS, SPECIALS, DVDs, BOOKS, FURNITURE

IS NOAH WYLE LEAVING ER?

August 16 2003
Paige Davis of
Trading Spaces;
Bob Hope

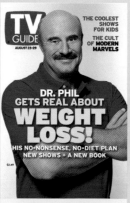

August 23 2003
Dr. Phil Gets Real About
Weight Loss

August 30 2003
Ellen DeGeneres and
Her Character, Dory, in
Finding Nemo

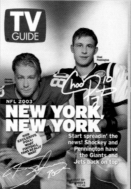

August 30 2003
Jeremy Shockey of the Giants and
Chad Pennington of the Jets

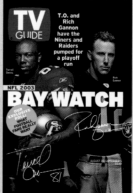

August 30 2003
Terrell Owens of the 49ers and
Rich Gannon of the Raiders

August 30 2003
Warren Sapp of the Buccaneers
and Rich Gannon of the Raiders

August 30 2003
Brian Urlacher of the Bears

August 30 2003
Jake Plummer of the Broncos

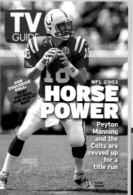

August 30 2003
Peyton Manning of the Colts

August 30 2003
Bill Parcells of the Cowboys

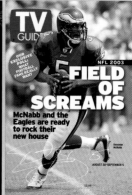

August 30 2003
Donovan McNabb of the Eagles

August 30 2003
Michael Vick of the Falcons

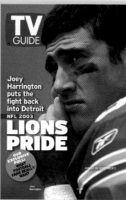

August 30 2003
Joey Harrington of the Lions

August 30 2003
Brett Favre of the Packers

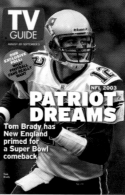

August 30 2003
Tom Brady of the Patriots

August 30 2003
Marshall Faulk of the Rams

August 30 2003
Champ Bailey of the Redskins

August 30 2003
Hines Ward of the Steelers

September 06 2003
David Boreanaz and James
Marsters of *Angel*; Jeff Probst
(*Survivor*); Jennifer Garner (*Alias*)

September 13 2003
Fall Preview

September 20 2003
Jennifer Aniston, David Schwimmer,
and Matt LeBlanc of
Friends

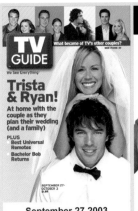

September 27 2003
Trista Rehn and
Ryan Sutter in
Trista & Ryan's Wedding

October 04 2003
Oprah Winfrey – Oprah
Opens Up!; Jessica Simpson
& Nick Lachey

October 11 2003
Rob Lowe of *West Wing*;
David Boreanaz and
James Marsters of *Angel*

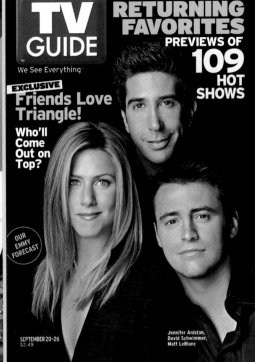

Jennifer Aniston,
David Schwimmer,
Matt LeBlanc

SEPTEMBER 20-26
$2.49

October 18 2003
Kiefer Sutherland and
Dennis Haysbert of
24

October 25 2003
David Smith and
Evan Marriott of
Joe Millionaire

October 25 2003
Keanu Reeves in
The Matrix Revolutions

Friends premiered on September 22, 1994 and
became the anchor of NBC's "Must See TV" Thursday
lineup. Like **Farrah Fawcett** before her, **Jennifer
Aniston**'s haircut became the most requested style in
salons across the country. The *Friends* parted ways
on May 6, 2004 with a two-hour series finale.

October 25 2003
Keanu Reeves in
The Matrix Revolutions
(3-D)

October 25 2003
Keanu Reeves in
The Matrix Revolutions
(3-D)

October 25 2003
Hugo Weaving and Keanu Reeves
in *Matrix Revolutions*
(3-D)

November 01 2003
Ashton Kutcher of
That 70's Show and *Punked*;
Ty Pennington

November 08 2003
Benjamin McKenzie and
Mischa Barton of *The O.C.*;
John Ritter

November 08 2003
The Cast of
8 Simple Rules

November 15 2003
Reba McEntire;
Judy Davis and James Brolin
as The Reagans

November 22 2003
Clay Aiken of
American Idol

November 22 2003
Ruben Studdard of
American Idol

November 29 2003
Jennifer Garner of *Alias*;
Art Carney

GREATEST TV MOMENTS OF 2003

WATCH OUR ABC SPECIAL DECEMBER 28TH

We See Everything™

WE DECORATED
WE BLUSHED
WE CRIED
WE LAUGHED
WE VOTED
WE GOT ALL MUSHY

TV Guide celebrated the end of 2003 by giving us two great covers and a TV special, *TV Guide: Greatest Moments of 2003*, which aired December 28, 2003. With **George Lopez** hosting and featuring a cavalcade of celebrities, the special polled America to honor the top television stars of 2003.

We enlarged both these covers so you can fully appreciate them. There's **Ruben** and **Clay** from *American Idol*, and **Paige Davis** of *Trading Spaces* in her wallpaper outfit. Remember **Trista** and **Ryan** getting married? Kisses between **Homer** and **Grady** on *The Simpsons*, **Joey** and **Rachel** on *Friends*, and **Britney** and **Madonna** on the *MTV Video Awards*. And we mourned **John Ritter**'s passing on September 11, 2003.

BEST & WORST OF 2003

AN ENTIRE YEAR OF TV IN JUST ONE MAGAZINE!

We See Everything™

WATCH OUR ABC SPECIAL DECEMBER 28TH

AMAZING MAKEOVERS!
WEIRD HOOKUPS!
SAD TIMES
BAD GIRLS!
SHOCKING SHOWDOWNS!
MADE-FOR-TV WEDDINGS!

DECEMBER 27-JANUARY 2

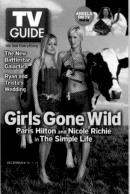

December 06 2003
Nicole Richie and Paris Hilton of *The Simple Life*; Emma Thompson in *Angels in America*

December 06 2003
Matt Kenseth

December 06 2003
Travis Kvapil

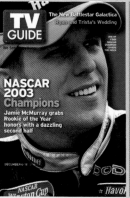

December 06 2003
Jamie McMurray

December 06 2003
Brian Vickers

December 13 2003
Survivor: Pearl Islands – The Final Five; Burton, Darrah, John, Sandra, and Lillian

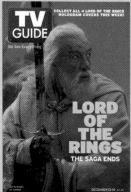

December 13 2003
Ian McKellen in *Lord of the Rings: The Return of the King*

December 13 2003
Viggo Mortensen in *Lord of the Rings: The Return of the King*

December 13 2003
Elijah Wood in *Lord of the Rings: The Return of the King*

December 13 2003
Gollum in *Lord of the Rings: The Return of the King*

December 20 2003
Kevin James and Leah Remini of *King of Queens*; George Eads; Sarah Jessica Parker; Tim McGraw

December 27 2003
Greatest TV Moments of 2003

December 27 2003
Best and Worst of 2003

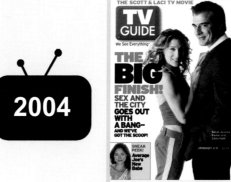

2004

January 03 2004
Sarah Jessica Parker and Chris
Noth of *Sex and the City*; Larissa
Meek of *Average Joe: Hawaii*

January 10 2004
We Salute the Best Military
Shows Ever!

January 10 2004
Mark Harmon of *NCIS*;
Nancy Kerrigan

January 17 2004
Sue, Alicia, and
Chapera Teammates of
All-Star Survivor

January 17 2004
Richard, Lex, and
Mogo Mogo Teammates
of *All-Star Survivor*

January 17 2004
Jerri, Rupert, and
Saboga Teammates of
All-Star Survivor

January 24 2004
Amber Tamblyn of
Joan of Arcadia

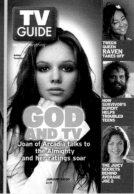

January 24 2004
Amber Tamblyn of *Joan of
Arcadia*; Raven; Rupert
Boneham; Larissa Meek

January 31 2004
David Boreanaz of
Angel

January 31 2004
Peyton Manning of the Colts

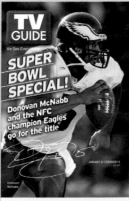

January 31 2004
Donovan McNabb of the Eagles

January 31 2004
Jake Delhomme of the Panthers

January 31 2004
Tom Brady of the Patriots

February 07 2004
Omarosa, Donald Trump, and
Ereka of *The Apprentice*; Meredith
Phillips of *The Bachelorette*

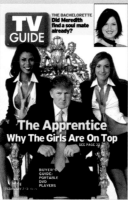

February 07 2004
Omarosa, Donald Trump, and
Ereka of *The Apprentice*; Meredith
Phillips of *The Bachelorette*

February 14 2004
NASCAR – Dual-Image Race
Cars; Dale Earnhardt Jr.; Jeff
Gordon; Kevin Harvick

February 14 2004
NASCAR – Dual-Image Race
Cars; Dale Earnhardt Jr.; Jeff
Gordon; Kevin Harvick

February 14 2004
NASCAR – Dual-Image Race
Cars; Dale Earnhardt Jr.; Jeff
Gordon; Kevin Harvick

227

February 14 2004
Parminder Nagra, Maura Tierney,
and Linda Cardelli of
ER

February 21 2004
Johnny Depp; Jennifer Aniston;
Sarah Jessica Parker –
Before They Were Stars!

February 21 2004
Ruben Studdard
and Simon Cowell of
American Idol

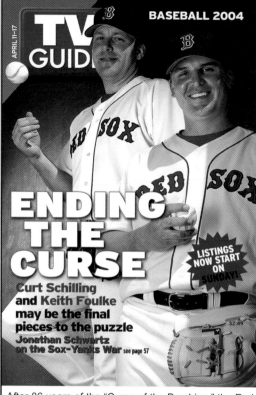

After 86 years of the "Curse of the Bambino," the Red
Sox won the World Series pennant in 2004, and
thanks to television, we got to see it. A feature movie
involving the Red Sox, *Fever Pitch*, happened to be
shooting at the time and captured the excitement of
the fans at that year's World Series on film.

February 28 2004
Viggo Mortensen; Orlando Bloom;
Johnny Depp – Oscar's
Year of the Hunks

March 06 2004
The Cast of *The Sopranos*:
Edie Falco, James Gandolfini,
Michael Imperioli,

Fold Out
Steve Buscemi, Drea de Matteo,
Dominic Chianese, Tony Sirico,
and Steven Van Zandt

March 13 2004
LaToya London, Diana DeGarmo,
and Matt Rogers of
American Idol

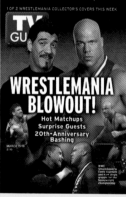

March 13 2004
Eddie Guerrero and
Kurt Angle of
WWE SmackDown!

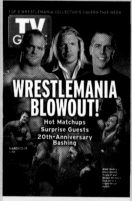

March 13 2004
Chris Benoit, Triple H, and
Shawn Michaels of
WWE RAW

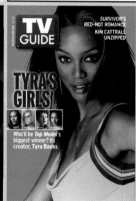

March 20 2004
Tyra Banks of *Top Model*; April
Wilkner; Shandi Sullivan; Yoanna
House; Mercedes Selba-Shorte

March 20 2004
Rob Mariano and Amber
Brkich of *Survivor*; Kim Catrall
of *Sex and the City*

March 20 2004
NCAAs: Carolina's Rashad
McCants

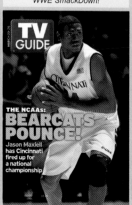

March 20 2004
NCAAs: Cincinnati's Jason Maxiell

March 20 2004
NCAAs: UCONN's Emeka Okafor

March 20 2004
NCAAs: Duke's Chris Duhon

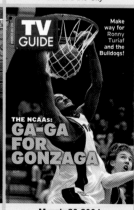

March 20 2004
NCAAs: Gonzaga's Ronny Turiaf

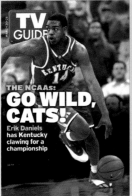

March 20 2004
NCAAs: Kentucky's Erik Daniels

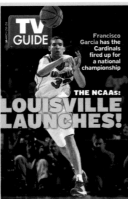

March 20 2004
NCAAs: Louisville's Francisco Garcia

March 20 2004
NCAAs: Pittsburgh's Carl Krauser

March 20 2004
NCAAs: St. Joseph's Jameer Nelson

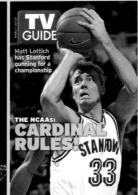

March 20 2004
NCAAs: Stanford's Matt Lottich

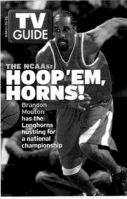

March 20 2004
NCAAs: Texas's Brandon Mouton

March 27 2004
Star Jones

March 27 2004
Star Jones; Sarah Michelle Gellar; William Petersen; Jim Caviezel

March 27 2004
Star Jones; Sarah Michelle Gellar; William Petersen; Jim Caviezel

April 03 2004
Where Are They Now?
(Special Eight Day Issue)

April 03 2004
Vladimir Guerrero of the Angels
(Special Eight Day Issue)

April 03 2004
Andy Pettitte and Roger Clemens of the Astros
(Special Eight Day Issue)

April 03 2004
Kerry Wood and Mark Prior of the Cubs
(Special Eight Day Issue)

April 03 2004
Josh Beckett of the Marlins
(Special Eight Day Issue)

April 03 2004
Jim Thorne of the Phillies
(Special Eight Day Issue)

April 03 2004
Ivan Rodriguez of the Tigers
(Special Eight Day Issue)

April 11 2004
Nick Lachey and Jessica Simpson

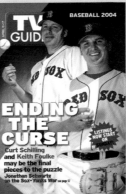

April 11 2004
Curt Schilling and Keith Foulke of the Red Sox

April 11 2004
Alex Rodriguez and Derek Jeter of the Yankees

April 18 2004
Jesse Palmer with Suzie and Trish of
The Bachelor

229

April 25 2004
Ty Pennington of *Extreme Makeover: Home Edition*; Rachel Luttrell; Jason Bateman

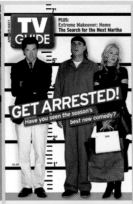

April 25 2004
Jason Bateman, Jeffrey Tambor, and Portia de Rossi of *Arrested Development*

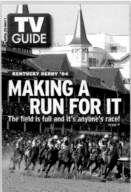

April 25 2004
Kentucky Derby '04

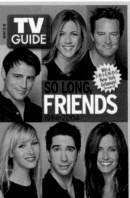

May 02 2004
The Cast of *Friends* – So Long, *Friends*

May 09 2004
Dick Van Dyke and Mary Tyler Moore of *The Dick Van Dyke Show*

May 16 2004
Nikki Cox and Josh Duhamel of *Las Vegas*

May 16 2004
Britney Spears – What It Might Cost to Look Like Britney

Fold Out
Makeover Madness!

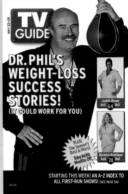

May 23 2004
Dr. Phil's Weight-Loss Success Stories!

May 30 2004
Sarah Michelle Gellar of *Buffy the Vampire Slayer*

May 30 2004
Leonard Nimoy and William Shatner of *Star Trek*

May 30 2004
David Duchovny and Gillian Anderson of *The X-Files*

May 30 2004
The Simpsons

June 06 2004
Brooke Burns of *North Shore*

June 06 2004
Brooke Burns of *North Shore*

June 13 2004
Peter Krause and Rachel Griffiths of *Six Feet Under*

June 13 2004
Kim Cattrall, Sarah Jessica Parker, Cynthia Nixon, and Kristin Davis of *Sex and the City*

June 20 2004
Dylan Walsh, Joely Richardson, and Julian McMahon of *Nip/Tuck*

June 27 2004
Rachel (*The Swan*); Rupert (*Survivor*); Trista & Ryan of (*Bachelorette*); Bill (*Apprentice*)

June 27 2004
Dale Earnhardt Jr.

July 04 2004
A Tribute to Elvis Presley:
The King

July 04 2004
A Tribute to Elvis Presley:
The King

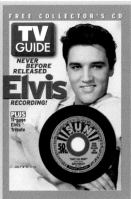

July 04 2004
A Tribute to Elvis Presley:
The King

July 04 2004
A Tribute to Elvis Presley:
The King

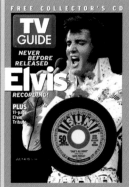

July 04 2004
A Tribute to Elvis Presley:
The King

July 11 2004
Will Ferrell in
Anchorman –
Move Over, Ted Baxter

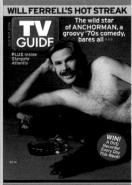

July 11 2004
Will Ferrell as
Ron Burgundy

Fold Out
in *Anchorman*

July 18 2004
Oprah Winfrey;
Brad Pitt & Jennifer Aniston;
Katie Couric

July 25 2004
Fantasia; The Donald;
Paris & Nicole – Cheers & Jeers:
Special Reality-TV Edition

August 01 2004
Beldar Conehead and
Captain Jean-Luc Picard –
25 Greatest Sci-Fi Legends

August 01 2004
George Jetson and
Seven of Nine –
25 Greatest Sci-Fi Legends

August 01 2004
ALF and Fox Mulder –
25 Greatest Sci-Fi Legends

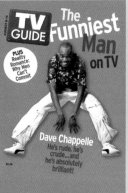

August 08 2004
Dave Chappelle of
Chapelle's Show

August 15 2004
Basketball Superstar,
Swin Cash

August 15 2004
Swimming Sensation,
Natalie Coughlin

August 15 2004
Decathlon World Champion,
Tom Pappas

August 15 2004
Prince of the Pool,
Michael Phelps

August 22 2004
Mel Gibson – The Secret Passion
of Mel Gibson

August 29 2004
Matt LeBlanc of
Joey

231

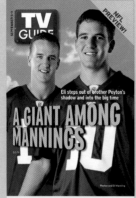

September 05 2004
Peyton and Eli Manning –
A Giant Among Mannings

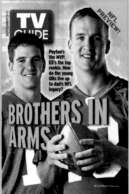

September 05 2004
Eli and Peyton Manning –
Brothers in Arms

September 05 2004
Eli and Peyton Manning –
The Manning Legacy

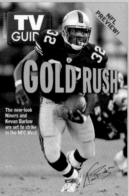

September 05 2004
Kevan Barlow of the 49ers

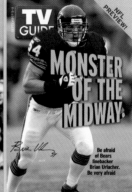

September 05 2004
Brian Urlacher of the Bears

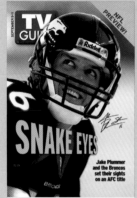

September 05 2004
Jake Plummer of the Broncos

September 05 2004
Roy Williams of the Cowboys

September 05 2004
Jevon Kearse and Terrell Owens
of the Eagles

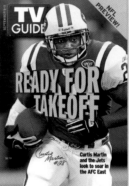

September 05 2004
Curtis Martin of the Jets

September 05 2004
Charles Rogers and Roy Williams
of the Lions

September 05 2004
Brett Favre of the Packers

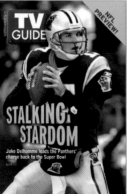

September 05 2004
Jake Delhomme of the Panthers

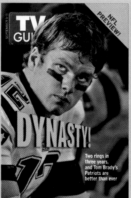

September 05 2004
Tom Brady of the Patriots

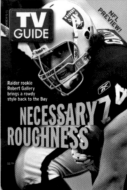

September 05 2004
Robert Gallery of the Raiders

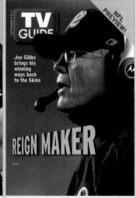

September 05 2004
Coach Joe Gibbs of the Redskins

September 05 2004
Ben Roethlisberger and Tommy
Maddox of the Steelers

September 12 2004
Heather Locklear of
LAX

September 12 2004
Heather Locklear of
LAX

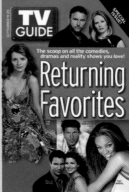

September 19 2004
*CSI; The O.C.; Will & Grace;
Extreme Makeover: Home Edition;
Top Model* – Returning Favorites

September 26 2004
Melina Kanakaredes and
Gary Sinise of
CSI: NY

October 03 2004
Maria, Donald Trump,
and Raj of
Apprentice 2

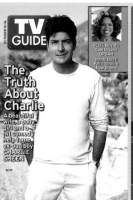

October 10 2004
Charlie Sheen of
Two and a Half Men;
Oprah Winfrey

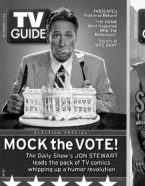

October 17 2004
Jon Stewart of
The Daily Show

October 24 2004
Dominic Monaghan, Evangeline
Lilly, and Matthew Fox of
Lost

October 31 2004
Peter Gallagher, Benjamin
McKenzie, and Adam Brody of
The O.C.

October 31 2004
Mischa Barton, Kelly Rowan,
and Rachel Bilson of
The O.C.

November 07 2004
Teri Hatcher, Eva Longoria, Marcia
Cross, and Felicity Huffman of
Desperate Housewives

November 07 2004
Shania Twain – Shania
Speaks Candidly

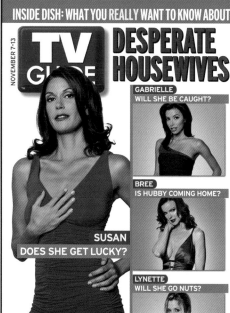

Desperate Housewives won two Screen Actors
Guild Awards while still in its first season. Three of
the "desperate housewives" were nominated for
Emmys and four for Golden Globes in 2005.
Felicity Huffman won the statue and **Teri Hatcher**
won the globe. The Scavo Brothers were #4 on
TV Guide's list of TV's 10 Biggest Brats.

November 14 2004
Clay Aiken: How Singing
Saved His Life

November 21 2004
Seinfeld Reunion

November 28 2004
Teri Hatcher and
James Denton of
Desperate Housewives

December 05 2004
The Beatles Appear on
The Ed Sullivan Show

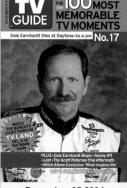

December 05 2004
Charles and Diana Wed

December 05 2004
Dale Earnhardt Dies at Daytona

December 05 2004
Elvis Stages Comeback Concert

December 05 2004
Kirk & Uhura Kiss on
Star Trek

December 12 2004
Happy Holidays from
The Simpsons

December 12 2004
Bart Simpson of
The Simpsons
(Lenticular)

December 12 2004
Homer and Maggie
The Simpsons
(Lenticular)

December 12 2004
The Simpsons
(Lenticular)

December 12 2004
Marge and Homer of
The Simpsons
(Lenticular)

December 19 2004
Matthew Fox of
Lost

December 19 2004
Evangeline Lilly of
Lost

December 26 2004
Stefan Vardon, Ty Pennington,
and Hydeia Broadbent of
Extreme Makeover: Home Edition

2005

January 02 2005
Anthony LaPaglia, Poppy
Montgomery, and Eric Close of
Without a Trace

January 09 2005
Kiefer Sutherland of
24

January 16 2005
Joan Rivers and Melissa Rivers;
Jennifer Garner; Johnny Depp;
Marcia Cross

January 23 2005
Eva Longoria and Jesse Metcalf of
Desperate Housewives; Jerry
Orbach; David Cassidy

January 30 2005
Naveen Andrews of
Lost

January 30 2005
Matthew Fox of
Lost

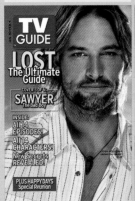

January 30 2005
Josh Holloway of
Lost

January 30 2005
Evangeline Lilly of
Lost

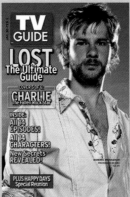

January 30 2005
Dominic Monaghan of
Lost

January 30 2005
Terry O'Quinn of
Lost

February 06 2005
Jennifer Garner of
Alias

February 13 2005
Johnny Carson (1966):
An Intimate Scrapbook

February 13 2005
Johnny Carson (1992):
An Intimate Scrapbook

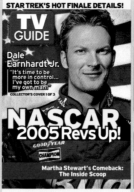

February 20 2005
Dale Earnhardt Jr.

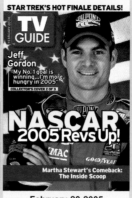

February 20 2005
Jeff Gordon

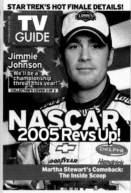

February 20 2005
Jimmie Johnson

February 27 2005
Gary Dourdan, Marg
Helgenberger, and George Eads
of *CSI*

March 06 2005
Rob Mariano and Amber
Brkich of *The Amazing Race*;
John Stamos

March 13 2005
Kirstie Alley of *Fat Actress*;
The Men of
Desperate Housewives

March 20 2005
Katee Sackhoff, Tricia Helfer, and
Grace Park of *Battlestar Galactica*;
Simon Cowell of *American Idol*

March 20 2005
Jill Hennessy of *Crossing
Jordan*; Simon Cowell of
American Idol

CSI began in 2000 and has been nominated for multiple Emmy awards every year since. It is based in Las Vegas and already has two spin-offs; *CSI: Miami* debuted in 2002 and *CSI: NY* in 2004. The show has sparked interest in criminal justice investigation, and students are rushing to enroll in training classes.

March 27 2005
Patricia Arquette of *Medium*;
Mark Harmon of *NCIS*

April 03 2005
Josh Holloway of
Lost

April 03 2005
Johnny Damon of the
Boston Red Sox

April 03 2005
Curt Schilling of the
Boston Red Sox

April 10 2005
Alexis Bledel and Matt
Czuchry of *Gilmore Girls*;
Seth Cohen

April 10 2005
Lauren Graham and Scott
Patterson of *Gilmore Girls*;
Seth Cohen

235

April 17 2005
Jolene Blalock, Scott Bakula,
and Connor Trinneer of
Star Trek: Enterprise

April 17 2005
Star Trek: Ultimate Tribute –
The First Officers

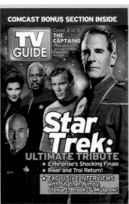

April 17 2005
Star Trek: Ultimate Tribute –
The Captains

April 17 2005
Star Trek: Ultimate Tribute –
The Heroic Crew

April 24 2005
Kiefer Sutherland of
24

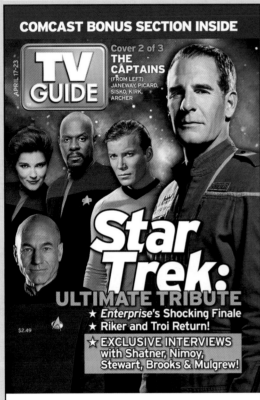

The original *Star Trek* premiered on September 8, 1966. Because of low ratings, NBC almost cancelled it after its second season, but diehard fans saved it. With four spinoffs and ten feature films, the *Star Trek* premise is still going strong and in 2004, **TV Guide** named it as the #1 Cult Show.

May 01 2005
Ewan McGregor and Hayden
Christensen in *Star Wars:
Episode III – Revenge of the Sith*

May 01 2005
Ewan McGregor and Hayden
Christensen in *Star Wars: Episode
III – Revenge of the Sith* (3-D)

May 01 2005
Hayden Christensen in *Star Wars:
Episode III – Revenge of the Sith*
(3-D)

May 01 2005
Natalie Portman in *Star Wars:
Episode III – Revenge of the Sith*
(3-D)

May 01 2005
Ian McDiarmid in *Star Wars:
Episode III – Revenge of the Sith*
(3-D)

May 01 2005
The Wookiees in *Star Wars:
Episode III – Revenge of the Sith*
(3-D)

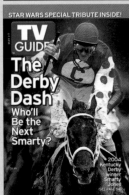

May 01 2005
The Derby Dash –
Smarty Jones, 2004 Winner

May 08 2005
Elvis Presley – Candid Moment,
1956

May 08 2005
Elvis Presley – Tampa Concert,
1955

May 08 2005
Elvis Presley – Rare Publicity Still,
1956

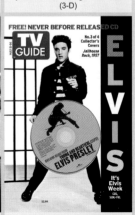

May 08 2005
Elvis Presley – Jailhouse Rock,
1957

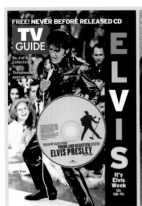

May 08 2005
Elvis Presley – The Comeback
Special, 1968

May 15 2005
Patrica Heaton and
Ray Romano of
Everybody Loves Raymond

May 15 2005
The Cast of
Everybody Loves Raymond –
Bye Ray!

THE BIG MOVIE GUIDE IS BACK
OVER **1,100** MOVIES REVIEWED & RATED

SUMMER
PREVIEW
19 NEW
SHOWS

Inside the Finale

LOST
Hot New Secrets From
the Show's Creators!
SNEAK PEEK of Next Season

CLOCKWISE: JOSH HOLLOWAY, HAROLD PERRINEAU,
MALCOLM DAVID KELLEY, DANIEL DAE KIM (WEDNESDAY ON ABC)

Lost debuted on 9/22/2004 and combined all the
elements needed for a hit show. It won the Best
Drama Emmy for its first season. Focusing on the
survivors of a plane crash who are stranded on a
mysterious island where "everything happens for a
reason," viewers are on the edge of their seats to
see what happens next.

May 22 2005
Carrie, Bo, Vonzell,
and Anthony of
American Idol

May 29 2005
Josh Holloway, Daniel Dae Kim,
Harold Perrineau, and Malcolm
David Kelley of *Lost*

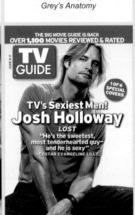

June 05 2005
Patrick Dempsey of
Grey's Anatomy

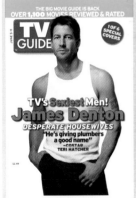

June 05 2005
James Denton of
Desperate Housewives

June 05 2005
Gary Dourdan of
CSI

June 05 2005
Josh Holloway of
Lost

June 05 2005
Hugh Laurie of
House

June 05 2005
Tom Westman of
Survivor

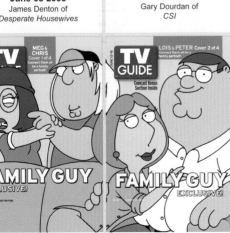

June 12 2005
Meg and Chris of
Family Guy

June 12 2005
Lois and Peter of
Family Guy

June 12 2005
Brian of
Family Guy

June 12 2005
Stewie of
Family Guy

SUMMER DIET SPECIAL

June 19 2005
Kelly Ripa – How She
Stays Sexy!

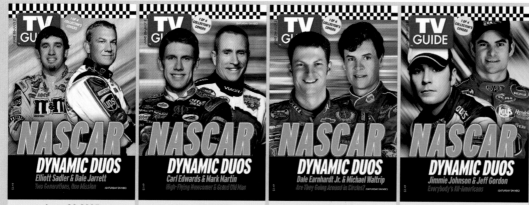

June 26 2005
Elliot Sadler & Dale Jarrett –
Two Generations, One Mission

June 26 2005
Carl Edwards & Mark Martin –
High-Flying Newcomer
& Grand Old Man

June 26 2005
Dale Earnhardt Jr. & Michael
Waltrip – Are They Going
Around in Circles?

June 26 2005
Jimmie Johnson & Jeff Gordon –
Everybody's All-Americans

July 03 2005
Ioan Gruffudd as
Mr. Fantastic in
Fantastic 4

July 03 2005
Jessica Alba as
The Invisible Woman in
Fantastic 4

July 03 2005
Michael Chiklis as
The Thing in
Fantastic 4

July 03 2005
Chris Evans as
The Human Torch in
Fantastic 4

July 03 2005
Julian McMahon as
Dr. Doom in
Fantastic 4

July 10 2005
Ben Browder, Tricia Helfer,
and Joe Flanigan –
Sci-Fi's Returning Favorites

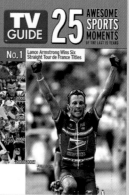
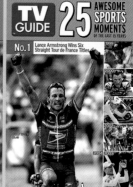

July 10 2005
Amanda Tapping and
Ben Browder of
Stargate SG-1

July 10 2005
Rachel Luttrell and
Joe Flanigan of
Stargate Atlantis

July 10 2005
James Calus and
Tricia Helfer of
Battlestar Galactica

July 17 2005
Lance Armstrong –
25 Awesome Sports Moments

July 17 2005
Lance Armstrong –
25 Awesome Sports Moments

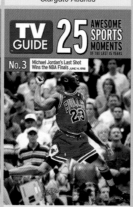

July 17 2005
Tiger Woods –
25 Awesome Sports Moments

July 17 2005
Michael Jordan –
25 Awesome Sports Moments

July 24 2005
Clay Aiken – The Intimate Truth:
Clay Opens Up

July 24 2005
Clay Aiken – The Intimate Truth:
Clay Opens Up

July 31 2005
Christopher Meloni and Mariska
Hargitay of *Law and Order: SVU*;
Indy Star Danica Patrick

July 31 2005
Indy Star Danica Patrick;
Christopher Meloni and Mariska
Hargitay of *Law and Order: SVU*

August 07 2005
Emily Proctor and David
Caruso of *CSI: Miami*;
Lucille Ball and Desi Arnaz

August 14 2005
John Lennon of
The Beatles

August 14 2005
Paul McCartney of
The Beatles

August 14 2005
George Harrison of
The Beatles

August 14 2005
Ringo Starr of
The Beatles

August 21 2005
Sela Ward and
Hugh Laurie of
House

August 28 2005
Yunjin Kim, Dominic Monaghan,
Evangline Lilly, and Jorge Garcia
of *Lost*; Peter Jennings

August 28 2005
Yunjin Kim, Dominic Monaghan,
Evangline Lilly, and Jorge Garcia
of *Lost*

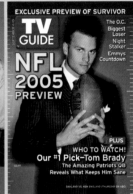

September 04 2005
Tom Brady of the Patriots

September 04 2005
Donovan McNabb of the Eagles
and Ben Roethlisberger of the
Steelers

September 11 2005
Bones; *Ghost Whisperer*; *E-Ring*;
Commander In Chief; *Everybody
Hates Chris*

September 11 2005
J. Love Hewitt; D. Boreanaz; M.
Stewart; C. Rock; B. Bratt; C.
Gugino; W. Miller; G. Davis

The original *Law & Order* premiered in 1990. Prior
to *CSI* spinning off into different cities, *Law & Order*
spun off into different branches of law enforcement.
Law & Order: Special Victims Unit appeared in 1999
and *Law & Order: Criminal Intent* in 2001. The third
spin-off, *Law & Order: Trial by Jury* showed up in
2005 but was cancelled after a brief 13 episodes.

September 18 2005
House; *Las Vegas*; *Without a Trace*;
Lost; *Grey's Anatomy* – Returning
Favorites

September 18 2005
House; *Las Vegas*; *Lost*; *Grey's
Anatomy*; *Without a Trace* –
Returning Favorites

September 25 2005
Marg Helgenberger, George
Eads, and Gary Dourdan
of *CSI*

September 25 2005
Robert David Hall, Jorja Fox, William Petersen, and Eric Szmanda of *CSI*

October 02 2005
Wentworth Miller of *Prison Break*

October 09 2005
The Cast of *Bernie Mac* as the Cast of *Good Times*

October 09 2005
Homer Simpson of *The Simpsons* as Fred Flintstone of *The Flintstones*

October 09 2005
Jennifer Love Hewitt of *Ghost Whisperer* as *The Flying Nun*

October 09 2005
Conan O'Brien of *Late Night* as Buffalo Bob of *The Howdy Doody Show*

October 09 2005
Kelly Ripa and Regis Philbin of *Live* as Jeannie and Major Nelson of *I Dream of Jeannie*

October 09 2005
Cast Members of *Scrubs* as Cast Members of *M*A*S*H*

October 09 2005
Greg Gumbel and Dan Marino of *The NFL Today* as Tubbs and Crockett of *Miami Vice*

October 09 2005
John Cryer and Charlie Sheen of *Two and a Half Men* as Felix and Oscar of *The Odd Couple*

October 09 2005
Reba McEntire of *Reba* as Lucy Ricardo of *I Love Lucy*

"That's why the Red Sox will never win the Series."
Christian Shepherd and Jack Shepherd,
Lost

Memorable TV Show Quotes from the 2000s

"I'm federal agent Jack Bauer, and today is the longest day of my life."
Jack Bauer, *24*

"You are the weakest link. Goodbye." Ann Robinson, *Weakest Link*

"Michael, I'm your big brother. I'll never be impressed with you."
George 'Gob' Bluth II, *Arrested Development*

"I'm wrong all the time. It's how I get to 'right.'" Gil Grissom, *CSI*

"I would like to give these kids a good home. In fact, there's one a few miles away from here... "
Bernie Mac, *The Bernie Mac Show*

"'Cult' is what a big congregation calls a little congregation."
Tom Baldwin, *The 4400*

Jake Harper: "You have to put a dollar in the swear jar. You said 'ass.'"
Charlie Harper: "Here's $20. That should cover me until lunch."
Two and a Half Men

"Massachusetts is a blue state. God has no place here."
Denny Crane, *Boston Legal*

"Write this down. E.M.E.T.I.B. Got it? Now, reverse it."
Sydney Bristow, *Alias*

The Tribute Covers

To mark the end of their digest era and their new beginning, **TV Guide** celebrated by having current stars recreate classic covers of the past. With so many shows and covers to choose from, we do not envy the person who had to make the decision of which covers to use.

Good Times ran from 1974 to 1979 and is perhaps most memorable for Jimmie Walker's "Dy-no-mite!" *The Flintstones* initially aired from 1960 to 1966 and the wacky stoneage characters also appeared in a number of TV movies. **TV Guide** chose the perfect person to portray *The Flying Nun* (1967 to 1970) – isn't there something kind of supernatural about a flying nun? Howdy Doody got his name because Bob Smith's ranch hand character on the radio show, *The Triple B Ranch*, would greet his sidekick, Elmer, with "Oh, hoho, howdy doody." Elmer's name was changed to Howdy Doody for TV and the original *The Howdy Doody Show* ran from 1947 to 1960. *M*A*S*H* first aired in 1972 and its finale in 1983 still holds the record for the largest series finale viewing audience. In 1984, *Miami Vice* appeared and by the end of the series run in 1990, men everywhere were wearing pastels, not wearing socks, and sporting 2-day stubble. Felix moved in with Oscar in 1970, and although *The Odd Couple* never made it to the Top 30, we still missed them when they left in 1975. **TV Guide** went national with an *I Love Lucy* cover so it's only fitting that the last digest cover be an *I Love Lucy* cover as well.

We're all sad to see the **TV Guide** digest go. We can't remember life without it, but we bet that in fifty years our children will say the same thing about the new version of **TV Guide**.

Kellita Smith, Jeremy Suarez, Dee Dee Davis, Camille Winbush, and Bernie Mac of *Bernie Mac* recreate the 1974 cover of Esther Rolle, Jimmie Walker, Ralph Carter, BerNadette Stanis, and John Amos of *Good Times*.

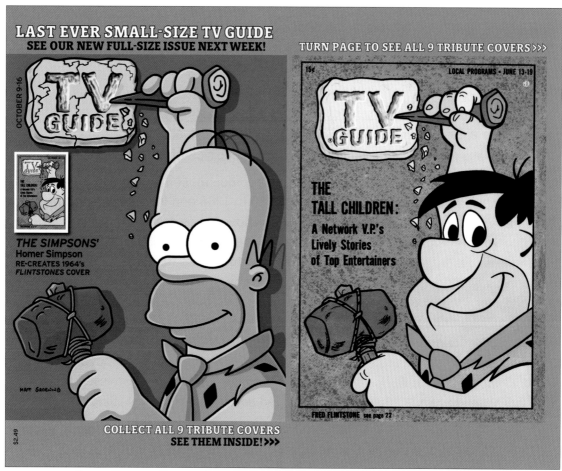

Homer Simpson of *The Simpsons* recreates Fred Flinstone of *The Flintstones*'s 1964 cover.

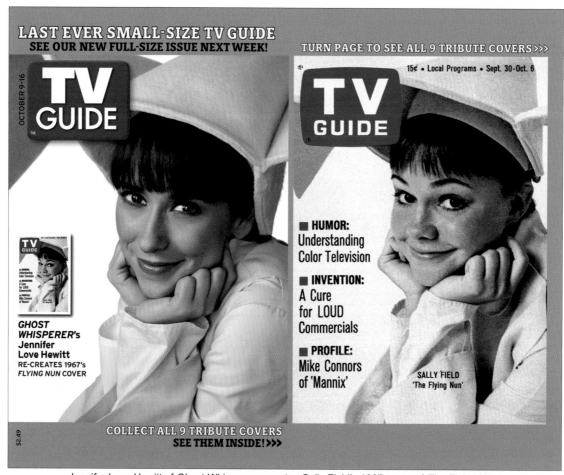

Jennifer Love Hewitt of *Ghost Whisperer* recreates Sally Field's 1967 cover of *The Flying Nun*.

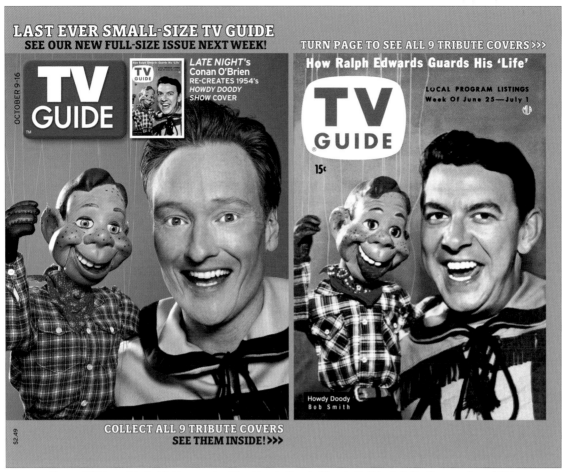

Conan O'Brien of *Late Night* recreates *The Howdy Doody Show*'s Buffalo Bob Smith cover from 1954.

Live's Regis Philbin and Kelly Ripa recreate Barbara Eden's and Larry Hagman's 1996 *I Dream of Jeannie* Cover.

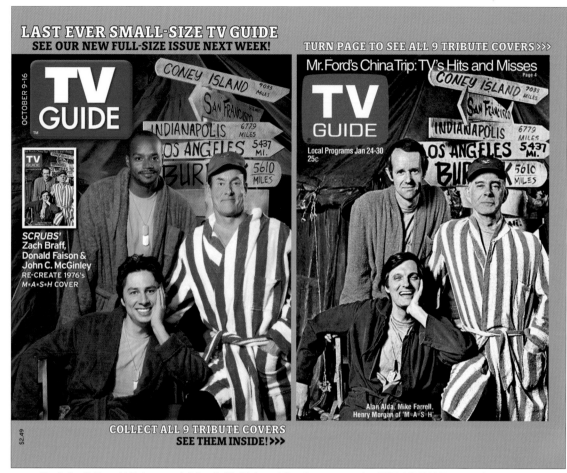

Zach Braff, Donald Faison, and John C. McGinley of *Scrubs* recreate the 1976 *M*A*S*H* cover of Alan Alda, Mike Farrell, and Harry Morgan.

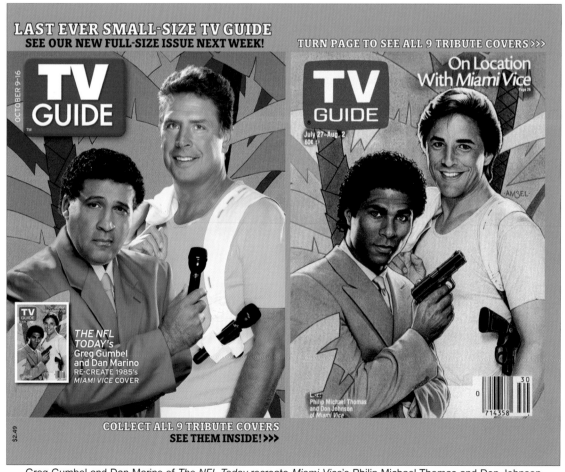

Greg Gumbel and Dan Marino of *The NFL Today* recreate *Miami Vice*'s Philip Michael Thomas and Don Johnson cover from 1985.

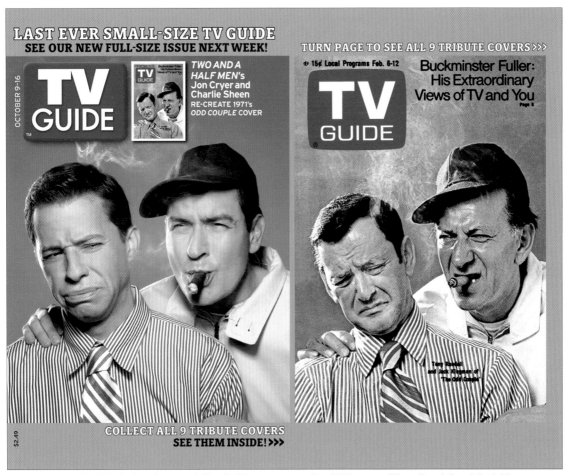

Two and a Half Men's Jon Cryer and Charlie Sheen recreate the 1971 cover of Tony Randall and Jack Klugman of *The Odd Couple.*

Reba McEntire of *Reba* recreates Lucille Ball's *I Love Lucy* commemorative cover from 2001.

Introducing...The New TV Guide!

ALL NEW!

TV GUIDE
™

October 17–23, 2005

TV Guide's
Extreme Makeover
Ty Pennington Breaks Out
the Big New *TV Guide*

Special
Price
99¢

> **This Week's Hottest TV**
39 Pages of Listings You'll Love!

Ty Pennington of *Extreme Makeover:
Home Edition* (Sunday on ABC)

EXCLUSIVE

ELLEN
A Day in My Life

LOST
The Creators Answer
Burning Questions!

CSI
Warrick's Secret
Wife Revealed

The First BIG TV Guide Cover!

Index and Value Guide

All values are for issues in mint condition.

Date . . . . .Caption . . . . .Value . . . .Page

1953

Date	Caption	Value	Page

1954

- [ ] 01-01-1954 . . .**Bing Crosby** – Why Bing Crosby Is Turning To TV $56 29
- [ ] 01-08-1954 . . .**Joan Caulfield** of *My Favorite Husband* $33 30
- [ ] 01-15-1954 . . .**Martha Raye** of *The Martha Raye Show* $32 30
- [ ] 01-22-1954 . . .**Jayne Meadows**, **Henry Morgan**, and **Joan Bennett** of *I've Got a Secret* $43 30
- [ ] 01-29-1954 . . .**Robert Montgomery** of *Robert Montgomery Presents* $38 30
- [ ] 02-05-1954 . . .**Jack Benny** of *The Jack Benny Program* $62 30
- [ ] 02-12-1954 . . .**Red Buttons** of *The Red Buttons Show* $32 30
- [ ] 02-19-1954 . . .**Ann Sothern** of *Private Secretary* $48 30
- [ ] 02-26-1954 . . .**Liberace** of *The Liberace Show* $25 30
- [ ] 03-05-1954 . . .**Marion Marlowe** and **Frank Parker** of *Arthur Godfrey and His Friends* . . $23 30
- [ ] 03-12-1954 . . .**Maria Riva** $28 30
- [ ] 03-19-1954 . . .**Groucho Marx** of *You Bet Your Life.* $144 30
- [ ] 03-26-1954 . . .**Jackie Gleason** of *The Jackie Gleason Show.* $79 30
- [ ] 04-02-1954 . . .**Eve Arden** of *Our Miss Brooks.* $62 30
- [ ] 04-09-1954 . . .**Charlie Applewhite** and **Milton Berle** of *The Milton Berle Show* $43 30
- [ ] 04-16-1954 . . .1954 Awards Issue $31 30
- [ ] 04-23-1954 . . .**Lucille Ball** of *I Love Lucy* $155 30
- [ ] 04-30-1954 . . .**Ben Alexander** and **Jack Webb** of *Dragnet* $62 31
- [ ] 05-07-1954 . . .**Harriet Nelson**, **Ricky Nelson**, and **David Nelson** of *Ozzie and Harriet* . . . $87 31
- [ ] 05-14-1954 . . .**Frank Sinatra** – Can Frank Make Good In TV? $87 31
- [ ] 05-21-1954 . . .**Patricia Benoit** and **Wally Cox** of *Mr. Peepers* $47 31
- [ ] 05-28-1954 . . .**Gale Storm** of *My Little Margie* $79 31
- [ ] 06-04-1954 . . .**Arthur Godfrey** – What Is Godfrey's Hold On Women? $39 31
- [ ] 06-11-1954 . . .**Ben Blue** and **Alan Young** of *The Saturday Night Revue.* $43 31
- [ ] 06-18-1954 . . .**Rise Stevens** and **Ed Sullivan** of *The Ed Sullivan Show* $48 31
- [ ] 06-25-1954 . . .**Bob Smith** and **Howdy Doody** of *The Howdy Doody Show.* $300 31
- [ ] 07-02-1954 . . .**Joan Davis** and **Jim Backus** of *I Married Joan* $60 31
- [ ] 07-09-1954 . . .**Arlene Francis** of *What's My Line?* $44 31
- [ ] 07-17-1954 . . .**Roy Rogers** of *The Roy Rogers Show* $275 31
- [ ] 07-24-1954 . . .**Jack Webb** and **Ann Robinson** of *Dragnet.* $30 31
- [ ] 07-31-1954 . . .**William Bendix** of *Life of Riley* $62 31
- [ ] 08-07-1954 . . .**Perry Como** of *The Perry Como Show* and Friends $51 31
- [ ] 08-14-1954 . . .**Jerry Lewis** and **Dean Martin** – Do Comics Hate Each Other? $140 31
- [ ] 08-21-1954 . . .**Jayne Meadows** of *I've Got a Secret* and
        Steve Allen of *The Steve Allen Show* $59 31
- [ ] 08-28-1954 . . .**Roxanne** of *Beat the Clock* $18 31
- [ ] 09-04-1954 . . .**Eddie Fisher** of *Coke Time* $28 31
- [ ] 09-11-1954 . . .**Betty Hutton** of *Satins and Spurs* $27 31
- [ ] 09-18-1954 . . .**Liberace** of *The Liberace Show.* $34 32
- [ ] 09-25-1954 . . .Fall Preview: 1954-1955 Shows $122 32
- [ ] 10-02-1954 . . .**Teresa Wright** and **Dick Powell** of *Climax!'s The Long Goodbye* $30 32
- [ ] 10-09-1954 . . .**Lucille Ball** of *I Love Lucy* $133 32
- [ ] 10-16-1954 . . .**Red Buttons** of *The Red Buttons Show* $27 32
- [ ] 10-23-1954 . . .**Walt Disney** of *Disneyland.* $247 32
- [ ] 10-30-1954 . . .**Barry Nelson** and **Joan Caulfield** of *My Favorite Husband.* $30 32
- [ ] 11-06-1954 . . .**Gracie Allen** and **George Burns** of *The Burns and Allen Show.* $79 32
- [ ] 11-13-1954 . . .**Joanne Rio** and **Liberace** of *The Liberace Show* $30 32
- [ ] 11-20-1954 . . .**Bebe Daniels** and **Ralph Edwards** of *This Is Your Life* $34 32
- [ ] 11-27-1954 . . .**Peter Lawford** and **Marcia Henderson** of *Dear Phoebe* $59 32
- [ ] 12-04-1954 . . .**George Gobel** of *The George Gobel Show.* $25 32
- [ ] 12-11-1954 . . .**Marion Marlowe** of *Arthur Godfrey and His Friends* $36 32
- [ ] 12-18-1954 . . .**Imogene Coca** of *The Imogene Coca Show.* $28 32
- [ ] 12-25-1954 . . .**The Nelson Family** of *Ozzie and Harriet* $122 32

1955

- [ ] 01-01-1955 . . .**Loretta Young** of *The Loretta Young Show* $71 32
- [ ] 01-08-1955 . . .**Arthur Godfrey** – Why Godfrey Doesn't Quit $32 32
- [ ] 01-15-1955 . . .**Bill Cullen**, **Jayne Meadows**, **Henry Morgan**, **Faye Emerson**,
        and **Garry Moore** of *I've Got a Secret* $36 32

1957

Date	Caption	Value	Page
☐ 03-16-1957	Your Guide To Television's Top Honors – *The Emmy Awards*	$15	39
☐ 03-23-1957	**Ernie Ford** of *The Ford Show*	$24	39
☐ 03-30-1957	**Julie Andrews** in Rodgers and Hammerstein's *Cinderella*	$30	39
☐ 04-06-1957	**Lawrence Welk** of *The Lawrence Welk Show*	$11	39
☐ 04-13-1957	**Nanette Fabray** of *Salute to Baseball*	$20	39
☐ 04-20-1957	**Loretta Young** of *The Loretta Young Show*	$27	39
☐ 04-27-1957	**Groucho Marx** of *You Bet Your Life*	$32	39
☐ 05-04-1957	**Hal March** and **Robert Strom** of *The $64,000 Question*	$10	39
☐ 05-11-1957	**James Arness** of *Gunsmoke*	$59	39
☐ 05-18-1957	**Esther Williams** of *Lux Video Theatre*	$26	39
☐ 05-25-1957	**Sid Caesar** of *Casesar's Hour*	$89	39
☐ 06-01-1957	**Ida Lupino** and **Howard Duff** of *Mr. Adams and Eve*	$34	40
☐ 06-08-1957	**Lassie**	$80	40
☐ 06-15-1957	**Red Skelton** of *The Red Skelton Show*	$31	40
☐ 06-22-1957	**Jack Bailey** of *Queen for a Day*	$20	40
☐ 06-29-1957	**Gale Storm** of *Oh! Susanna*	$34	40
☐ 07-06-1957	**Dorothy Kilgallen**, **Bennett Cerf**, **Arlene Francis**, and **John Daly** of *What's My Line?*	$38	40
☐ 07-13-1957	**Gail Davis** of *Annie Oakley*	$57	40
☐ 07-20-1957	**Julius La Rosa** of *The Julius La Rosa Show*	$11	40
☐ 07-27-1957	**Garry Moore** of *I've Got A Secret*	$13	40
☐ 08-03-1957	**Cleo** of *The People's Choice*	$44	40
☐ 08-10-1957	**Ann B. Davis** and **Bob Cummings** of *Love That Bob!*	$15	40
☐ 08-17-1957	**Phil Silvers** of *The Phil Silvers Show*	$78	40
☐ 08-24-1957	**Marjorie Lord** and **Danny Thomas** of *The Danny Thomas Show*	$11	40
☐ 08-31-1957	**Clint Walker** of *Cheyenne*	$75	40
☐ 09-07-1957	**Janette Davis** and **Arthur Godfrey** of *Arthur Godfrey and His Friends*	$21	40
☐ 09-14-1957	Fall Preview: 1957-1958 Shows	$127	40
☐ 09-21-1957	**Pat Boone** of *The Pat Boone Show*	$24	40
☐ 09-28-1957	**Gracie Allen** and **George Burns** of *The Burns and Allen Show*	$57	40
☐ 10-05-1957	**Joan Caulfield** of *Sally*	$13	40
☐ 10-12-1957	This Is The Week To Watch	$27	40
☐ 10-19-1957	**Loretta Young** of *The Loretta Young Show*	$27	41
☐ 10-26-1957	**Peter Lawford** and **Phyllis Kirk** of *The Thin Man*	$20	41
☐ 11-02-1957	**Lucille Ball** of *I Love Lucy*	$96	41
☐ 11-09-1957	**James Garner** of *Maverick*	$80	41
☐ 11-16-1957	**Patti Page** of *The Patti Page Show*	$18	41
☐ 11-23-1957	**Mary Martin** in *Annie Get Your Gun*	$15	41
☐ 11-30-1957	**Alfred Hitchcock** of *Alfred Hitchcock Presents*	$57	41
☐ 12-07-1957	**Dinah Shore** of *The Dinah Shore Show*	$30	41
☐ 12-14-1957	**Walt Disney** of *Disneyland*	$110	41
☐ 12-21-1957	Greetings	$26	41
☐ 12-28-1957	**Ricky Nelson** of *Ozzie and Harriet*	$78	41

1958

Date	Caption	Value	Page
☐ 01-04-1958	**Lawrence Welk** of *The Lawrence Welk Show*	$22	41
☐ 01-11-1958	**Gisele MacKenzie** of *Your Hit Parade*	$11	41
☐ 01-18-1958	**John Payne** of *The Restless Gun*	$59	41
☐ 01-25-1958	**Sid Caesar** and **Imogene Coca** of *Sid Caesar Invites You*	$26	41
☐ 02-01-1958	**Walter Winchell** of *The Walter Winchell File*	$15	42
☐ 02-08-1958	**Peggy King** and **Tab Hunter** in *Hallmark Hall of Fame's Hans Brinker*	$18	42
☐ 02-15-1958	A Great Week	$12	42
☐ 02-22-1958	**Rosemary Clooney** of *The Rosemary Clooney Show*	$23	42
☐ 03-01-1958	**Lassie**	$67	42
☐ 03-08-1958	**Arthur Godfrey** of *Arthur Godfrey and His Friends*	$11	42
☐ 03-15-1958	**Amanda Blake** and **James Arness** of *Gunsmoke*	$64	42
☐ 03-22-1958	**Perry Como** of *The Perry Como Show*	$24	42
☐ 03-29-1958	**Tennessee Ernie Ford** of *The Ford Show*	$14	42
☐ 04-05-1958	**Gale Storm** of *The Gale Storm Show*	$37	42
☐ 04-12-1958	**Hugh O'Brian** of *Wyatt Earp*	$56	42
☐ 04-19-1958	**Polly Bergen** of *The Polly Bergen Show*	$31	42

Date	Caption	Value	Page
04-26-1958	**Guy Williams** of *Zorro*	$131	42
05-03-1958	**Shirley Temple** of *Shirley Temple Theatre*	$60	42
05-10-1958	**Richard Boone** of *Have Gun, Will Travel*	$66	42
05-17-1958	**Danny Thomas** of *The Danny Thomas Show*	$23	42
05-24-1958	**Dick Clark** of *American Bandstand*	$95	42
05-31-1958	**Phyllis Kirk** of *The Thin Man*	$13	42
06-07-1958	**Pat Boone** of *The Pat Boone Show*	$15	42
06-14-1958	**Jane Wyatt** and **Robert Young** of *Father Knows Best*	$34	42
06-21-1958	**Ed Sullivan** of *The Ed Sullivan Show*	$28	43
06-28-1958	**Jerry Mathers** of *Leave It to Beaver*	$131	43
07-05-1958	**Bill Cullen** of *The Price Is Right*	$37	43
07-12-1958	**Lucille Ball** of *The Lucy-Desi Comedy Hour*	$87	43
07-19-1958	**Dale Robertson** of *Wells Fargo*	$56	43
07-26-1958	**Paula Raymond** and **Marvin Miller** of *The Millionaire*	$33	43
08-02-1958	**Walter Brennan** of *The Real McCoys*	$27	43
08-09-1958	**Steve Lawrence** and **Eydie Gorme** of *The Steve Lawrence and Eydie Gorme Show*	$37	43
08-16-1958	**Robert Horton** and **Ward Bond** of *Wagon Train*	$57	43
08-23-1958	**Edie Adams** and **Janet Blair** of *The Chevy Show*	$14	43
08-30-1958	**Bud Collyer**, **Polly Bergen**, and **Kitty Carlisle** of *To Tell the Truth*	$26	43
09-06-1958	**Arthur Godfrey** of *Arthur Godfrey and His Friends*	$14	43
09-13-1958	**Kathy, Dianne, Peggy**, and **Janet Lennon**, and **Lawrence Welk** of *The Lawrence Welk Show*	$11	43
09-20-1958	Fall Preview 1958-1959 Shows	$90	43
09-27-1958	**Garry Moore** of *I've Got a Secret*	$36	43
10-04-1958	**Dick Clark** of *American Bandstand*	$44	43
10-11-1958	**Barrie Chase** and **Fred Astaire** of *An Evening with Fred Astaire*	$23	43
10-18-1958	**Perry Como** of *The Perry Como Show*	$34	43
10-25-1958	**George Burns** of *The George Burns Show*	$56	43
11-01-1958	**Jack Paar** of *The Jack Paar Show*	$21	43
11-08-1958	**Loretta Young** of *The Loretta Young Show*	$31	44
11-15-1958	**Warner Anderson** and **Tom Tully** of *The Lineup*	$31	44
11-22-1958	**Ronald and Nancy Reagan** in *General Electric Theater's A Turkey for the President*	$44	44
11-29-1958	**Victor Borge** of *Comedy and Music*	$15	44
12-06-1958	**James Arness** of *Gunsmoke*	$56	44
12-13-1958	**Danny Thomas** of *The Danny Thomas Show*	$14	44
12-20-1958	Special Holiday Issue	$43	44
12-27-1958	**David Nelson** and **Ricky Nelson** of *Ozzie and Harriet*	$78	44

1959

Date	Caption	Value	Page
01-03-1959	**Lola Albright** and **Craig Stevens** of *Peter Gunn*	$26	44
01-10-1959	**Milton Berle** of *The Milton Berle Show*	$61	44
01-17-1959	**James Garner** and **Jack Kelly** of *Maverick*	$57	44
01-24-1959	**Red Skelton** of *The Red Skelton Show*	$31	44
01-31-1959	**George Gobel** of *The George Gobel Show*	$11	44
02-07-1959	**Johnny Crawford** and **Chuck Connors** of *The Rifleman*	$75	44
02-14-1959	**Alfred Hitchcock** of *Alfred Hitchcock Presents*	$56	44
02-21-1959	**Barbara Hale** and **Raymond Burr** of *Perry Mason*	$66	45
02-28-1959	**Richard Boone** of *Have Gun, Will Travel*	$66	45
03-07-1959	**Walter Brennan** of *The Real McCoys*	$24	45
03-14-1959	**Arthur Godfrey** of *Arthur Godfrey and His Friends*	$13	45
03-21-1959	**Ann Sothern** of *The Ann Sothern Show*	$26	45
03-28-1959	**Ernie Ford** of *The Ford Show*	$14	45
04-04-1959	**Efrem Zimbalist Jr.** and **Roger Smith** of *77 Sunset Strip*	$56	45
04-11-1959	**Ward Bond** of *Wagon Train*	$56	45
04-18-1959	**Dinah Shore** of *The Dinah Shore Show*	$46	45
04-25-1959	**Dick Powell**	$27	45
05-02-1959	**Hugh O'Brian** of *Wyatt Earp*	$56	45
05-09-1959	**Edward Byrnes** of *77 Sunset Strip*	$41	45
05-16-1959	**Loretta Young** of *The Loretta Young Show*	$23	45

Date	Caption	Value	Page
☐ 05-23-1959	**Bob Hope**	$45	45
☐ 05-30-1959	**Steve McQueen** of *Wanted: Dead or Alive*	$131	45
☐ 06-06-1959	**Gale Storm** of *Oh! Susanna*	$31	45
☐ 06-13-1959	**Pat Boone** of *The Pat Boone Show*	$24	46
☐ 06-20-1959	**Robert Young** and **Lauren Chapin** of *Father Knows Best*	$38	46
☐ 06-27-1959	**Lloyd Bridges** of *Sea Hunt*	$56	46
☐ 07-04-1959	**Jon Provost** and **Lassie** of *Lassie*	$111	46
☐ 07-11-1959	**Lola Albright** and **Craig Stevens** of *Peter Gunn*	$22	46
☐ 07-18-1959	**Janet Blair** of *The Blair and Raitt Show*	$22	46
☐ 07-25-1959	**John Russell** of *Lawman*	$56	46
☐ 08-01-1959	**Dave Garroway** of *Today*	$12	46
☐ 08-08-1959	**Donna Reed** of *The Donna Reed Show*	$30	46
☐ 08-15-1959	**Lawrence Welk** of *The Lawrence Welk Show*	$24	46
☐ 08-22-1959	**Bess Myerson**, **Henry Morgan**, **Betsy Palmer**, and **Bill Cullen** of *I've Got A Secret*	$24	46
☐ 08-29-1959	**Dick Clark** of *American Bandstand*	$31	46
☐ 09-05-1959	**James Garner** and **Jack Kelly** of *Maverick*	$56	46
☐ 09-12-1959	**Arthur Godfrey** of *Arthur Godfrey and His Friends*	$26	46
☐ 09-19-1959	Fall Preview: 1959-1960 Shows	$77	46
☐ 09-26-1959	**Abby Dalton** and **Jackie Cooper** of *Hennessey*	$24	46
☐ 10-03-1959	**June Allyson** of *The June Allyson Show*	$12	46
☐ 10-10-1959	**Robert Taylor** of *The Detectives*	$26	46
☐ 10-17-1959	**Ingrid Bergman** in *The Turn of the Screw*	$26	46
☐ 10-24-1959	**Jay North** of *Dennis the Menace*	$56	46
☐ 10-31-1959	**Fred Astaire** and **Barrie Chase** of *Astaire Time*	$20	47
☐ 11-07-1959	**Jack Benny** of *The Jack Benny Program*	$59	47
☐ 11-14-1959	**Perry Como** of *The Perry Como Show*	$26	47
☐ 11-21-1959	**Clint Walker** of *Cheyenne*	$59	47
☐ 11-28-1959	**Art Carney**: Special This Week	$14	47
☐ 12-05-1959	**Dwayne Hickman**, **Gayle Polayes**, and **Joan Chandler** of *Dobie Gillis*	$28	47
☐ 12-12-1959	**Danny Thomas** of *The Danny Thomas Show*	$26	47
☐ 12-19-1959	Merry Christmas	$25	47
☐ 12-26-1959	**Loretta Young** of *The Loretta Young Show*	$27	47

1960

Date	Caption	Value	Page
☐ 01-02-1960	**James Arness**, **Amanda Blake**, **Dennis Weaver**, and **Milburn Stone** of *Gunsmoke*	$56	48
☐ 01-09-1960	**Jane Wyatt** and **Elinor Donahue** of *Father Knows Best*	$38	48
☐ 01-16-1960	**Cliff Arquette** of *The Charley Weaver Show*	$13	48
☐ 01-23-1960	**Kathleen Nolan** and **Walter Brennan** of *The Real McCoys*	$36	48
☐ 01-30-1960	**Garry Moore** of *The Garry Moore Show*	$9	48
☐ 02-06-1960	**Richard Boone** of *Have Gun, Will Travel*	$56	48
☐ 02-13-1960	**Craig Stevens** and **Lola Albright** of *Peter Gunn* with **John Vivyan** and **Pippa Scott** of *Mr. Lucky*	$27	48
☐ 02-20-1960	**Red Skelton** of *The Red Skelton Show*	$46	48
☐ 02-27-1960	**Robert Stack** of *The Untouchables*	$38	48
☐ 03-05-1960	**Jay North** of *Dennis The Menace*	$45	49
☐ 03-12-1960	**Chuck Connors** of *The Rifleman*	$73	49
☐ 03-19-1960	**Raymond Burr** and **Barbara Hale** of *Perry Mason*	$56	49
☐ 03-26-1960	**Donna Reed** of *The Donna Reed Show*	$23	49
☐ 04-02-1960	**Ernie Ford** of *The Ford Show*	$14	49
☐ 04-09-1960	**Efrem Zimbalist Jr.** of *77 Sunset Strip*	$15	49
☐ 04-16-1960	**Ann Sothern** of *The Ann Sothern Show*	$38	49
☐ 04-23-1960	**Robert Crawford**, **John Smith**, **Robert Fuller**, and **Hoagy Carmichael** of *Laramie*	$66	49
☐ 04-30-1960	**June Lockhart**, **Jon Provost**, and **Lassie** of *Lassie*	$56	49
☐ 05-07-1960	*Frank Sinatra's Welcome Home Party for **Elvis Presley*	$157	49
☐ 05-14-1960	**Ernie Kovacs** and **Edie Adams** of *The Ernie Kovacs Show*	$38	49
☐ 05-21-1960	**Gene Barry** of *Bat Masterson*	$56	49
☐ 05-28-1960	**Poncie Ponce** and **Connie Stevens** of *Hawaiian Eye*	$33	49
☐ 06-04-1960	**Darren McGavin** of *Riverboat*	$66	49

Date	Caption	Value	Page
06-11-1960	**Noreen Corcoran**, **John Forsythe**, and **Sammee Tong** of *Bachelor Father*	$24	49
06-18-1960	**Gardner McKay** of *Adventures in Paradise*	$31	49
06-25-1960	**Dan Blocker**, **Lorne Greene**, **Pernell Roberts**, and **Michael Landon** of *Bonanza*	$111	50
07-02-1960	**Lawrence Welk** of *The Lawrence Welk Show*	$12	50
07-09-1960	**David Brinkley** and **Chet Huntley** of *NBC News*	$15	50
07-16-1960	**Lucille Ball** of *The Lucy-Desi Comedy Hour*	$74	50
07-23-1960	**John Daly** of *What's My Line?*	$10	50
07-30-1960	**Ruta Lee** and **Michael Connors** of *Tightrope*	$21	50
08-06-1960	**Esther Williams** in *Esther Williams at Cypress Gardens*	$13	50
08-13-1960	**Nick Adams** of *The Rebel*	$56	50
08-20-1960	**Betsy Palmer** of *I've Got a Secret*	$19	50
08-27-1960	**Roger Smith**, **Efrem Zimbalist Jr.**, **Edd Byrnes**, and **Richard Long** of *77 Sunset Strip*	$56	50
09-03-1960	**Arlene Francis** of *What's My Line?*	$18	50
09-10-1960	**Dick Clark** of *American Bandstand*	$38	50
09-17-1960	**June Allyson** and **Dick Powell**	$33	50
09-24-1960	Fall Preview: 1960-1961 Shows	$124	50
10-01-1960	**Dinah Shore** of *The Dinah Shore Chevy Show*	$44	50
10-08-1960	**Arthur Godfrey** of *Candid Camera*	$30	50
10-15-1960	**Marion Lorne** and **Carol Burnett** of *The Garry Moore Show*	$13	50
10-22-1960	**Debbie Reynolds**	$33	50
10-29-1960	**Danny Kaye** in a Special This Week	$32	50
11-05-1960	**Loretta Young** of *Letter to Loretta*	$30	50
11-12-1960	**Fred MacMurray** of *My Three Sons*	$20	51
11-19-1960	**Ward Bond** of *Wagon Train*	$56	51
11-26-1960	**Abby Dalton** of *Hennesey* and Friends	$13	51
12-03-1960	**Shirley Temple** of *The Shirley Temple Show*	$56	51
12-10-1960	**Amanda Blake** and **James Arness** of *Gunsmoke*	$56	51
12-17-1960	**Sebastian Cabot**, **Anthony George**, and **Doug McClure** of *Checkmate*	$41	51
12-24-1960	Christmas	$31	51
12-31-1960	**Dorothy Provine** of *The Roaring 20's*	$23	51

1961

Date	Caption	Value	Page
01-07-1961	**Richard Boone** of *Have Gun, Will Travel*	$57	51
01-14-1961	**Perry Como** of *The Perry Como Show*	$32	51
01-21-1961	**Barbara Stanwyck** of *The Barbara Stanwyck Show*	$24	51
01-28-1961	**Ron Howard** and **Andy Griffith** of *The Andy Griffith Show*	$132	51
02-04-1961	**Eric Fleming** and **Clint Eastwood** of *Rawhide*	$85	51
02-11-1961	**Lola Albright** and **Craig Stevens** of *Peter Gunn*	$24	51
02-18-1961	**Nanette Fabray** of *Westinghouse Playhouse*	$24	51
02-25-1961	**Dorothy Collins**, **Allen Funt**, and **Arthur Godfrey** of *Candid Camera*	$27	51
03-04-1961	**Raymond Burr** of *Perry Mason*	$57	51
03-11-1961	**Robert Stack** of *The Untouchables*	$38	51
03-18-1961	**Marjorie Lord** of *The Danny Thomas Show*	$35	51
03-25-1961	**Alfred Hitchcock** of *Alfred Hitchcock Presents*	$38	52
04-01-1961	**Roger Smith** of *77 Sunset Strip*	$22	52
04-08-1961	**Lori Martin** and **King** of *National Velvet*	$31	52
04-15-1961	**Mitch Miller** of *Sing Along with Mitch*	$12	52
04-22-1961	**Garry Moore** of *The Garry Moore Show*	$64	52
04-29-1961	**Rod Taylor** of *Hong Kong*	$36	52
05-06-1961	**Donna Reed** of *The Donna Reed Show*	$28	52
05-13-1961	**Lorne Greene** of *Bonanza*	$24	52
05-20-1961	**Walter Brennan** and **Richard Crenna** of *The Real McCoys*	$19	52
05-27-1961	**Ronald Reagan** and **Dorothy Malone** of *G. E. Theater*	$25	52
06-03-1961	**Paul Burke** and **Horace McMahon** of *Naked City*	$13	52
06-10-1961	**Nanette Fabray** and **Efrem Zimbalist Jr.** – Two of the *Award Show* Stars	$27	52
06-17-1961	**Lawrence Welk** of *The Lawrence Welk Show*	$18	52
06-24-1961	**John McIntire** and **Robert Horton** of *Wagon Train*	$50	52
07-01-1961	**Betty**, **Wilma**, **Fred**, and **Barney** of *The Flintstones*	$99	52
07-08-1961	**Harry Morgan** and **Cara Williams** of *Pete and Gladys*	$25	52

1962

1963

1964

1965

1969

Date . . . . .Caption . . . . .Value . . . .Page

70'S (1970 - 1971)

1970

- [ ] 01-03-1970 . . .Here Come the '70s! How They Will Change the Way You Live. $12 78
- [ ] 01-10-1970 . . .**Fred MacMurray** and **Beverly Garland** of *My Three Sons* $18 78
- [ ] 01-17-1970 . . .**Don Mitchell, Barbara Anderson, Don Galloway,**
      and **Raymond Burr** of *Ironside* $18 78
- [ ] 01-24-1970 . . .**Tom Jones** in *This Is Tom Jones* $22 78
- [ ] 01-31-1970 . . .**Debbie Reynolds** of *The Debbie Reynolds Show* $12 78
- [ ] 02-07-1970 . . .**Elizabeth Montgomery** and **Dick Sargent** of *Bewitched* $42 78
- [ ] 02-14-1970 . . .**Linda Harrison, Laraine Stephens**, and **Karen Jensen** of *Bracken's World*. . . .$18 78
- [ ] 02-21-1970 . . .**James Daly** and **Chad Everett** of *Medical Center*. $19 78
- [ ] 02-28-1970 . . .**Clarence Williams III, Michael Cole**, and **Peggy Lipton** of *The Mod Squad*. . . .$20 78
- [ ] 03-07-1970 . . .The *Hee Haw* Group: They Have Last Laugh $15 79
- [ ] 03-14-1970 . . .**Diahann Carroll** of *Julia* $7 79
- [ ] 03-21-1970 . . .**Jackie Gleason** of *The Jackie Gleason Show* $19 79
- [ ] 03-28-1970 . . .**Dan Rowan** and **Dick Martin** of *Rowan and Martin's Laugh-In* $19 79
- [ ] 04-04-1970 . . .The Cast of *The Brady Bunch* $105 79
- [ ] 04-11-1970 . . .**Carol Burnett** of *The Carol Burnett Show* $23 79
- [ ] 04-18-1970 . . .**Burl Ives, James Farentino**, and **Joseph Campanella** of *The Bold Ones*. $28 79
- [ ] 04-25-1970 . . .**Raquel Welch** and **John Wayne** in *Raquel!*. $25 79
- [ ] 05-02-1970 . . .**Glen Campbell** of *The Glen Campbell Goodtime Hour* $11 79
- [ ] 05-09-1970 . . .**David Frost** of *The David Frost Show* $11 79
- [ ] 05-16-1970 . . .**Vice President Spiro Agnew** – Another Challenge to the Television Industry . . .$14 79
- [ ] 05-23-1970 . . .**Tricia Nixon** with **Mike Wallace** and **Harry Reasoner** $21 79
- [ ] 05-30-1970 . . .**Julie Sommars** of *The Governor and J.J.* $10 79
- [ ] 06-06-1970 . . .**Robert Young** of *Marcus Welby, M.D.* $10 79
- [ ] 06-13-1970 . . .**Johnny Cash** of *The Johnny Cash Show*. $11 79
- [ ] 06-20-1970 . . .**Susan Neher, Joyce Menges, John Forsythe,**
      and **Melanie Fullerton** of *To Rome With Love* $15 79
- [ ] 06-27-1970 . . .**Liza Minnelli** Does a Special $15 79
- [ ] 07-04-1970 . . .**Miyoshi Umeki, Brandon Cruz**, and **Bill Bixby**
      of *The Courtship of Eddie's Father*. $26 79
- [ ] 07-11-1970 . . .The Cast of *The Beverly Hillbillies*. $25 79
- [ ] 07-18-1970 . . .*The Golddiggers* in London $25 79
- [ ] 07-25-1970 . . .The Cast of *Mayberry R.F.D.* $18 80
- [ ] 08-01-1970 . . .**Chet Huntley** of *The Huntley-Brinkley Report* $9 80
- [ ] 08-08-1970 . . .**Ted Bessel** and **Marlo Thomas** of *That Girl* $21 80
- [ ] 08-15-1970 . . .**Johnny Carson** of *The Tonight Show* $30 80
- [ ] 08-22-1970 . . .**Ken Curtis, Milburn Stone, James Arness,**
      and **Amanda Blake** of *Gunsmoke* $24 80
- [ ] 08-29-1970 . . .**Eddie Albert** of *Green Acres*. $23 80
- [ ] 09-05-1970 . . .**Richard Burton, Lucille Ball** and **Elizabeth Taylor** $23 80
- [ ] 09-12-1970 . . .Fall Preview: Special Issue $47 80
- [ ] 09-19-1970 . . .**Mary Tyler Moore** of *The Mary Tyler Moore Show*. $30 80
- [ ] 09-26-1970 . . .**Lloyd Haines, Denise Nicholad, Karen Valentine,**
      and **Michael Constantine** of *Room 222* $23 80
- [ ] 10-03-1970 . . .**Red Skelton** of *The Red Skelton Show* $20 80
- [ ] 10-10-1970 . . .**Herschel Bernardi** of *Arnie*. $11 80
- [ ] 10-17-1970 . . .The Cast of *The Partridge Family* $60 80
- [ ] 10-24-1970 . . .**Don Knotts** of *The Don Knotts Show* $27 80
- [ ] 10-31-1970 . . .**Mike Connors** of *Mannix* $42 80
- [ ] 11-07-1970 . . .**Renne Jarrett, John Fink**, and **Celeste Holm** of *Nancy*. $10 80
- [ ] 11-14-1970 . . .**Christopher George** of *The Immortal* $20 80
- [ ] 11-21-1970 . . .**Sally Marr** – What It Takes To Be a Starlet in the '70s $11 80
- [ ] 11-28-1970 . . .**John Wayne**'s $2,000,000 Special $19 80
- [ ] 12-05-1970 . . .**Dick Cavett** of *The Dick Cavett Show*. $11 80
- [ ] 12-12-1970 . . .**Ed Sullivan** and **The Muppets** in Christmas Show $20 81
- [ ] 12-19-1970 . . .Holiday Preview. $25 81
- [ ] 12-26-1970 . . .**Diahann Carroll** and **Fred Williamson** of *Julia* $10 81

1971

- [ ] 01-02-1971 . . .Remember 1970? $15 81
- [ ] 01-09-1971 . . .**Andy Griffith** of *Headmaster* $30 81

1972

Date	Caption	Value	Page
☐ 01-29-1972	**David Janssen** of *O'Hara, U.S. Treasury*	$39	84
☐ 02-05-1972	**Raymond Burr** and **Elizabeth Baur** of *Ironside*	$25	84
☐ 02-12-1972	**Arthur Hill** of *Owen Marshall, Counselor at Law*	$6	84
☐ 02-19-1972	**President Nixon** and **En-lai Chou**	$31	84
☐ 02-26-1972	**Mary Tyler Moore** of *The Mary Tyler Moore Show*	$26	84
☐ 03-04-1972	**Johnny Carson** of *The Tonight Show*	$20	84
☐ 03-11-1972	**James Brolin** and **Robert Young** of *Marcus Welby, M.D.*	$9	84
☐ 03-18-1972	**Sonny** and **Cher Bono** of *The Sonny & Cher Comedy Hour*	$27	84
☐ 03-25-1972	**Peter Falk** of *Columbo*	$19	84
☐ 04-01-1972	**Glenn Ford** of *Cade's County*	$20	84
☐ 04-08-1972	TV Political Coverage: Fair or Biased?	$14	84
☐ 04-15-1972	Astronauts **Thomas K. Mattingly**, **Charles M. Duke**, and **John W. Young**	$9	85
☐ 04-22-1972	**Don Rickles** of *The Don Rickles Show*	$13	85
☐ 04-29-1972	**Susan Saint James** and **Rock Hudson** of *McMillan & Wife*	$18	85
☐ 05-06-1972	**Sandy Duncan** of *Funny Face*	$14	85
☐ 05-13-1972	**Demond Wilson** and **Redd Foxx** of *Sanford and Son*	$24	85
☐ 05-20-1972	**Efrem Zimbalist Jr.** of *The FBI* and **J. Edgar Hoover** of The FBI	$7	85
☐ 05-27-1972	**Carroll O'Connor** and **Jean Stapleton** of *All in the Family*	$25	85
☐ 06-03-1972	**Rod Serling** of *Night Gallery*	$35	85
☐ 06-10-1972	**Doris Day** of *The Doris Day Show*	$27	85
☐ 06-17-1972	**Julie London** of *Emergency!*	$23	85
☐ 06-24-1972	**Mike Connors** of *Mannix*	$23	85
☐ 07-01-1972	**Carol Burnett** of *The Carol Burnett Show*	$11	85
☐ 07-08-1972	**Merv Griffin** of *The Merv Griffin Show*	$7	85
☐ 07-15-1972	**David Cassidy** of *The Partridge Family*	$45	85
☐ 07-22-1972	Producer **Jack Webb**, **Martin Milner**, and **Kent McCord** of *Adam-12*	$49	85
☐ 07-29-1972	All About *Love, American Style*	$23	85
☐ 08-05-1972	*War and Peace* Comes To Television	$7	86
☐ 08-12-1972	**Leonardo Da Vinci**: Unusual Drama Series Starts This Week	$7	86
☐ 08-19-1972	**Chad Everett** of *Medical Center*	$15	86
☐ 08-26-1972	The Olympics	$11	86
☐ 09-02-1972	**Jack Klugman** and **Tony Randall** of *The Odd Couple*	$33	86
☐ 09-09-1972	Fall Preview: Special Issue	$27	86
☐ 09-16-1972	**Yul Brynner** and **Samantha Eggar** in *Anna and the King*	$11	86
☐ 09-23-1972	**George Peppard** of *Banacek*	$10	86
☐ 09-30-1972	**Meredith Baxter** and **David Birney** of *Bridget Loves Bernie*	$15	86
☐ 10-07-1972	The Cast of *Bonanza*	$37	86
☐ 10-14-1972	**Robert Conrad** of *Assignment: Vienna*	$11	86
☐ 10-21-1972	**Carroll O'Connor** and **Cloris Leachman** star in *Of Thee I Sing*	$19	86
☐ 10-28-1972	**Snoopy, Charlie Brown**, and **Woodstock**	$28	86
☐ 11-04-1972	**John Wayne**: He Learned to Love TV	$24	86
☐ 11-11-1972	**Allistair Cooke**'s *America*	$12	86
☐ 11-18-1972	**Beatrice Arthur** of *Maude*	$19	86
☐ 11-25-1972	**Doug McClure**, **Tony Franciosa**, and **Hugh O'Brian** of *Search*	$21	86
☐ 12-02-1972	**Mike Douglas** of *The Mike Douglas Show*	$11	86
☐ 12-09-1972	**Julie Andrews** of *The Julie Andrews Hour*	$18	86
☐ 12-16-1972	The **Duke and Duchess of Windsor** – Television Recalls the Love Affair of the Century	$9	86
☐ 12-23-1972	Christmas	$27	87
☐ 12-30-1972	**Barbara Walters** of *Today*	$10	87

1973

Date	Caption	Value	Page
☐ 01-06-1973	**Richard Nixon**, **Leonid Brezhnev**, **Chou En-Lai**, and **Mark Spitz**	$14	87
☐ 01-13-1973	China – Inside The Forbidden City	$11	87
☐ 01-20-1973	**Bob Newhart** and **Suzanne Pleshette** of *The Bob Newhart Show*	$19	87
☐ 01-27-1973	**Sam Melville**, **Georg Stanford Brown**, and **Michael Ontkean** of *The Rookies*	$15	87
☐ 02-03-1973	**Bill Cosby** of *The New Bill Cosby Show*	$14	87
☐ 02-10-1973	**John Calvin**, **Paul Lynde**, and **Jane Actman** of *The Paul Lynde Show*	$36	87
☐ 02-17-1973	**Susan Saint James** and **Rock Hudson** of *McMillan & Wife*	$15	87
☐ 02-24-1973	The Cast of *M*A*S*H*	$52	87

1975

1977

1978

1985

1987

Date	Caption	Value	Page
10-10-1987	Cast Members of *Growing Pains*; **Michael J. Fox** of *Family Ties*; **Bob Newhart** of *Newhart*	$15	131
10-17-1987	**Dolly Parton** of *Dolly*	$14	131
10-24-1987	**Bruce Willis** and **Cybill Shepherd** of *Moonlighting*	$22	131
10-31-1987	**Courteney Cox** and **Michael J. Fox** of *Family Ties*	$14	131
11-07-1987	**Jacqueline Bisset** and **Armand Assante** in *Napoleon and Josephine: A Love Story*	$9	131
11-14-1987	**Ted Danson** and **Kirstie Alley** of *Cheers*	$14	131
11-21-1987	**Linda Gray**, **Kenny Rogers**, and **Bruce Boxleitner** in *Gambler III*	$22	131
11-28-1987	**David Birney** and **Meredith Baxter Birney** in *The Long Journey Home*	$7	131
12-05-1987	**Connie Sellecca** in *Downpayment on Murder*	$14	131
12-12-1987	**John Ritter** of *Hooperman*	$7	131
12-19-1987	**Keshia Knight Pulliam** in *The Little Match Girl*	$10	131
12-26-1987	**Amanda Peterson**, **Trey Ames**, and **Richard Kiley** of *A Year in the Life*	$22	131

1988

Date	Caption	Value	Page
01-02-1988	The Women of *Falcon Crest*	$13	131
01-09-1988	**Emma Samms** of *Dynasty*	$7	131
01-16-1988	**Sharon Gless** and **Tyne Daly** of *Cagney and Lacey*	$7	131
01-23-1988	Campaign '88	$7	132
01-30-1988	**Priscilla Beaulieu Presley** – My Life With **Elvis**	$37	132
02-06-1988	**Jaclyn Smith** and **Robert Wagner** in *Windmills of the Gods*	$18	132
02-13-1988	The Winter Olympic Games	$10	132
02-20-1988	**Pierce Brosnan** and **Deborah Raffin** in *Noble House*	$23	132
02-27-1988	**Cheryl Ladd** in *Bluegrass*	$14	132
03-05-1988	**Oprah Winfrey** of *The Oprah WInfrey Show*	$5	132
03-12-1988	*I Love Lucy, M*A*S*H, ALF, and Cheers* – Is TV Getting Better or Worse?	$36	132
03-19-1988	**Philip Michael Thomas** and **Don Johnson** of *Miami Vice*	$14	132
03-26-1988	**Sheree J. Wilson** of *Dallas*	$14	132
04-02-1988	**Kirk Cameron** and **Tracey Gold** of *Growing Pains*	$15	132
04-09-1988	**Harry Hamlin** of *L.A. Law*	$10	132
04-16-1988	**Tim Reid** and **Daphne Maxwell Reid** of *Frank's Place*	$7	132
04-23-1988	**Jason Bateman** of *Valerie's Family*	$9	132
04-30-1988	**Dr. Ruth Westheimer** and *The Golden Girls*	$15	132
05-07-1988	**Richard Chamberlain** and **Jaclyn Smith** in *The Bourne Identity*	$14	132
05-14-1988	**Lesley Stahl**; **Sam Donaldson**; **Chris Wallace** – Beat The Press	$5	133
05-21-1988	**Princess Diana** and **Prince Charles** – Why We're So Taken with British Royalty	$22	133
05-28-1988	**Brian Bonsall** and **Michael J. Fox** of *Family Ties*	$14	133
06-04-1988	**Carl Lewis** and **Donna de Varona**; **Howard Cosell**; **Al Michaels** – Stars and Strife at ABC Sports	$5	133
06-11-1988	**Mel Harris**, **Brittany Craven**, and **Ken Olin** of *thirtysomething*	$14	133
06-18-1988	The 1988 Network News All-Star Team	$5	133
06-25-1988	Olympics; **Tom Selleck**; **Oliver North**; *Cheers* – The Best and Worst We Saw	$14	133
07-02-1988	**Delta Burke**, **Annie Potts**, **Dixie Carter**, and **Jean Smart** of *Designing Women*	$14	133
07-09-1988	The Cast of *Head of the Class*	$14	133
07-16-1988	**Kim Alexis** and **Nicollette Sheridan** – The Six Most Beautiful Women on TV	$14	133
07-23-1988	How TV is Shaking Up the American Family	$10	133
07-30-1988	**Leann Hunley** – Was She Right To Walk Away from *Dynasty*?	$5	133
08-06-1988	**Susan Lucci**; **Peter Barton** & **Lauralee Bell**; **Drake Hogestyn**; **Tristan Rogers** – Daytime Soaps	$7	133
08-13-1988	*ALF*	$21	133
08-20-1988	**Johnny Depp** and **Holly Robinson** of *21 Jump Street*	$14	133
08-27-1988	**Mariel Hemingway** in *Steal the Sky*	$5	133
09-03-1988	**Kaye Lani Rafko**; **Phoebe Mills**; *Peanuts*; **Charlie Sheen**	$5	133
09-10-1988	**Kaye Lani Rafko** – Inside the Mind of Miss America	$5	133
09-17-1988	Olympics '88 Viewers Guide	$9	133
09-24-1988	Cast Members of *The Cosby Show*	$9	133
10-01-1988	Fall Preview: Special Issue	$15	134

1989

1991

1994

Date	Caption	Value	Page

1995

☐ 01-07-1995 . . .**Oprah Winfrey** – "I Feel I'm Finally Growing Up" . . . . $5 . . .154

☐ 01-14-1995 . . .**Kate Mulgrew**, **Tim Russ**, and **Robert Beltran** of *Star Trek: Voyager* . . . . $13 . . .154

☐ 01-21-1995 . . .*The Wayans Bros.*; **Delta Burke**; **Julia Campbell**;
            John Leguizamo; **Richard Grieco** – Winter Preview . . . . $7 . . .154

☐ 01-28-1995 . . .Super Bowl Spectacular . . . . $9 . . .154

☐ 02-04-1995 . . .**Jerry Seinfeld** of *Seinfeld*; **Roseanne** . . . . $11 . . .154

☐ 02-11-1995 . . .**Heather Locklear** in *Texas Justice* . . . . $10 . . .154

☐ 02-18-1995 . . .**Sally Field** in *A Woman of Independent Means* . . . . $9 . . .154

☐ 02-25-1995 . . .**George Clooney** of *ER* . . . . $13 . . .154

☐ 03-04-1995 . . .Parents' Guide to Kids' TV . . . . $13 . . .154

☐ 03-11-1995 . . .**Gillian Anderson** and **David Duchovny** of *The X-Files* . . . . $46 . . .154

☐ 03-18-1995 . . .**Roseanne**; **Tim Allen**; **Oprah**; **Jerry Seinfeld** –
            TV's 10 Most Powerful Stars. . . . . $7 . . .154

☐ 03-25-1995 . . .**David Letterman** – Dave Does the Oscars . . . . $6 . . .155

☐ 04-01-1995 . . .**Jenny Jones**, **Jerry Springer**, **Ricki Lake**, and
            Montel Williams – Are Talk Shows Out of Control? . . . . $7 . . .155

☐ 04-08-1995 . . .**Jennie Garth** of *Beverly Hills, 90210* . . . . $10 . . .155

☐ 04-15-1995 . . .**Fran Drescher** of *The Nanny* . . . . $10 . . .155

☐ 04-22-1995 . . .**Susan Lucci** in *Seduced and Betrayed* . . . . $5 . . .155

☐ 04-29-1995 . . .**Kate Mulgrew**, **Courtney Thorne- Smith**, and **Roxanne Hart** – Boss Ladies. . . $13 . . .155

☐ 05-06-1995 . . .**Jane Seymour** and **Joe Lando** of *Dr. Quinn, Medicine Woman* . . . . $10 . . .155

☐ 05-13-1995 . . .**Naomi Judd**, **Wynonna Judd**, and **Ashley Judd** . . . . $9 . . .155

☐ 05-20-1995 . . .**Gail O'Grady** and **Sharon Lawrence** of *NYPD Blue* . . . . $13 . . .155

☐ 05-27-1995 . . .**Pamela Anderson** of *Baywatch* . . . . $7 . . .155

☐ 06-03-1995 . . .**Larry King** of *Larry King Live*; **Connie Chung** . . . . $5 . . .155

☐ 06-10-1995 . . .Summer Preview: Your Guide to the Hot New Shows . . . . $10 . . .155

☐ 06-17-1995 . . .**Brett Butler** of *Grace Under Fire*; **Bryant Gumbel** of *Today* . . . . $9 . . .155

☐ 06-24-1995 . . .**Jason David Frank** of *Mighty Morphin Power Rangers* . . . . $6 . . .155

☐ 07-01-1995 . . .**Victoria Principal** in *Dancing in the Dark* . . . . $5 . . .155

☐ 07-08-1995 . . .**Cal Ripken Jr.** – Baseball's Best Hope;
            Jerry Seinfeld and **Shoshanna Lonstein** . . . . $6 . . .155

☐ 07-15-1995 . . .**Jennifer Lien** and **Ethan Phillips** of *Star Trek: Voyager* . . . . $13 . . .156

☐ 07-22-1995 . . .**Dean Cain** of *Lois and Clark: The New Adventures of Superman* . . . . $13 . . .156

☐ 07-29-1995 . . .**Josie Bissett** of *Melrose Place* . . . . $15 . . .156

☐ 08-05-1995 . . .**Tom Selleck** Talks Tough . . . . $6 . . .156

☐ 08-12-1995 . . .**Cybill Shepherd** and **Jimmy Smits** – Best Dressed Stars . . . . $9 . . .156

☐ 08-19-1995 . . .**Regis Philbin** of *Live with Regis & Kathie Lee* . . . . $5 . . .156

☐ 08-26-1995 . . .**Tiffani-Amber Thiessen** and **Brian Austin Green** of *Beverly Hills, 90210* . . . . . . $5 . . .156

☐ 08-26-1995 . . .Tennessee QB **Peyton Manning** . . . . $13 . . .156

☐ 08-26-1995 . . .University of Florida QB **Danny Wuerffel** . . . . $13 . . .156

☐ 08-26-1995 . . .Alabama tackle **Shannon Brown**; Auburn tailback **Stephen Davis** . . . . $13 . . .156

☐ 08-26-1995 . . .**Stephen Davis**; **Peyton Manning**; **Steve Taneyhill**; **Moe Williams** . . . . $13 . . .156

☐ 09-02-1995 . . .**Boomer Esiason** of the Jets; **Dave Brown** of the Giants . . . . $13 . . .156

☐ 09-02-1995 . . .**Vinny Testaverde** of the Browns; **Jeff Blake** of the Bengals . . . . $13 . . .156

☐ 09-02-1995 . . .**Steve Young** of the 49ers; **Jeff Hostetler** of the Raiders . . . . $13 . . .156

☐ 09-02-1995 . . .**Steve Young** of the 49ers . . . . $13 . . .156

☐ 09-02-1995 . . .**Chris Zorich** of the Bears . . . . $13 . . .156

☐ 09-02-1995 . . .**Jim Kelly** of the Bills . . . . $13 . . .156

☐ 09-02-1995 . . .**John Elway** of the Broncos . . . . $13 . . .156

☐ 09-02-1995 . . .**Trent Dilfer** of the Buccaneers . . . . $13 . . .156

☐ 09-02-1995 . . .**Steve Bono** of the Chiefs . . . . $13 . . .156

☐ 09-02-1995 . . .**Troy Aikman** of the Cowboys . . . . $13 . . .157

☐ 09-02-1995 . . .**Dan Marino** of the Dolphins . . . . $13 . . .157

☐ 09-02-1995 . . .**Ricky Watters** of the Eagles . . . . $13 . . .157

☐ 09-02-1995 . . .**Jeff George** of the Falcons . . . . $13 . . .157

☐ 09-02-1995 . . .**Steve Beuerlein** of the Jaguars . . . . $13 . . .157

☐ 09-02-1995 . . .**Barry Sanders** of the Lions . . . . $13 . . .157

☐ 09-02-1995 . . .**Haywood Jeffires** of the Oilers . . . . $13 . . .157

☐ 09-02-1995 . . .**Brett Favre** of the Packers . . . . $13 . . .157

☐ 09-02-1995 . . .**Frank Reich** of the Panthers . . . . $13 . . .157

Date	Caption	Value	Page
☐ 05-09-1998	**Julia Louis-Dreyfus** of *Seinfeld*	$24	175
☐ 05-09-1998	**Michael Richards** of *Seinfeld*	$24	175
☐ 05-16-1998	**Julia Roberts**	$11	175
☐ 05-23-1998	**Tom Hanks**; **Jim Carrey**; **Drew Barrymore** – Summer Movie Preview!	$15	175
☐ 05-30-1998	**Frank Sinatra**	$12	175
☐ 06-06-1998	**Magic Johnson** of *The Magic Hour*	$11	175
☐ 06-13-1998	**Jensen Ackles**, **Laura Wright**, and **Ingo Rademacher** – Summer Soaps Preview	$10	176
☐ 06-20-1998	**David Duchovny** of *The X-Files*	$28	176
☐ 06-20-1998	**Gillian Anderson** of *The X-Files*	$20	176
☐ 06-27-1998	**Taylor Hanson**, **Zac Hanson**, and **Isaac Hanson** (42 Different Variations)	$10	176
☐ 07-04-1998	**Matt Lauer** of Today (Multiple Variations)	$6	176
☐ 07-11-1998	TV's 50 Greatest Sports Moments	$11	176
☐ 07-18-1998	**Brandy Norwood** of *Moesha*; **Phil Hartman** of *NewsRadio*	$9	176
☐ 07-25-1998	**Jerry Mathers**; **Johnny Carson**; **Ted Nugent**; **Mary Hart**; **Soupy Sales** – TV Confidential!	$10	176
☐ 08-01-1998	**Drew Carey** of *Whose Line Is It Anyway?*	$13	176
☐ 08-08-1998	The 50 Greatest Movies on TV and Video	$13	176
☐ 08-15-1998	**Princess Diana**	$14	176
☐ 08-22-1998	**Joe Mantegna**, **Ray Liotta**, **Angus Macfadyen**, **Bobby Slayton**, and **Don Cheadle** in *The Rat Pack*	$20	176
☐ 08-22-1998	**Vivica A. Fox** of *Getting Personal* and **Thomas Gibson** of *Dharma & Greg*	$13	176
☐ 08-29-1998	**Steve Young** of the 49ers; **Jeff George** of the Raiders	$12	176
☐ 08-29-1998	**Glenn Foley** of the Jets; **Danny Kanell** of the Giants	$12	176
☐ 08-29-1998	**Steve Young** of the 49ers	$12	176
☐ 08-29-1998	**Erik Kramer** of the Bears	$12	176
☐ 08-29-1998	**Carl Pickens** of the Bengals	$12	176
☐ 08-29-1998	**Bruce Smith** of the Bills	$12	176
☐ 08-29-1998	**John Elway** of the Broncos	$23	176
☐ 08-29-1998	**Trent Dilfer** of the Buccaneers	$12	177
☐ 08-29-1998	**Jake Plummer** of the Cardinals	$12	177
☐ 08-29-1998	**Ryan Leaf** of the Chargers	$12	177
☐ 08-29-1998	**Kimble Anders** of the Chiefs	$12	177
☐ 08-29-1998	**Peyton Manning** of the Colts	$12	177
☐ 08-29-1998	**Troy Aikman** of the Cowboys	$12	177
☐ 08-29-1998	**Dan Marino** of the Dolphins	$12	177
☐ 08-29-1998	**Bobby Hoying** of the Eagles	$12	177
☐ 08-29-1998	**Jamal Anderson** of the Falcons	$12	177
☐ 08-29-1998	**Danny Kanell** of the Giants	$12	177
☐ 08-29-1998	**Mark Brunell** of the Jaguars	$12	177
☐ 08-29-1998	**Glenn Foley** of the Jets	$12	177
☐ 08-29-1998	**Barry Sanders** of the Lions	$12	177
☐ 08-29-1998	**Steve McNair** of the Oilers	$12	177
☐ 08-29-1998	**Brett Favre** of the Packers	$27	177
☐ 08-29-1998	**Kenny Collins** of the Panthers	$12	177
☐ 08-29-1998	**Drew Bledsoe** of the Patriots	$12	177
☐ 08-29-1998	**Jeff George** of the Raiders	$12	177
☐ 08-29-1998	**Isaac Bruce** of the Rams	$12	177
☐ 08-29-1998	**Michael Jackson** of the Ravens	$12	177
☐ 08-29-1998	**Gus Frerotte** of the Redskins	$12	178
☐ 08-29-1998	**Billy Joe Hobert** of the Saints	$12	178
☐ 08-29-1998	**Joey Galloway** of the Seahawks	$12	178
☐ 08-29-1998	**Jerome Betts** of the Steelers	$12	178
☐ 08-29-1998	**Brad Johnson** of the Vikings	$12	178
☐ 09-05-1998	*Ally McBeal*; *Frasier*; *Cosby*; *The Practice*; *ER*; *Buffy the Vampire Slayer* – Returning Favorites	$30	178
☐ 09-12-1998	Fall Preview: Special Issue	$11	178
☐ 09-19-1998	**Tim Allen** of *Home Improvement*	$41	178
☐ 09-19-1998	**Faith Hill** – Bold New Women of Country Music	$21	178
☐ 09-19-1998	**LeAnn Rimes** – Bold New Women of Country Music	$10	178
☐ 09-19-1998	**Shania Twain** – Bold New Women of Country Music	$26	178

☐ 06-24-2000 . . .*The Real World* – Brave New World $10 195
☐ 06-24-2000 . . .**Kobe Bryant** of the Lakers $9 195
☐ 06-24-2000 . . .**Rick Fox** of the Lakers $9 195
☐ 06-24-2000 . . .**Shaquille O'Neal** of the Lakers. $9 195
☐ 06-24-2000 . . .**Glen Rice** of the Lakers $9 195
☐ 07-01-2000 . . .**Judy Garland** in *The Wizard of Oz* $10 195
☐ 07-01-2000 . . .**Ray Bolger** in *The Wizard of Oz* $14 195
☐ 07-01-2000 . . .**Jack Haley** in *The Wizard of Oz* $25 195
☐ 07-01-2000 . . .**Bert Lahr** in *The Wizard of Oz* $13 195
☐ 07-08-2000 . . .**Jenna Lewis**, **Rudy Boesch**, **Kelly Wigglesworth**,
        and **Susan Hawk** of *Survivor* $11 195
☐ 07-08-2000 . . .**Steve Young** of the 49ers (Passing) $9 196
☐ 07-08-2000 . . .**Steve Young** of the 49ers (Running) $9 196
☐ 07-08-2000 . . .**Andres Galarraga** of the Braves $9 196
☐ 07-08-2000 . . .**Chipper Jones** of the Braves $9 196
☐ 07-08-2000 . . .**Mark McGwire** of the Cardinals $9 196
☐ 07-08-2000 . . .**Randy Johnson** of the Diamondbacks. $9 196
☐ 07-08-2000 . . .**Pedro Martinez** of the Red Sox $9 196
☐ 07-08-2000 . . .**Ken Griffey Jr.** of the Reds. $9 196
☐ 07-15-2000 . . .**Halle Berry** as Storm in *X-Men* $20 196
☐ 07-15-2000 . . .**Hugh Jackman** as Wolverine in *X-Men* $20 196
☐ 07-15-2000 . . .**Famke Janssen** as Jean Grey in *X-Men*. $20 196
☐ 07-15-2000 . . .**James Marsden** as Cyclops in *X-Men* $20 196
☐ 07-15-2000 . . .**Anna Paquin** as Rogue in *X-Men*. $20 196
☐ 07-15-2000 . . .**Patrick Stewart** as Professor Charles Francis Xavier in *X-Men* $20 196
☐ 07-22-2000 . . .**Martin Sheen** in *The West Wing*. $21 196
☐ 07-29-2000 . . .**Claudia Black** of *Farscape* $36 196
☐ 07-29-2000 . . .**Roxann Dawson** of *Star Trek: Voyager* $36 196
☐ 07-29-2000 . . .**Gigi Edgley** of *Farscape*. $36 196
☐ 07-29-2000 . . .**Katherine Heigl** of *Roswell*. $36 196
☐ 07-29-2000 . . .**Virginia Hey** of *Farscape* $36 196
☐ 07-29-2000 . . .**Renee O'Connor** of *Xena: Warrior Princess* $36 197
☐ 07-29-2000 . . .**Jeri Ryan** of *Star Trek: Voyager* $36 197
☐ 07-29-2000 . . .**Xenia Seeberg** of *Lexx* $36 197
☐ 08-05-2000 . . .**Clint Eastwood** – From *Rawhide* to *Space Cowboys* . . . . $15 . . .197
☐ 08-12-2000 . . .**Dale Earnhardt** $25 197
☐ 08-12-2000 . . .**Bill Elliott** $25 197
☐ 08-12-2000 . . .**Ricky Rudd** $25 197
☐ 08-12-2000 . . .**Rusty Wallace**. $25 197
☐ 08-19-2000 . . .**The Kat** of the WWF $10 197
☐ 08-19-2000 . . .**Chris Jericho** of the WWF $18 197
☐ 08-19-2000 . . .**Kurt Angle** of the WWF $18 197
☐ 08-19-2000 . . .**Rikishi** of the WWF $18 197
☐ 08-26-2000 . . .**Christina Aguilera** $26 197
☐ 08-26-2000 . . .**Metallica** $26 197
☐ 08-26-2000 . . .**'N Sync** $10 197
☐ 08-26-2000 . . .**Sisqo** $10 197
☐ 08-26-2000 . . .**The Wayans** $12 197
☐ 09-02-2000 . . .**Dennis Miller** of *Monday Night Football* $10 197
☐ 09-02-2000 . . .**Jerry Rice** of the 49ers $12 197
☐ 09-02-2000 . . .**Rob Johnson** of the Bills $12 197
☐ 09-02-2000 . . .**Terrell Davis** of the Broncos $12 198
☐ 09-02-2000 . . .**Tim Couch** of the Browns $12 198
☐ 09-02-2000 . . .**Troy Aikman** of the Cowboys $12 198
☐ 09-02-2000 . . .**Donovan McNabb** of the Eagles $12 198
☐ 09-02-2000 . . .**Charlie Batch** of the Lions $12 198
☐ 09-02-2000 . . .**Brett Favre** of the Packers $12 198
☐ 09-02-2000 . . .**Steve Beuerlein** of the Panthers $12 198
☐ 09-02-2000 . . .**Drew Bledsoe** of the Patriots $12 198
☐ 09-02-2000 . . .**Rich Gannon** of the Raiders. $12 198
☐ 09-02-2000 . . .**Kurt Warner** of the Rams $12 198

	Date	Caption	Value	Page
☐	05-26-2001	**Backstreet Boys**	$20	204
☐	05-26-2001	**Nick Carter** of **Backstreet Boys**	$20	204
☐	05-26-2001	**Howie Dorough** of **Backstreet Boys**	$20	204
☐	05-26-2001	**Brian Littell** of **Backstreet Boys**	$20	205
☐	05-26-2001	**A.J. McLean** of **Backstreet Boys**	$20	205
☐	05-26-2001	**Kevin Richardson** of **Backstreet Boys**	$20	205
☐	06-02-2001	**Laila Ali** and **Jacquelyn Frazier-Lyde**	$5	205
☐	06-09-2001	**Tiger Woods** – His Shot At Making History (Close-Up/Swinging)	$19	205
☐	06-09-2001	**Tiger Woods** – His Shot At Making History (Close-Up)	$19	205
☐	06-09-2001	**Tiger Woods** – His Shot At Making History (Walking)	$19	205
☐	06-09-2001	**Tiger Woods** – His Shot At Making History (Swinging)	$19	205
☐	06-16-2001	**Bill O'Reilly** of *The O'Reilly Factor*	$5	205
☐	06-16-2001	**Kobe Bryant** of the Lakers	$13	205
☐	06-16-2001	**Rick Fox** of the Lakers	$13	205
☐	06-16-2001	**Robert Horry** of the Lakers	$13	205
☐	06-16-2001	**Derek Fisher** of the Lakers	$13	205
☐	06-16-2001	**Horace Grant** of the Lakers	$13	205
☐	06-16-2001	**Shaquille O'Neal** of the Lakers	$13	205
☐	06-23-2001	The Women of *ER*	$5	205
☐	06-30-2001	**Jerry Seinfeld**	$6	206
☐	07-07-2001	**Juliet Mills**, **McKenzie Westmore**, and **Galen Gering** of *Passions*	$9	206
☐	07-07-2001	**McKenzie Westmore**, **Galen Gering**, and **Juliet Mills** of *Passions*	$30	206
☐	07-07-2001	**Bozo The Clown** Signs Off	$20	206
☐	07-14-2001	**Julianna Margulies** in *The Mists of Avalon*	$9	206
☐	07-21-2001	A Tribute to **Chet Atkins**	$12	206
☐	07-21-2001	**Angelica** of *Rugrats*	$12	206
☐	07-21-2001	**Chuckie** of *Rugrats*	$12	206
☐	07-21-2001	**Lil** and **Phil** of *Rugrats*	$12	206
☐	07-21-2001	**Tommy** of *Rugrats*	$12	206
☐	07-28-2001	**Glenn Shadix** as Senator Nado and **Michael Clarke Duncan** as Attar in *Planet of the Apes*	$14	206
☐	07-28-2001	**Tim Roth** as General Thade in *Planet of the Apes*	$14	206
☐	07-28-2001	**Mark Wahlberg** as Astronaut Leo Davidson in *Planet of the Apes*	$9	206
☐	07-28-2001	**Estella Warren** as Daena in *Planet of the Apes*	$14	206
☐	07-28-2001	**Helena Bonham Carter** as Ari in *Planet of the Apes*	$14	206
☐	07-28-2001	**Lisa Marie** as Nova and **Kris Kristofferson** as Karubi in *Planet of the Apes*	$14	207
☐	08-04-2001	**Danny Masterson** of *That '70s Show*	$14	207
☐	08-04-2001	**Mila Kunis** of *That '70s Show*	$14	207
☐	08-04-2001	**Ashton Kutcher** of *That '70s Show*	$14	207
☐	08-04-2001	**Topher Grace** of *That '70s Show*	$14	207
☐	08-04-2001	**Laura Prepon** of *That '70s Show*	$15	207
☐	08-04-2001	**Wilmer Valderrama** of *That '70s Show*	$14	207
☐	08-11-2001	**Justin & Britney; Sarah Michelle & Freddie; Katie & Chris; Jessica & Michael**	$12	207
☐	08-18-2001	**Kelly Ripa** of *Live with Regis & Kelly*	$11	207
☐	08-25-2001	**Dominic Keating** as Lt. Malcolm Reed, **Connor Trinneer** as Chief Engineer Charles "Trip" Tucker III, and **Linda Park** as Ensign Hoshi Sato of *Enterprise*	$11	207
☐	08-25-2001	**Scott Bakula** as Captain Jonathan Archer of *Enterprise*	$11	207
☐	08-25-2001	**Jolene Blalock** as Vulcan Sub-Commander T'Pol of *Enterprise*	$11	207
☐	08-25-2001	**Jolene Blalock** and **Scott Bakula** of *Enterprise*	$11	207
☐	08-25-2001	**Anthony Montgomery** as Ensign Travis Mayweather and **John Billingsley** as Dr. Phlox of *Enterprise*	$11	207
☐	09-01-2001	**Peyton Manning** of the Colts and **Daunte Culpepper** of the Vikings	$15	207
☐	09-01-2001	**Donovan McNabb** of the Eagles	$15	207
☐	09-01-2001	**Marshall Faulk** of the Rams	$15	207
☐	09-01-2001	**Lavar Arrington** of the Redskins	$15	208
☐	09-01-2001	**Jerome Bettis** of the Steelers	$15	208
☐	09-08-2001	*Ally McBeal*; *The West Wing*; *Buffy the Vampire Slayer*; *Once and Again*; *Boston Public*; *Judging Amy*	$10	208

Date	Caption	Value	Page
☐ 04-20-2002	**Avery Brooks** of *Star Trek: Deep Space Nine*	$23	214
☐ 04-20-2002	**Nana Visitor** and **Alexander Siddig** of *Star Trek: Deep Space Nine*	$23	214
☐ 04-20-2002	**Armin Shimerman** of *Star Trek: Deep Space Nine*	$23	214
☐ 04-20-2002	**Cirroc Lofton** and **Colm Meaney** of *Star Trek: Deep Space Nine*.	$23	214
☐ 04-20-2002	**Roxann Dawson** and **Robert Duncan McNeill** of *Star Trek: Voyager*	$23	214
☐ 04-20-2002	**Jennifer Lien** and **Ethan Phillips** of *Star Trek: Voyager*	$23	214
☐ 04-20-2002	**Robert Picardo** of *Star Trek: Voyager*	$23	214
☐ 04-20-2002	**Kate Mulgrew** of *Star Trek: Voyager*.	$23	215
☐ 04-20-2002	**Robert Beltran** of *Star Trek: Voyager*.	$23	215
☐ 04-20-2002	**Jeri Ryan** of *Star Trek: Voyager*	$23	215
☐ 04-20-2002	**Tim Russ** and **Garrett Wang** of *Star Trek: Voyager*.	$23	215
☐ 04-20-2002	**John Billingsley** and **Linda Park** of *Enterprise*	$23	215
☐ 04-20-2002	**Jolene Blalock** and **Connor Trinneer** of *Enterprise*	$23	215
☐ 04-20-2002	**Scott Bakula** of *Enterprise*	$23	215
☐ 04-20-2002	**Anthony Montgomery** and **Dominic Keating** of *Enterprise*	$23	215
☐ 04-20-2002	**Alice Krige** of *Star Trek: Voyager*	$23	215
☐ 04-20-2002	**Ricardo Montalban** of *Star Trek*	$23	215
☐ 04-20-2002	**John de Lancie** of *Star Trek: The Next Generation*	$23	215
☐ 04-27-2002	**Spider-Man** by **John Romita**	$18	215
☐ 04-27-2002	**Spider-Man** by **John Romita Jr.**	$18	215
☐ 04-27-2002	**Spider-Man** by **Mark Bagley**	$18	215
☐ 04-27-2002	**Spider-Man** by **Alex Ross**	$18	215
☐ 04-27-2002	**Tobey Maguire** in *Spider-Man*	$18	215
☐ 05-04-2002	*The Tonight Show*; *Sopranos*; *I Love Lucy*; *The Dick Van Dyke Show*; *Simpsons*; *Cosby Show*.	$9	215
☐ 05-11-2002	**Hayden Christensen** and **Ewan McGregor** in *Star Wars: Episode II – Attack of the Clones* (3-D)	$15	215
☐ 05-11-2002	**Natalie Portman** and **Hayden Christensen** in *Star Wars: Episode II - Attack of the Clones* (3-D)	$15	215
☐ 05-11-2002	**Hayden Christensen** in *Star Wars: Episode II – Attack of the Clones* (3-D)	$15	215
☐ 05-11-2002	*Dinotopia*	$7	216
☐ 05-18-2002	**Gillian Anderson** and **David Duchovny** of *The X-Files*	$8	216
☐ 05-18-2002	**Robert Patrick** and **Annabeth Gish** of *The X-Files*.	$8	216
☐ 05-25-2002	**Alex Michel** and **Amanda Marsh** of *The Bachelor*	$6	216
☐ 06-01-2002	**Ashley Judd**	$6	216
☐ 06-08-2002	**Jennifer Aniston** of *Friends*	$24	216
☐ 06-08-2002	**Courtney Cox Arquette** of *Friends*	$24	216
☐ 06-08-2002	**Lisa Kudrow** of *Friends*	$24	216
☐ 06-08-2002	**Matt LeBlanc** of *Friends*	$24	216
☐ 06-08-2002	**Matthew Perry** of *Friends*	$24	216
☐ 06-08-2002	**David Schwimmer** of *Friends*.	$24	216
☐ 06-15-2002	50 Greatest **TV Guide** Covers.	$9	216
☐ 06-22-2002	**Alexis Bledel** and **Lauren Graham** of *Gilmore Girls*	$7	216
☐ 06-22-2002	**Alexis Bledel** and **Lauren Graham** of *Gilmore Girls* (Additional Lettering).	$7	216
☐ 06-29-2002	**Sarah Jessica Parker** of *Sex and the City*.	$6	216
☐ 07-06-2002	**Catherine Bell** and **David James Elliott** of *JAG*.	$10	216
☐ 07-06-2002	**P. Diddy** & **Jennifer Lopez**; **Gideon Yago** & **Kelly Osbourne**; **Tobey Maguire** & **Nicole Kidman**	$11	216
☐ 07-13-2002	Contestants **Jim Verraros**, **Tamyra Gray**, and **Ryan Starr** of *American Idol*	$6	216
☐ 07-20-2002	50 Worst Shows of All Time.	$9	216
☐ 07-27-2002	**Kelly Ripa** and **Regis Philbin** of *Live with Regis & Kelly*.	$6	216
☐ 08-03-2002	**Charlie Brown** of *Peanuts* and **Angelica Pickles** of *Rugrats*	$8	217
☐ 08-03-2002	**Daffy Duck** (as Duck Dodgers) and Cadet **Porky Pig** with the **Powerpuff Girls**	$22	217
☐ 08-03-2002	**Homer Simpson** with **Rocky** and **Bullwinkle**	$22	217
☐ 08-03-2002	**Popeye** and **SpongeBob SquarePants**	$22	217
☐ 08-10-2002	**Leah Remini**, **Kevin James**, and **Jerry Stiller** of *The King of Queens*.	$6	217
☐ 08-10-2002	**Winona Ryder** – The Strange Case of Winona Ryder	$12	217
☐ 08-10-2002	**Stacey Dales-Schuman**, **Vicky Bullett**, and **Chamique Holdsclaw**	$6	217
☐ 08-17-2002	**Elvis Presley** – Elvis Forever!	$7	217
☐ 08-17-2002	**Elvis Presley** – Elvis Forever! (3-D)	$15	217

Date	Caption	Value	Page
08-17-2002	**Elvis Presley** – Elvis Forever! (3-D) (Gyrating)	$15	217
08-17-2002	**Elvis Presley** – Elvis Forever! (3-D) (Kiss)	$15	217
08-24-2002	**James Gandolfini** of *The Sopranos*	$8	217
08-24-2002	**Edie Falco** of *The Sopranos*	$18	217
08-31-2002	**Donovan McNabb** of the Eagles and **Tom Brady** of the Patriots	$19	217
08-31-2002	**Rich Gannon** of the Raiders and **Jeff Garcia** of the 49ers	$18	217
08-31-2002	**Brian Urlacher** of the Bears	$19	217
08-31-2002	**Emmitt Smith** of the Cowboys	$18	218
08-31-2002	**Brett Favre** of the Packers	$19	218
08-31-2002	**Kordell Stewart** of the Steelers	$18	218
09-07-2002	**Reba McEntire** (*Reba*), **Christopher Meloni** (*Law & Order: SVU*), and **Julie Bowen** (*ER*)	$7	218
09-14-2002	**Bill Bellamy, Ashley Scott, Kiele Sanchez, David Caruso,** and **Gail O'Grady** – Fall Preview	$13	218
09-21-2002	**Jennifer Garner** of *Alias* (Animal Print Dress)	$7	218
09-21-2002	**Jennifer Garner** of *Alias*	$7	218
09-21-2002	**Jennifer Garner** of *Alias* (White Dress/Pearls)	$7	218
09-21-2002	**Ernie Harwell** – Detroit's Sports Legend Signs Off	$15	218
09-28-2002	**Henry Simmmons** of *NYPD Blue* and **Kim Cattrall** of *Sex and the City* (Close-Up)	$9	218
09-28-2002	**Henry Simmmons** of *NYPD Blue* and **Kim Cattrall** of *Sex and the City*	$9	218
10-05-2002	**Don Francisco** of *Sabado Gigante*	$12	218
10-05-2002	The Cast of *Everybody Loves Raymond*	$6	218
10-05-2002	**Unitas** Forever – A Tribute by **Barry Levinson**	$12	218
10-12-2002	**Maura Tierney, Noah Wyle, Goran Visnjic,** and **Mehki Phife** of *ER*	$6	218
10-19-2002	**Oprah Winfrey, Ozzy Osbourne, Drew Carey, Katie Couric,** and **David Letterman**	$6	218
10-26-2002	The Cast of *Friends*	$6	219
11-09-2002	**Pierce Brosnan** in *Die Another Day* (JFK's Lost Ship)	$22	219
11-09-2002	**Pierce Brosnan** in *Die Another Day*	$22	219
11-09-2002	**Halle Berry** in *Die Another Day*	$14	219
11-09-2002	**Pierce Brosnan** and **Halle Berry** in *Die Another Day*	$20	219
11-02-2002	**Shania Twain** – Shania's Back!	$6	219
11-16-2002	**Heidi Klum** – The Victoria's Secret Fashion Show	$10	219
11-16-2002	**Tyra Banks** – The Victoria's Secret Fashion Show	$10	219
11-16-2002	**Heidi Klum** and **Tyra Banks** – The Victoria's Secret Fashion Show	$10	219
11-23-2002	**Gregory Smith, Brittany Snow, David Gallagher,** and **Kathy Cuoco** – Generation Now	$24	219
11-23-2002	**Paul McCartney**	$6	219
11-30-2002	*Austin Powers*; *The Lord of the Rings*; *Shrek*; *The Godfather*, *Sex and the City*	$10	219
11-30-2002	**Catherine Dent** and **Anton Yelchin** in *Taken*	$10	219
12-07-2002	**Patrick Stewart** and **Brent Spiner** of *Star Trek Nemesis* (3-D)	$15	219
12-07-2002	**Patrick Stewart** in *Star Trek Nemesis* (3-D)	$15	219
12-07-2002	The U.S.S. Enterprise of *Star Trek Nemesis* (3-D) (Side View)	$15	219
12-07-2002	The U.S.S. Enterprise of *Star Trek Nemesis* (3-D)	$15	219
12-07-2002	**Ten Danson** of *Becker*	$9	219
12-14-2002	**Greg Biffle**	$13	219
12-14-2002	**Mike Bliss**	$13	219
12-14-2002	**Ryan Newman**	$13	220
12-14-2002	**Tony Stewart**	$14	220
12-14-2002	*The Simpsons*; **Jennifer Garner** of *Alias*; **Matthew Perry** of *Friends*; The Cast of *Seinfeld*	$6	220
12-21-2002	**Shaquille O'Neal** of the Lakers	$6	220
12-28-2002	**Holly Marie Combs** of *Charmed*	$12	220
12-28-2002	**Rose McGowan** of *Charmed*	$12	220
12-28-2002	**Alyssa Milano** of *Charmed*	$12	220
12-28-2002	**Rose McGowan, Holly Marie Combs,** and **Alyssa Milano** of *Charmed*	$30	220

Date . . . . .Caption . . . . .Value . . . .Page

00's (2003)

2003